[redacted]

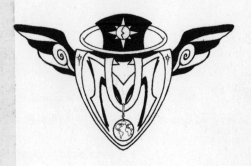

ALSO AVAILABLE FROM ⊂TOKYOPOP.

MANGA

For more information visit www.TOKYOPOP.com

*INDICATES 100% AUTHENTIC MANGA (RIGHT-TO-LEFT FORMAT)

CINE-MANGA™

NOVELS

TOKYOPOP KIDS

ART BOOKS

ANIME GUIDES

062703

SHUTTERBOX

Book One:
Orientation, Damien, Adrien, and the Running of the Hyperpans

BY

TAVISHA
AND
RIKKI SIMONS

TOKYOPOP®
LOS ANGELES • TOKYO • LONDON

Tavisha/Wired Psyche - Story & Illustrations
Rikki Simons - Writer, tones & letters
Tavisha & Rikki Simons - Front cover
Patrick Hook - Graphic Designer
Paul Morrissey - Associate Editor
Tim Beedle - Copy Editor
Mark Paniccia - Editor

Jill Freshney - Managing Editor
Antonio DePietro - Production Coordinator
Jennifer Miller - Production Manager
Matt Alford - Art Director
Jeremy Ross - Editorial Director
Ron Klamert - VP of Production
John Parker - President & C.O.O.
Stuart Levy - Publisher & C.E.O.

Email: editor@TOKYOPOP.com
Come visit us online at www.TOKYOPOP.com

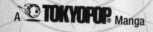

A TOKYOPOP® Manga

TOKYOPOP Inc.
5900 Wilshire Blvd. Suite 2000
Los Angeles, CA 90036

ISBN: 1-59182-361-7

First TOKYOPOP printing: September 2003
10 9 8 7 6 5 4 3 2 1
Printed in the USA

AN INTRODUCTION BY THE WIRED PSYCHE

For some time now, we here in this afterlife have been searching for a human capable of describing our tale to you in the mortal world below. We beseeched our usual throng of clients, hasty poets, nepotistic philosophers, horrid comedians, and so forth...but being that our realm here within the ninth level of imperception is only communicable to you in the shortest bursts of time, the usual clients failed us in a most spectacular fashion.

The five senses are inside humans, humans are inside the nine dimensions, the nine dimensions are inside the universe, and the universe is inside the infinite multiverse...and as such, an artist cursed with a nearly schizophrenic sense of their own work was needed to translate our tale in full. A comic book artist, we soon discovered, was the only person truly capable of fully receiving us. Thus, we have whispered our tale to Tavisha for many years, and she has been so kind as to force her husband's hand in writing it all down. Here now, is the first of six chapters revealing the true story of how our realm was changed forever by the addition of one small mortal girl to our Merridiah University. May the telling of the tale further free you from the corruption of the banshees and the otherwise sad horror of living.

Eternally Nocturnally Yours,
The Inhabitants of Merridiah,
speaking through this Wired Psyche

CHAPTER ONE:

IT IS

TRANSMUNDANE

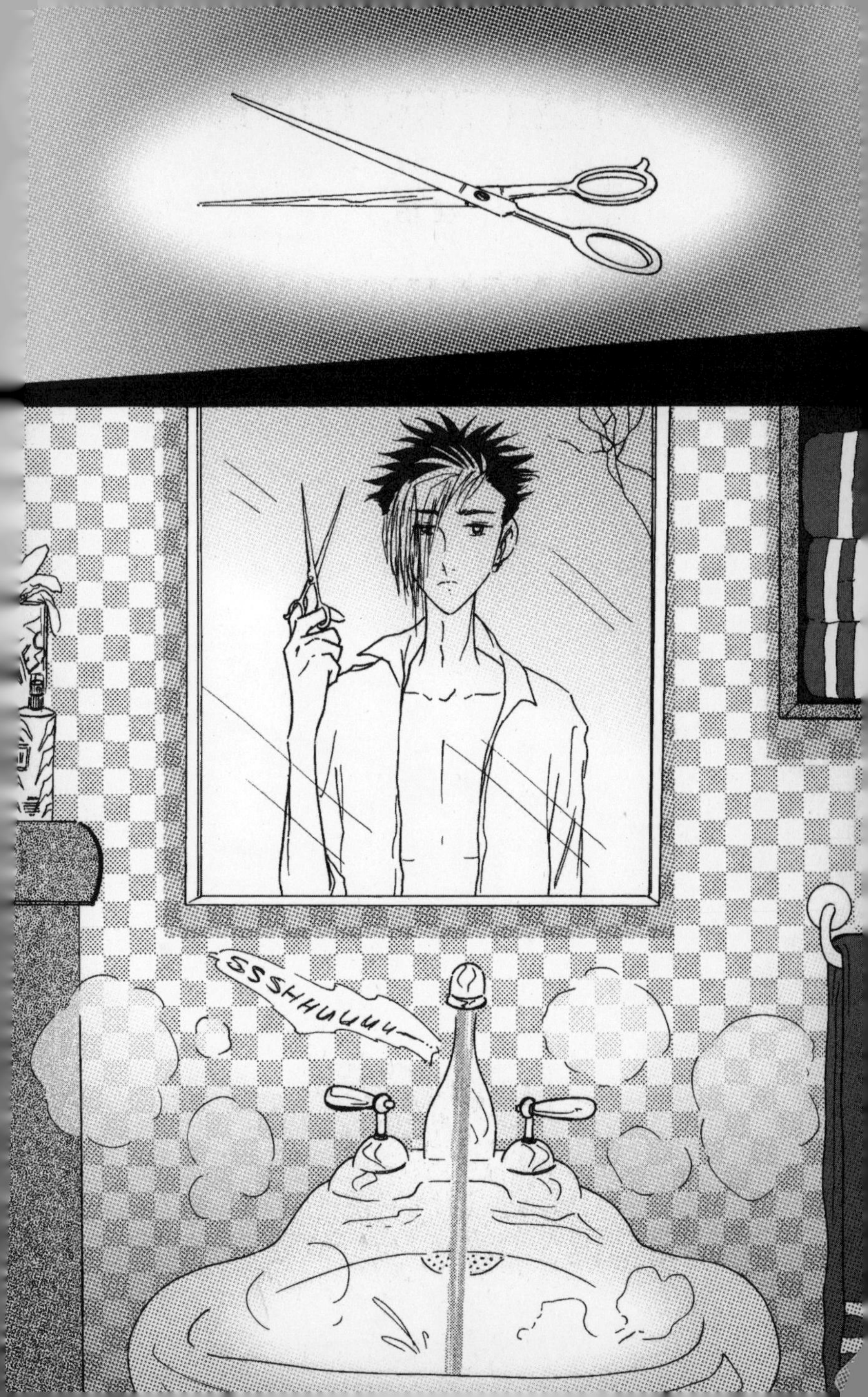
SSSHHUUUU—

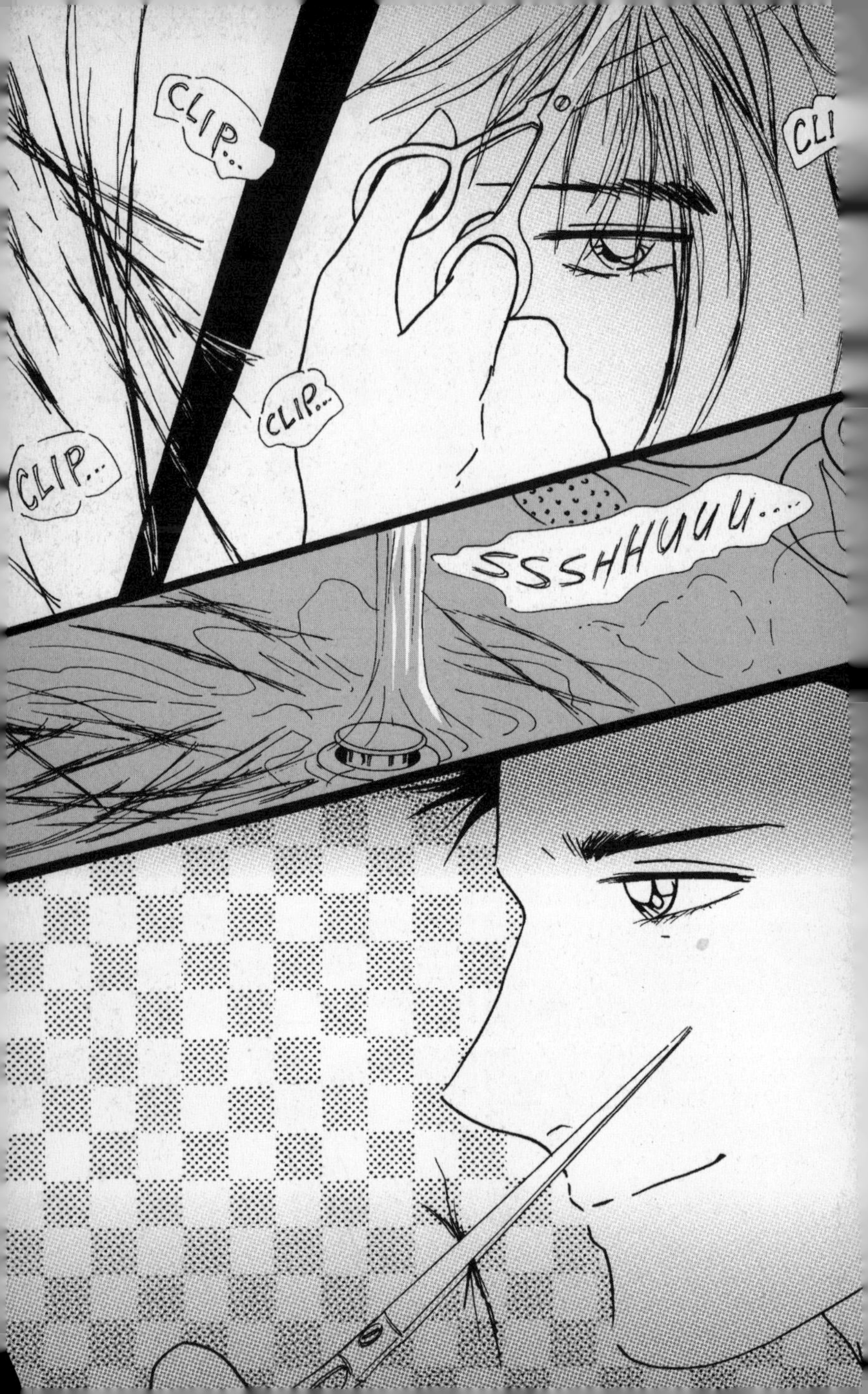
CLIP...
CLIP...
CLIP...
CLI
SSSHHUUU....

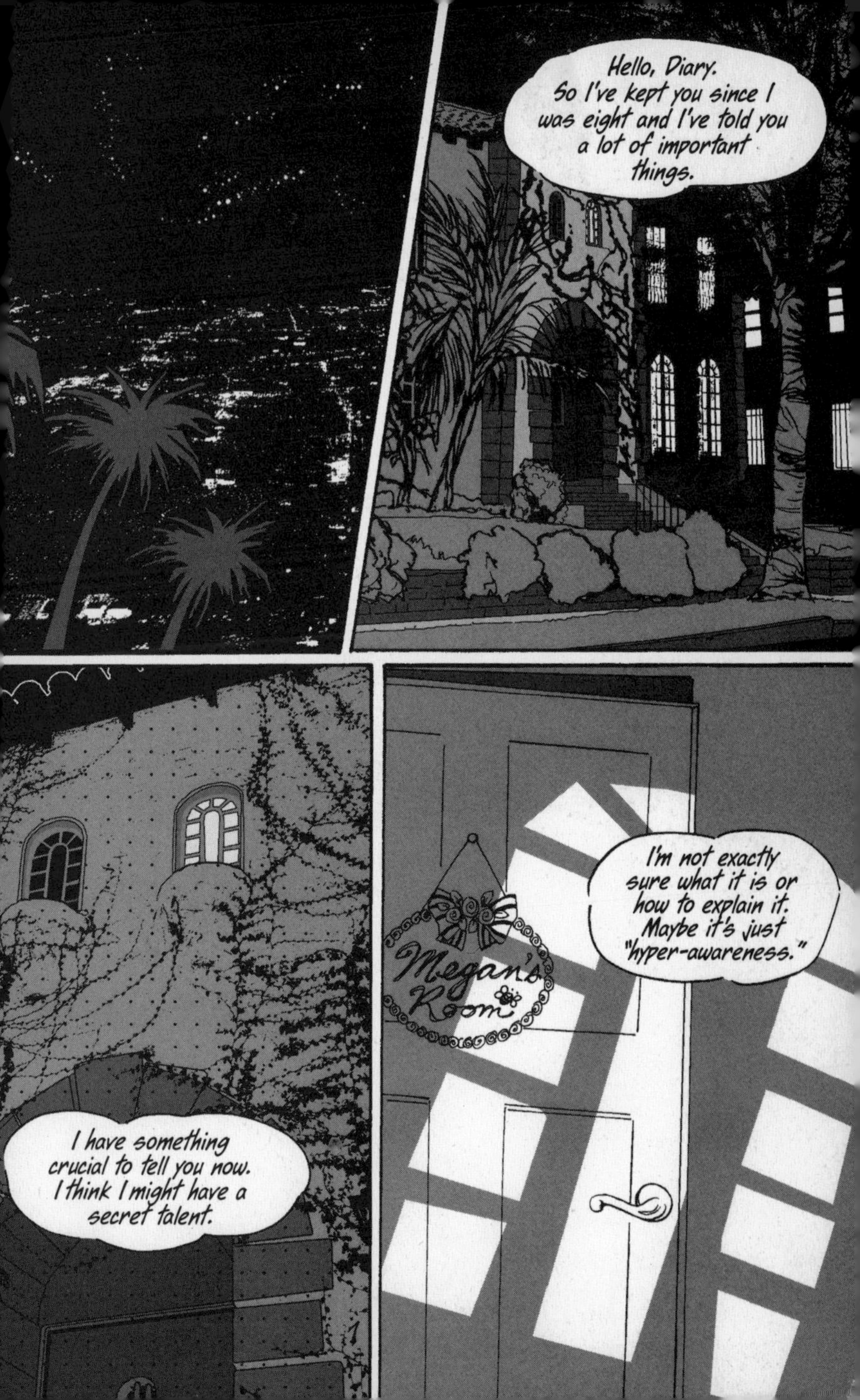
Hello, Diary. So I've kept you since I was eight and I've told you a lot of important things.
I have something crucial to tell you now. I think I might have a secret talent.
Megan's Room
I'm not exactly sure what it is or how to explain it. Maybe it's just "hyper-awareness."

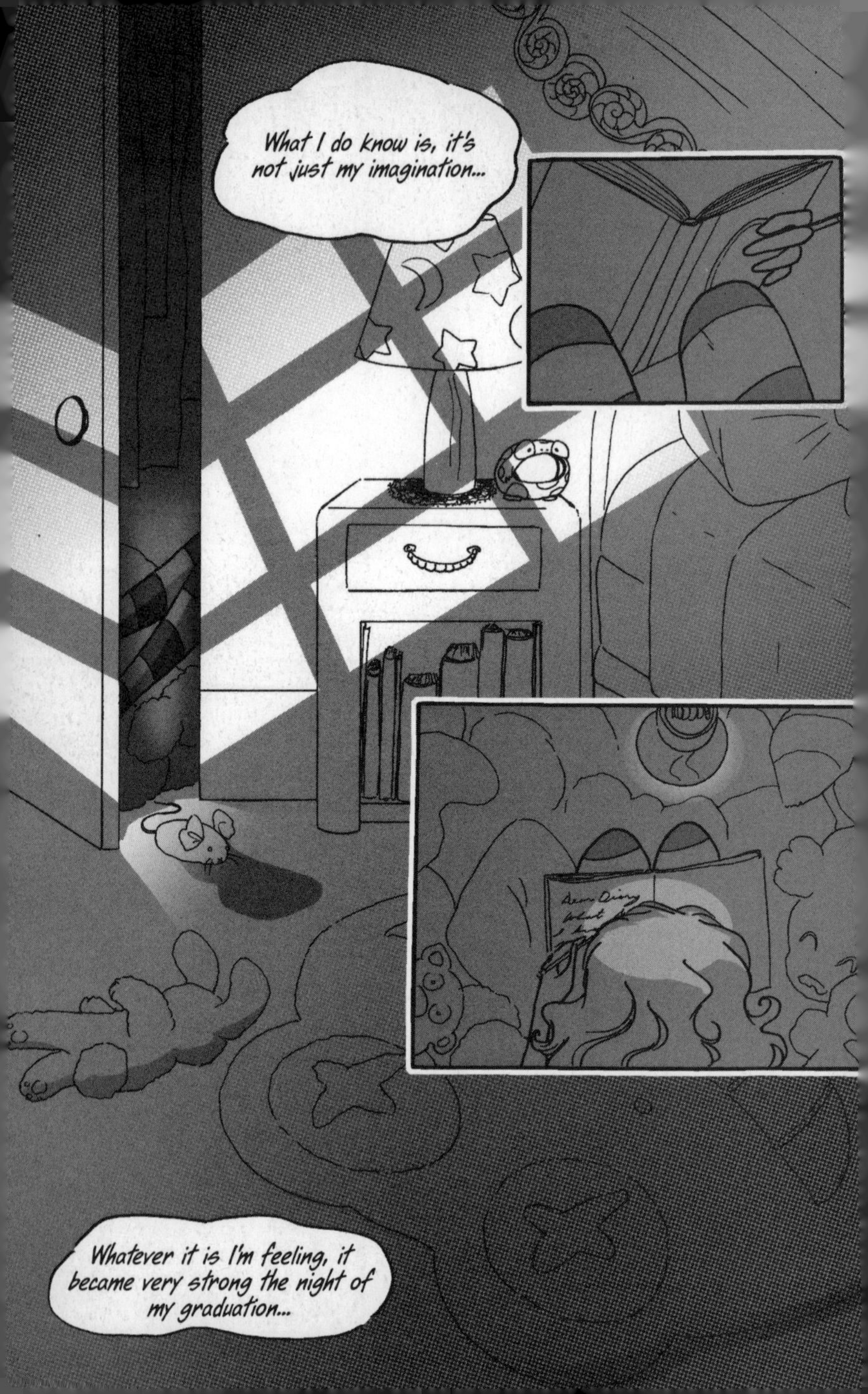
What I do know is, it's not just my imagination...
Whatever it is I'm feeling, it became very strong the night of my graduation...

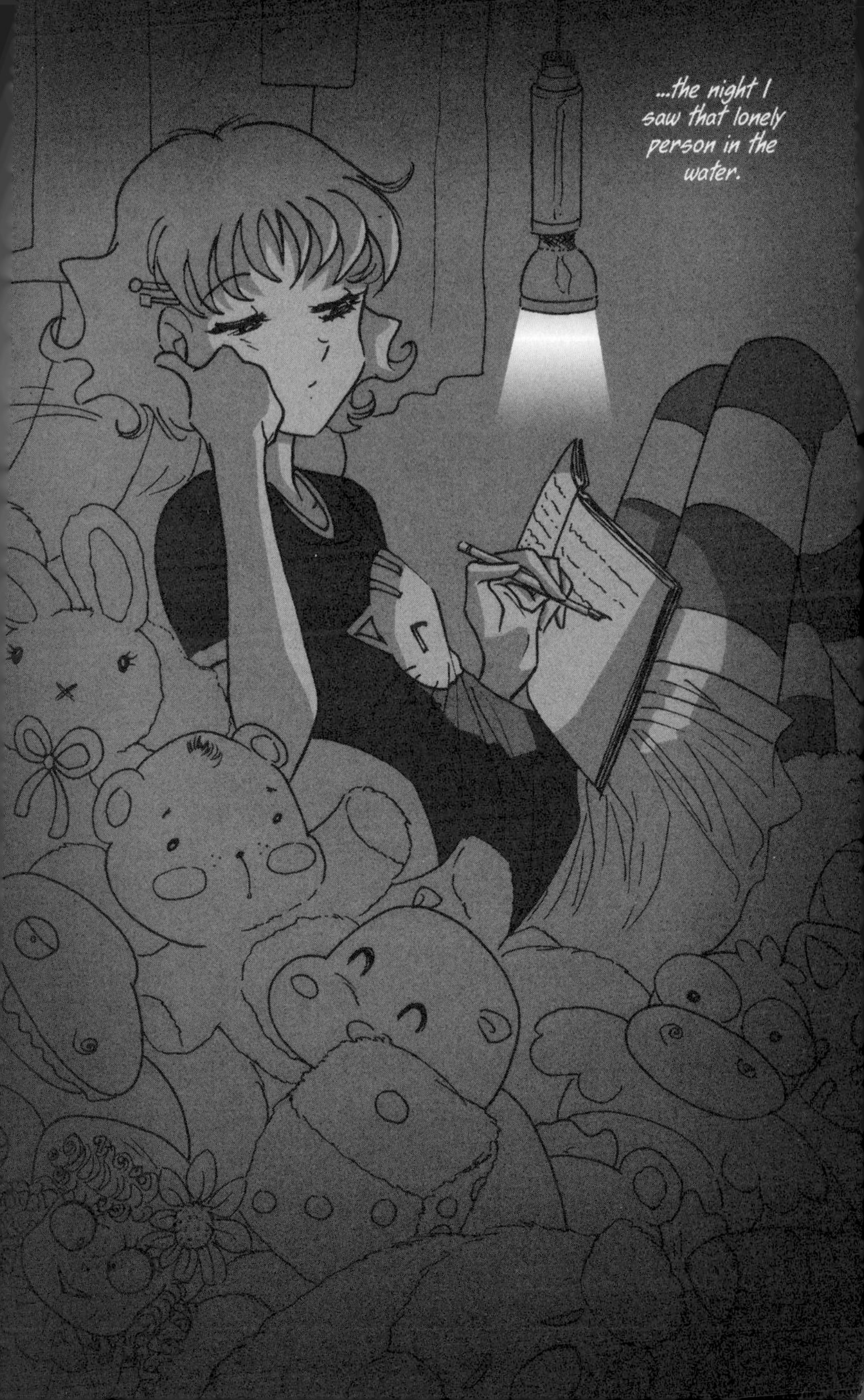
...the night I saw that lonely person in the water.

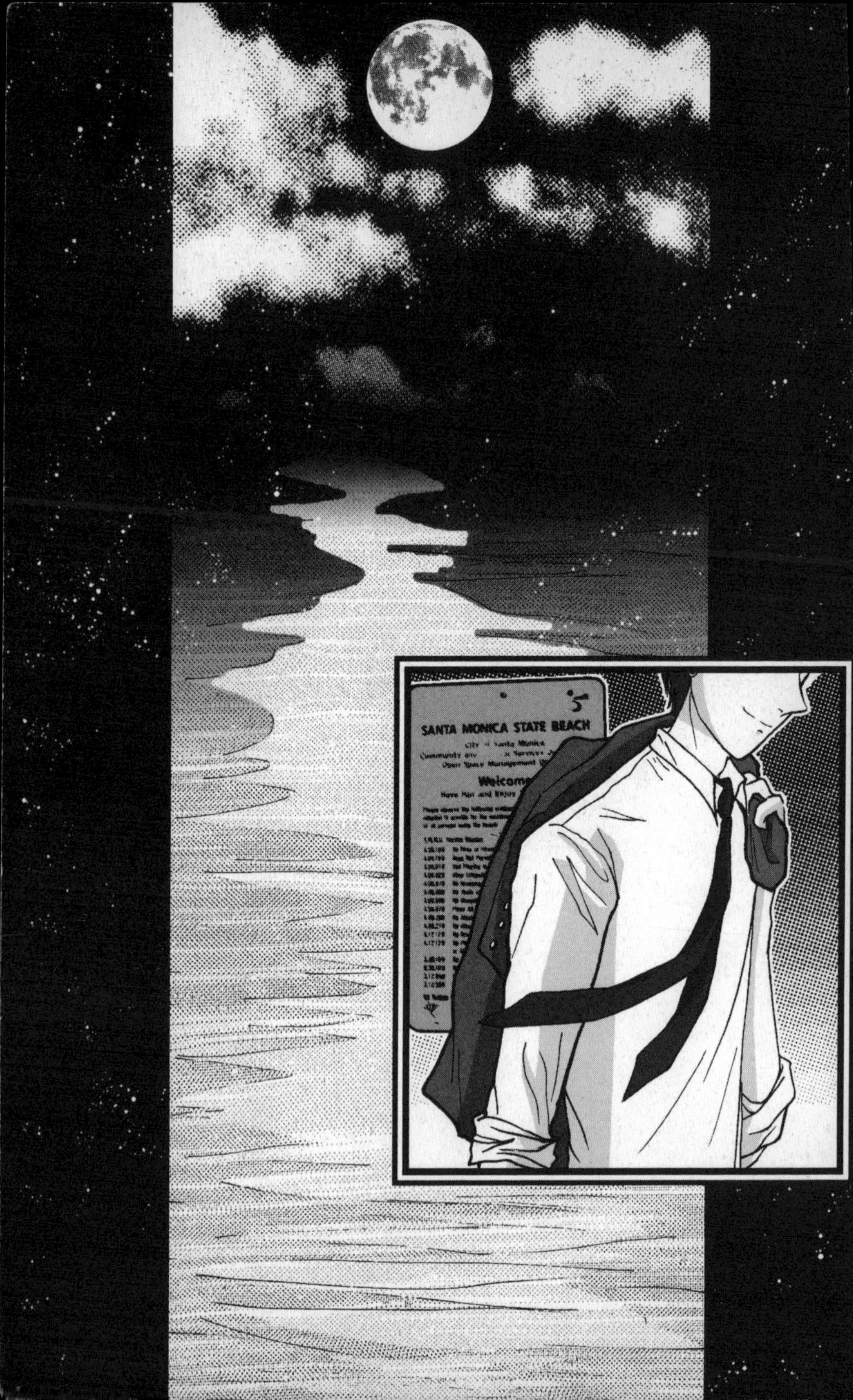
SANTA MONICA STATE BEACH

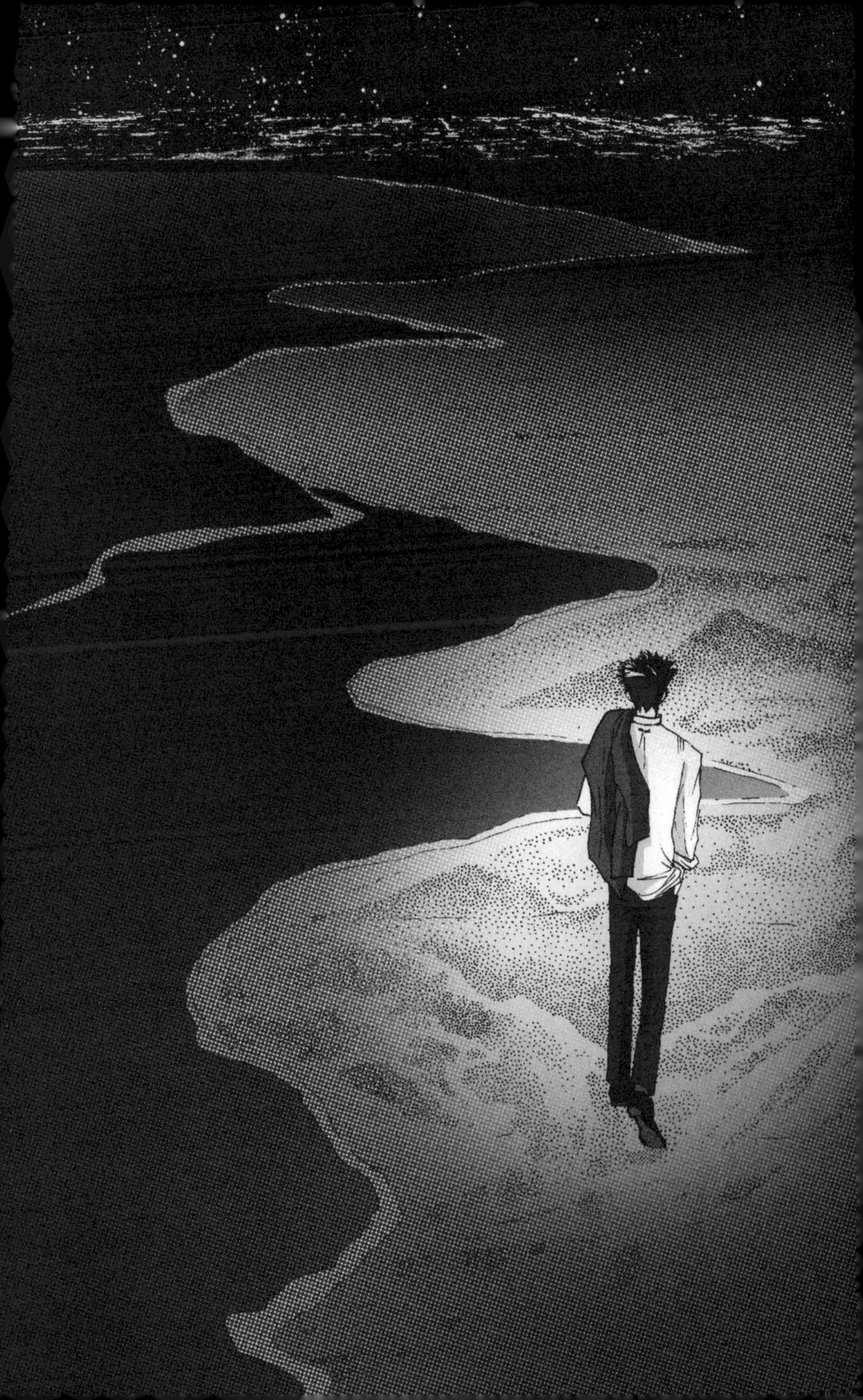

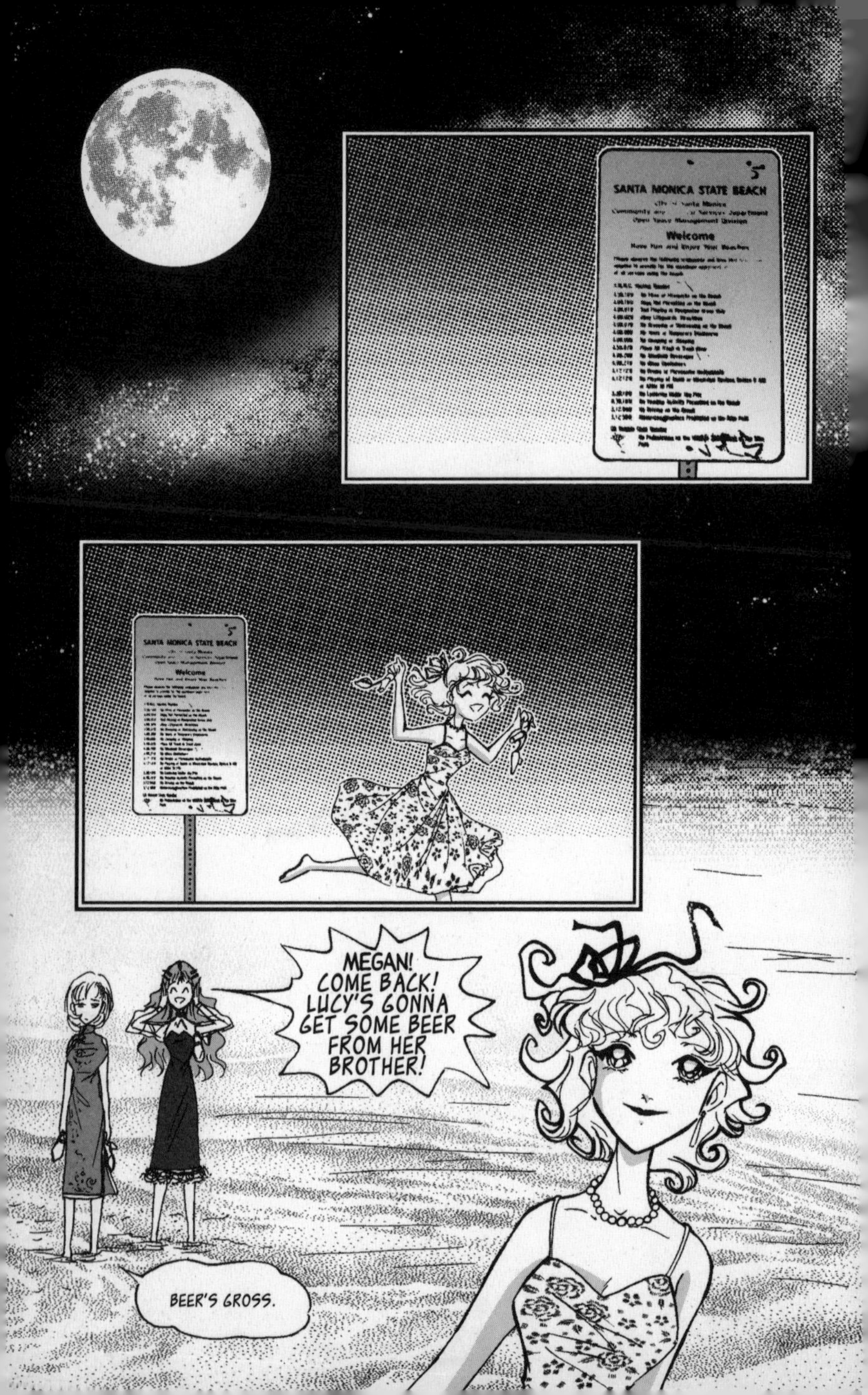
SANTA MONICA STATE BEACH
Welcome
SANTA MONICA STATE BEACH
Welcome
MEGAN! COME BACK! LUCY'S GONNA GET SOME BEER FROM HER BROTHER!
BEER'S GROSS.

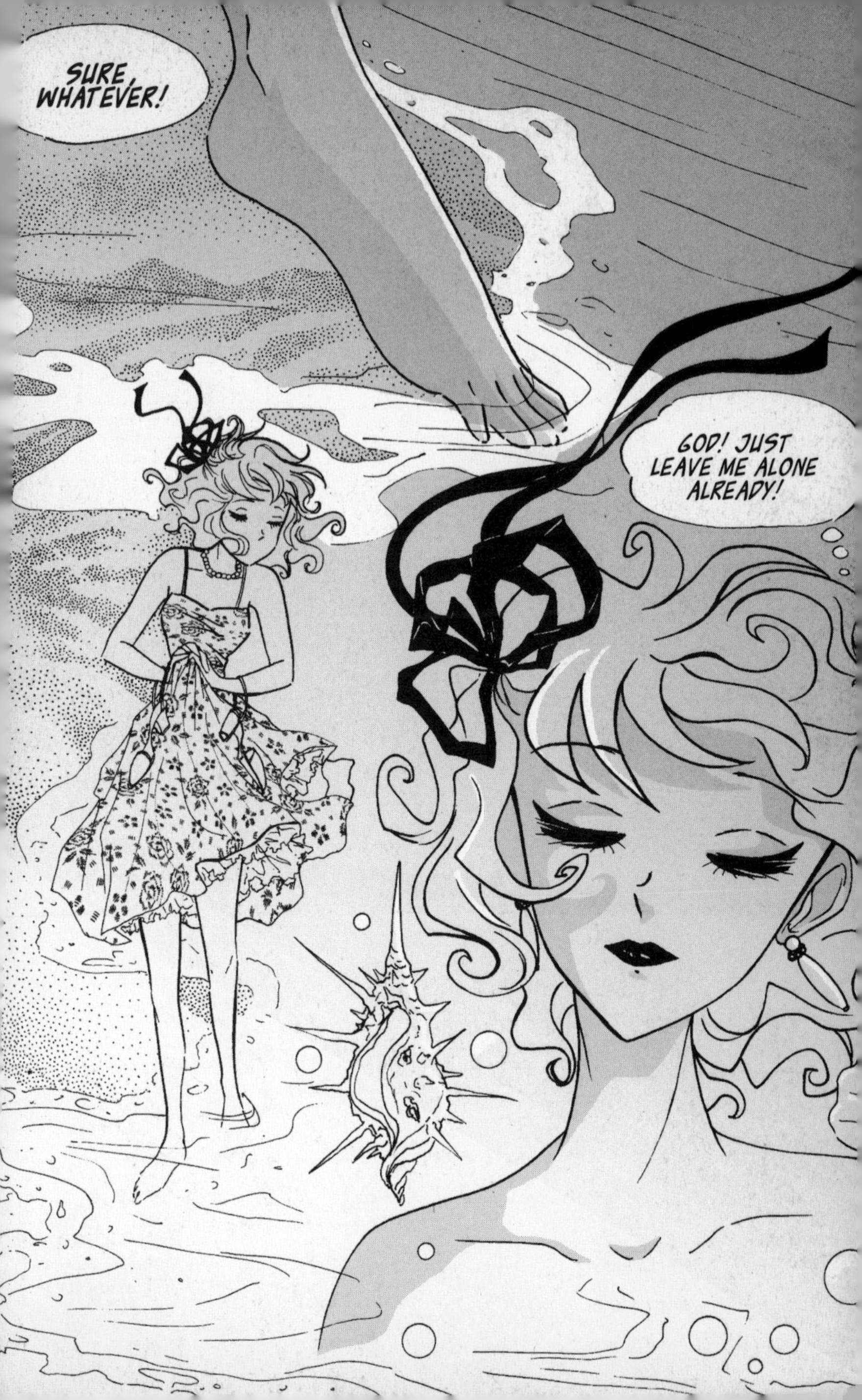
SURE, WHATEVER!
GOD! JUST LEAVE ME ALONE ALREADY!

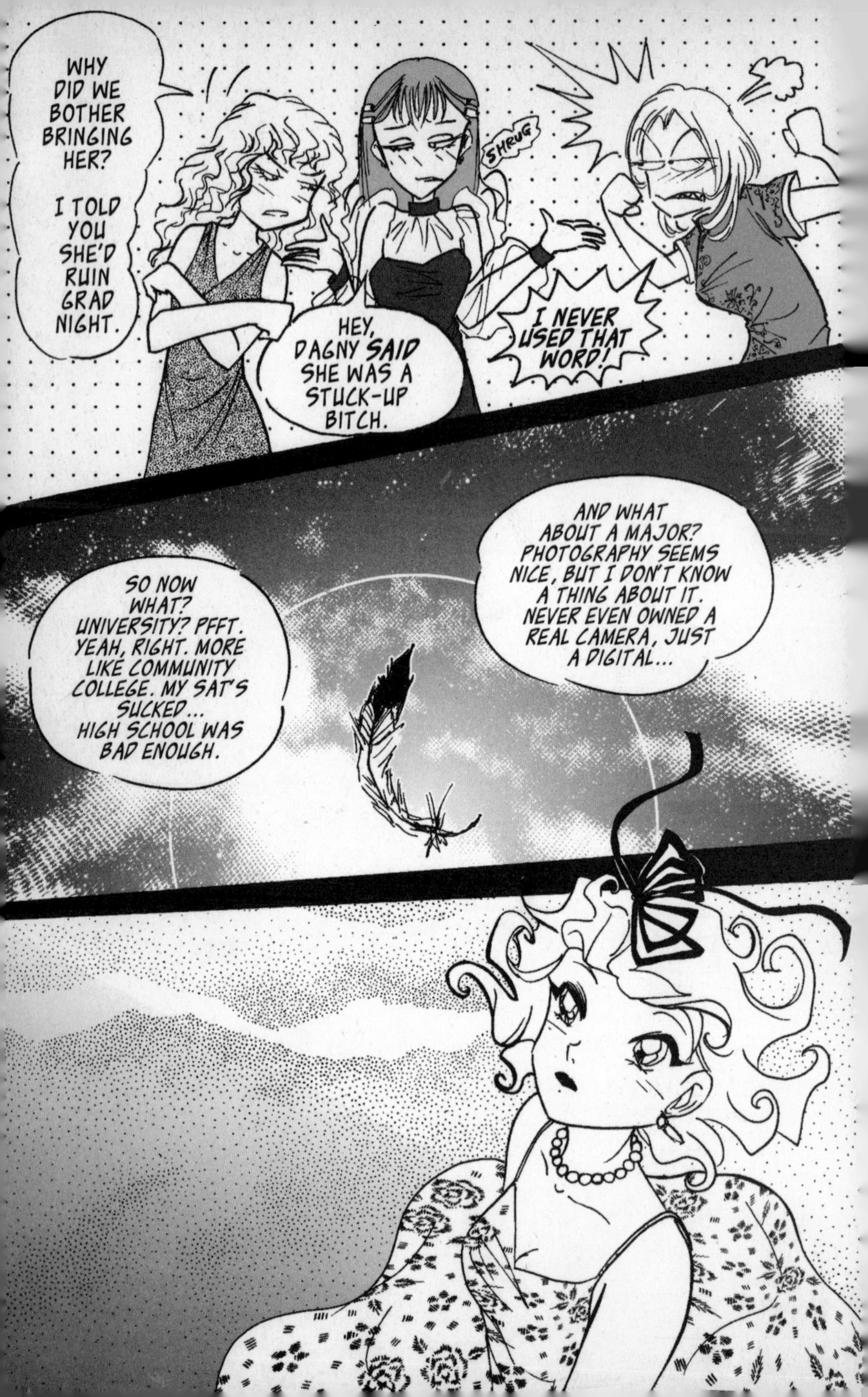
WHY DID WE BOTHER BRINGING HER?
I TOLD YOU SHE'D RUIN GRAD NIGHT.
SHRUG
HEY, DAGNY SAID SHE WAS A STUCK-UP BITCH.
I NEVER USED THAT WORD!
SO NOW WHAT? UNIVERSITY? PFFT. YEAH, RIGHT. MORE LIKE COMMUNITY COLLEGE. MY SAT'S SUCKED... HIGH SCHOOL WAS BAD ENOUGH.
AND WHAT ABOUT A MAJOR? PHOTOGRAPHY SEEMS NICE, BUT I DON'T KNOW A THING ABOUT IT. NEVER EVEN OWNED A REAL CAMERA, JUST A DIGITAL...

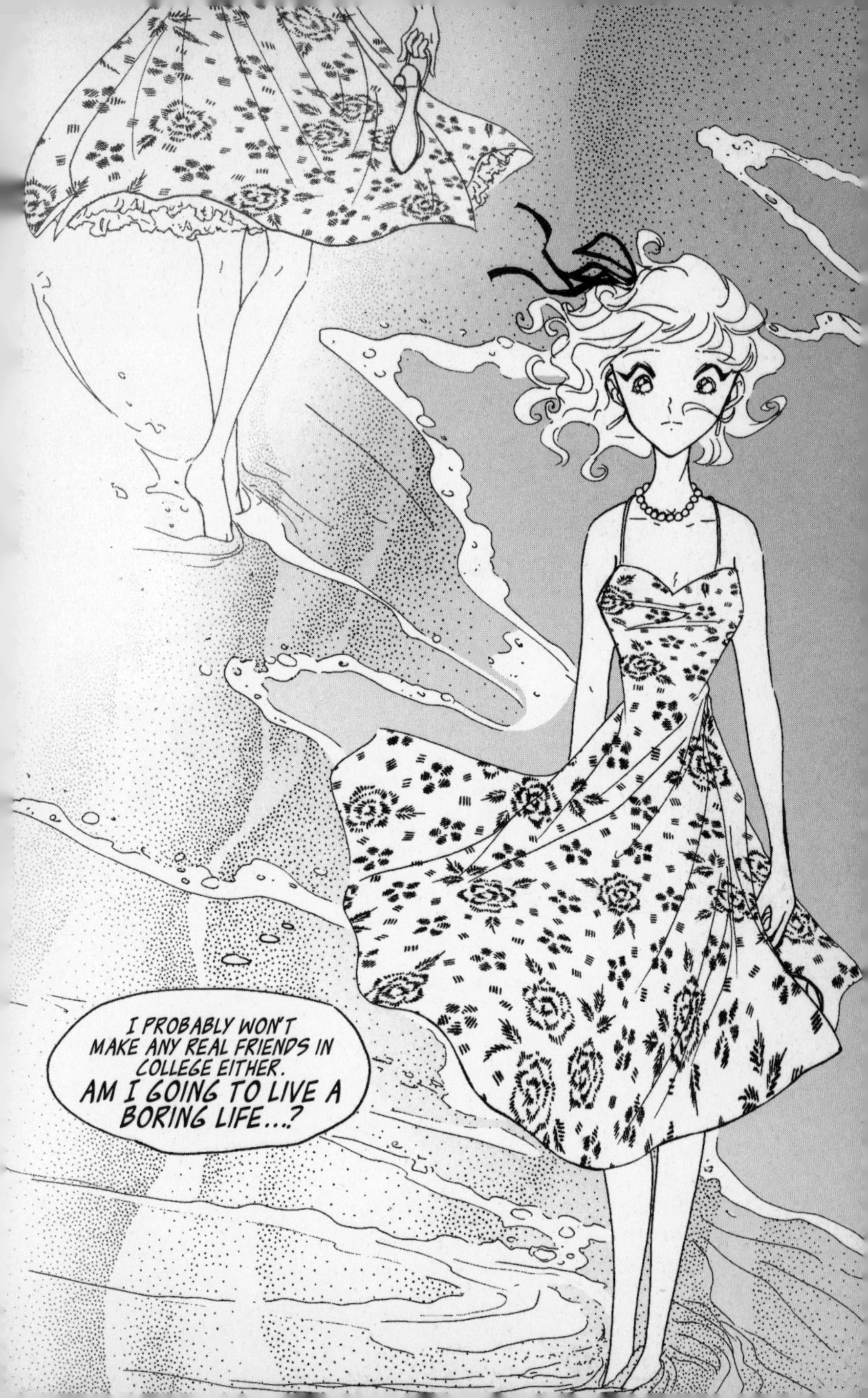
I PROBABLY WON'T MAKE ANY REAL FRIENDS IN COLLEGE EITHER. AM I GOING TO LIVE A BORING LIFE...?

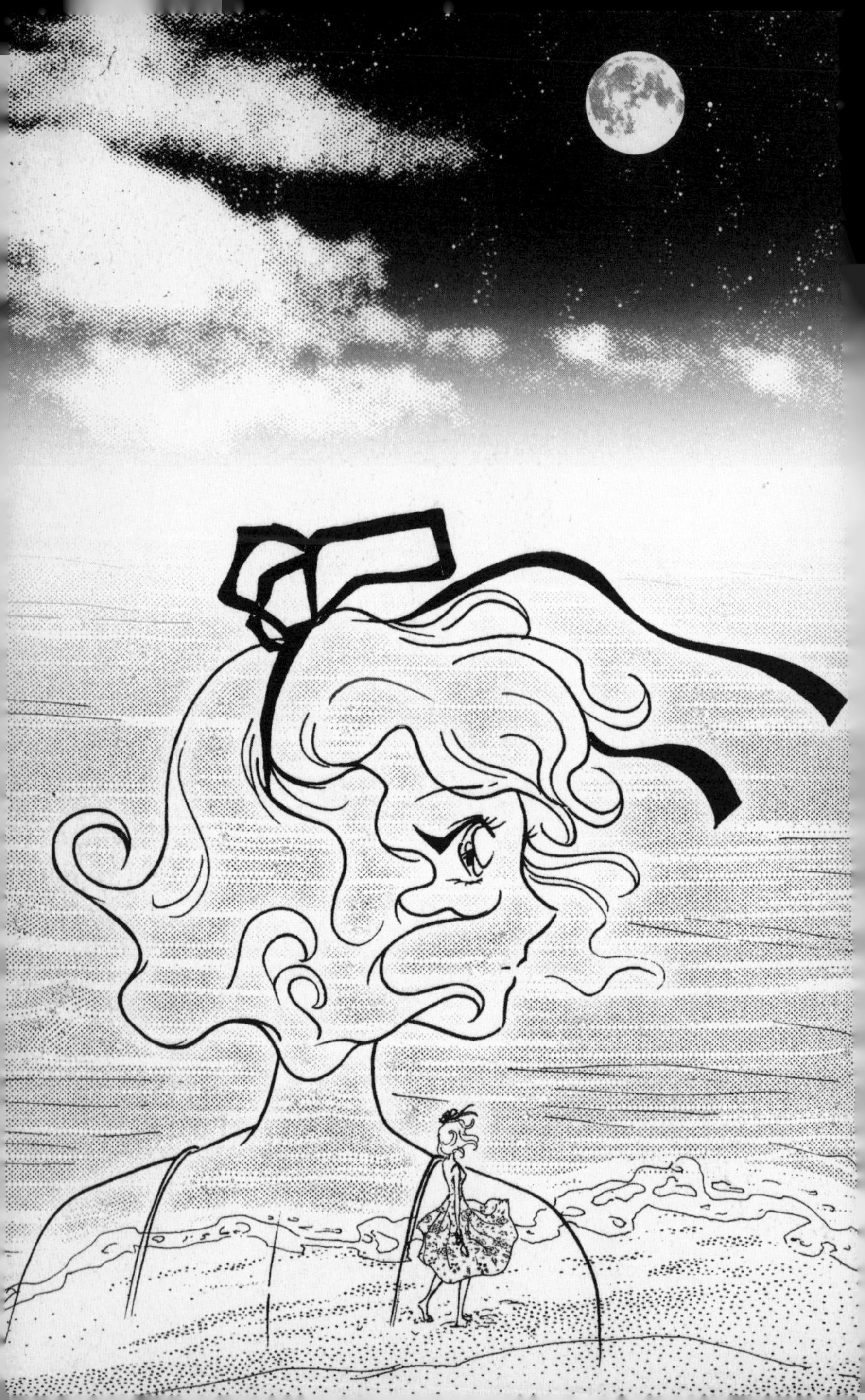

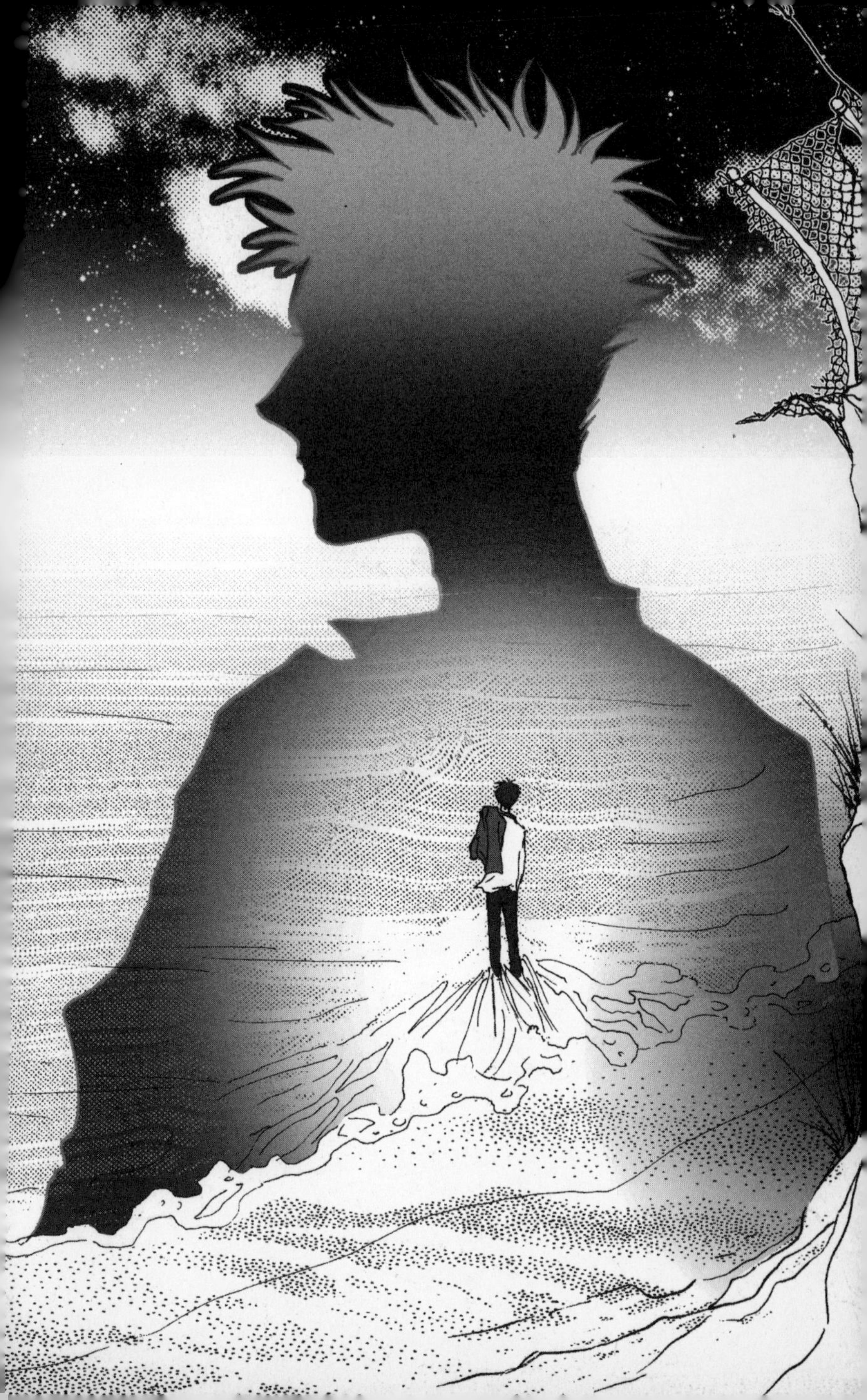

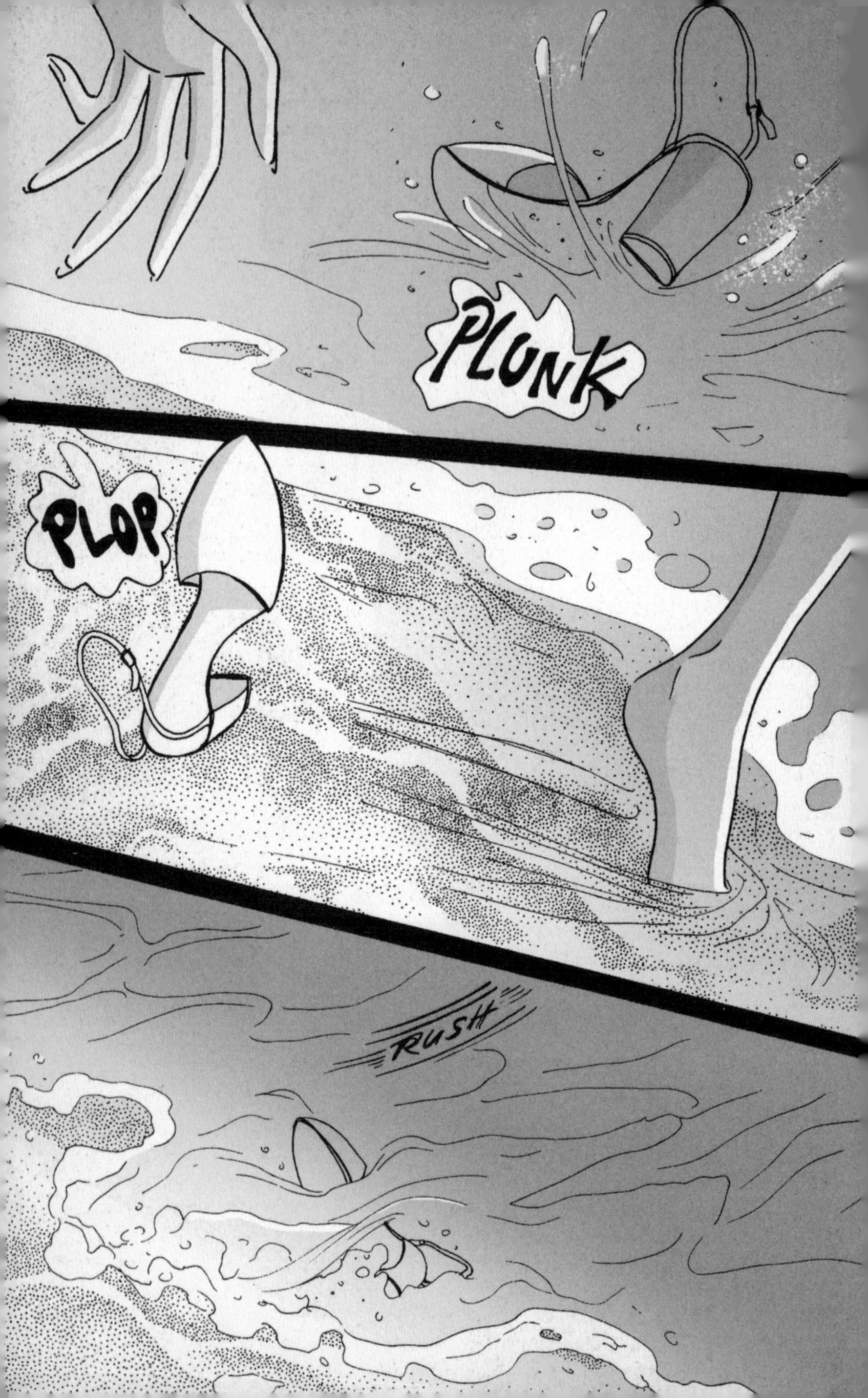
PLUNK
PLOP
RUSH

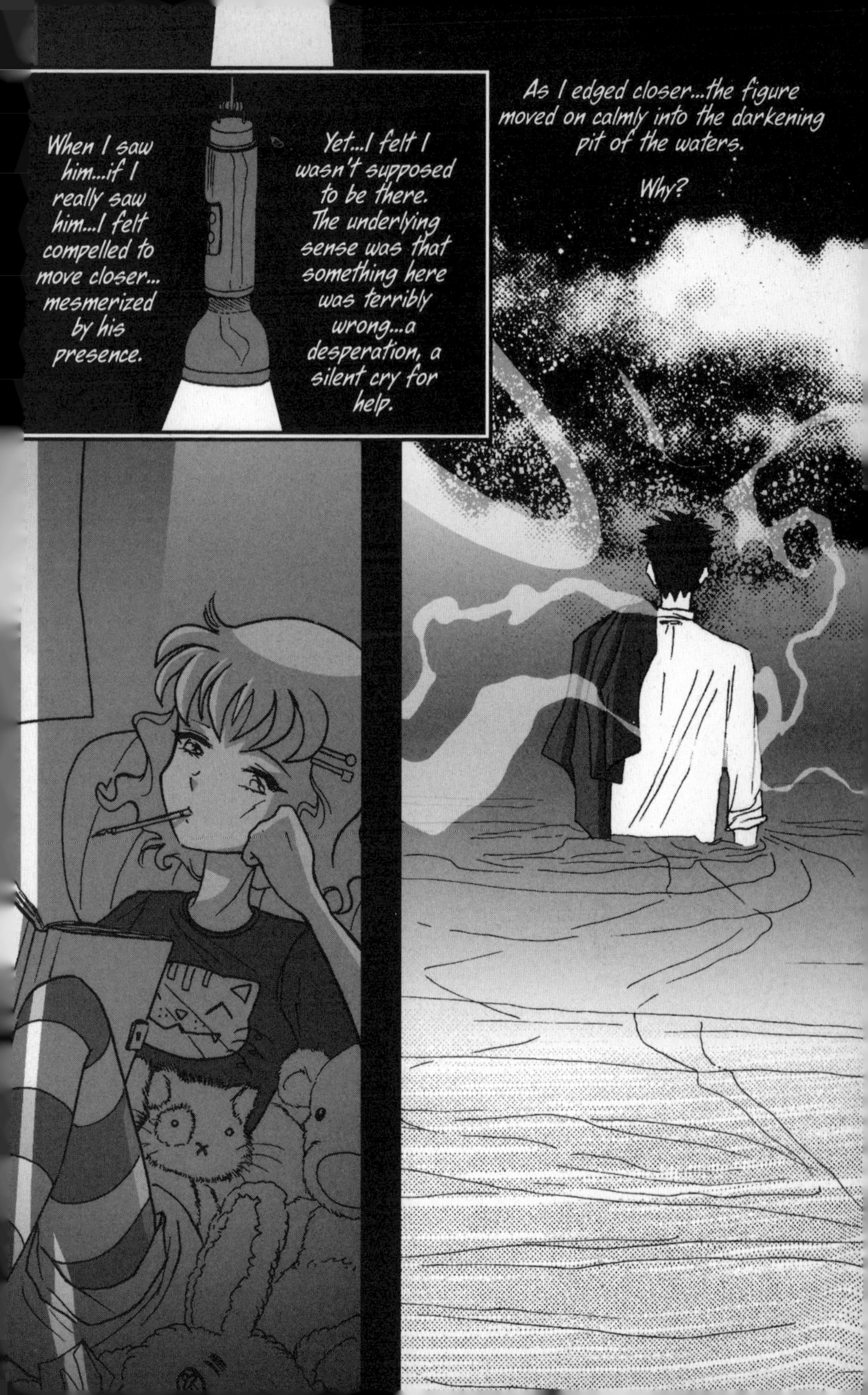
When I saw him...if I really saw him...I felt compelled to move closer... mesmerized by his presence.
Yet...I felt I wasn't supposed to be there. The underlying sense was that something here was terribly wrong...a desperation, a silent cry for help.
As I edged closer...the figure moved on calmly into the darkening pit of the waters.
Why?

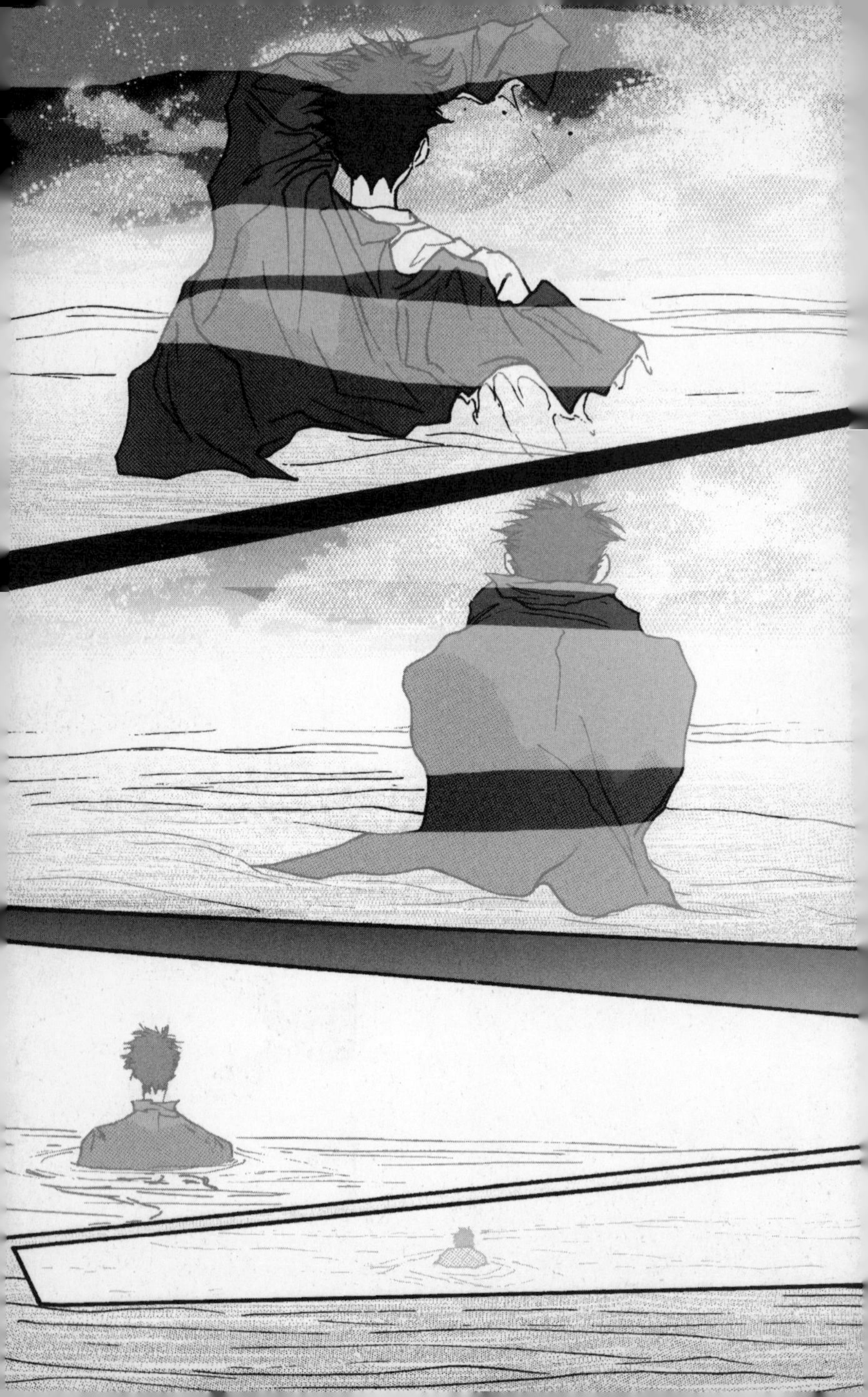

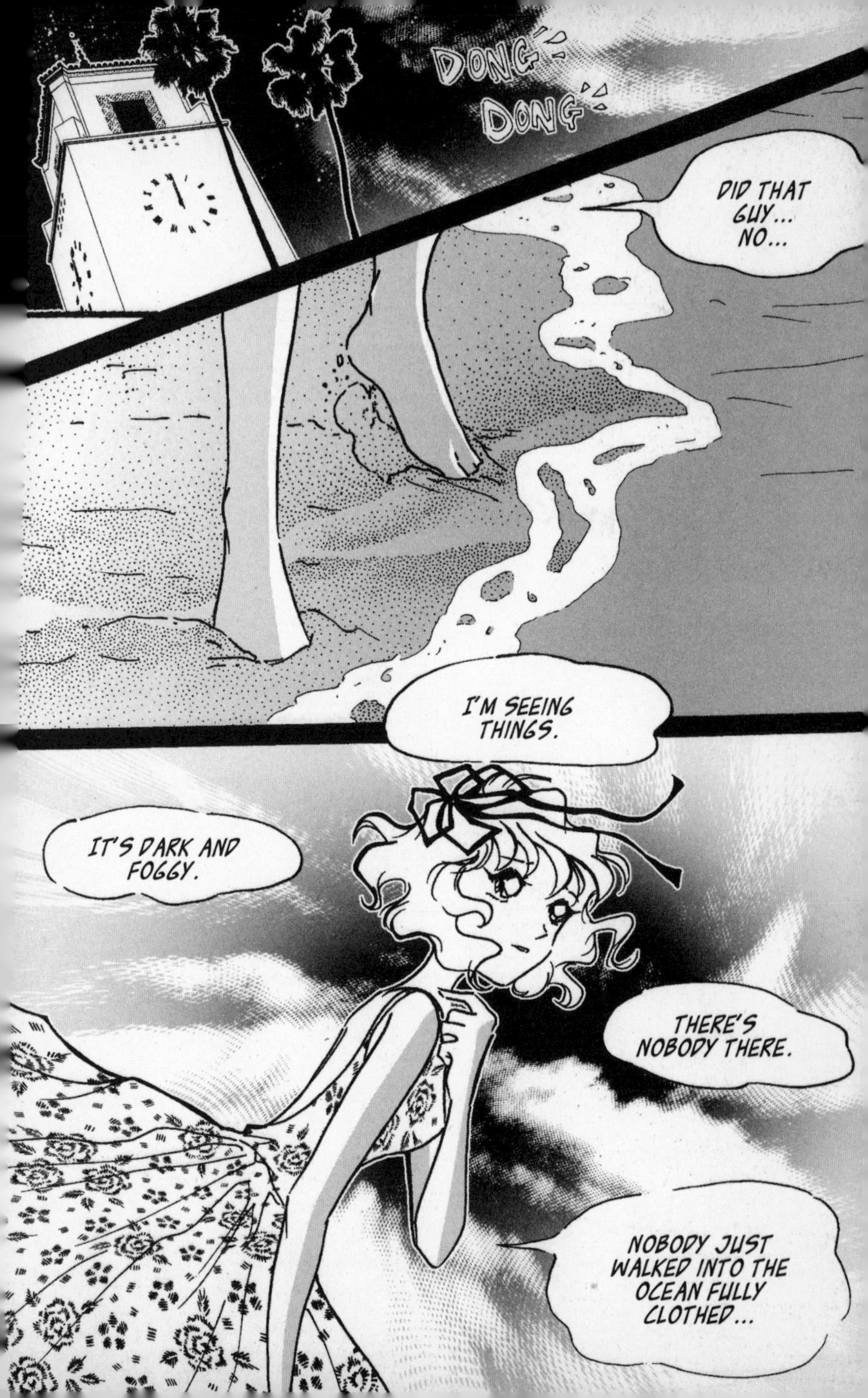
DONG DONG
DID THAT GUY... NO...
I'M SEEING THINGS.
IT'S DARK AND FOGGY.
THERE'S NOBODY THERE.
NOBODY JUST WALKED INTO THE OCEAN FULLY CLOTHED...

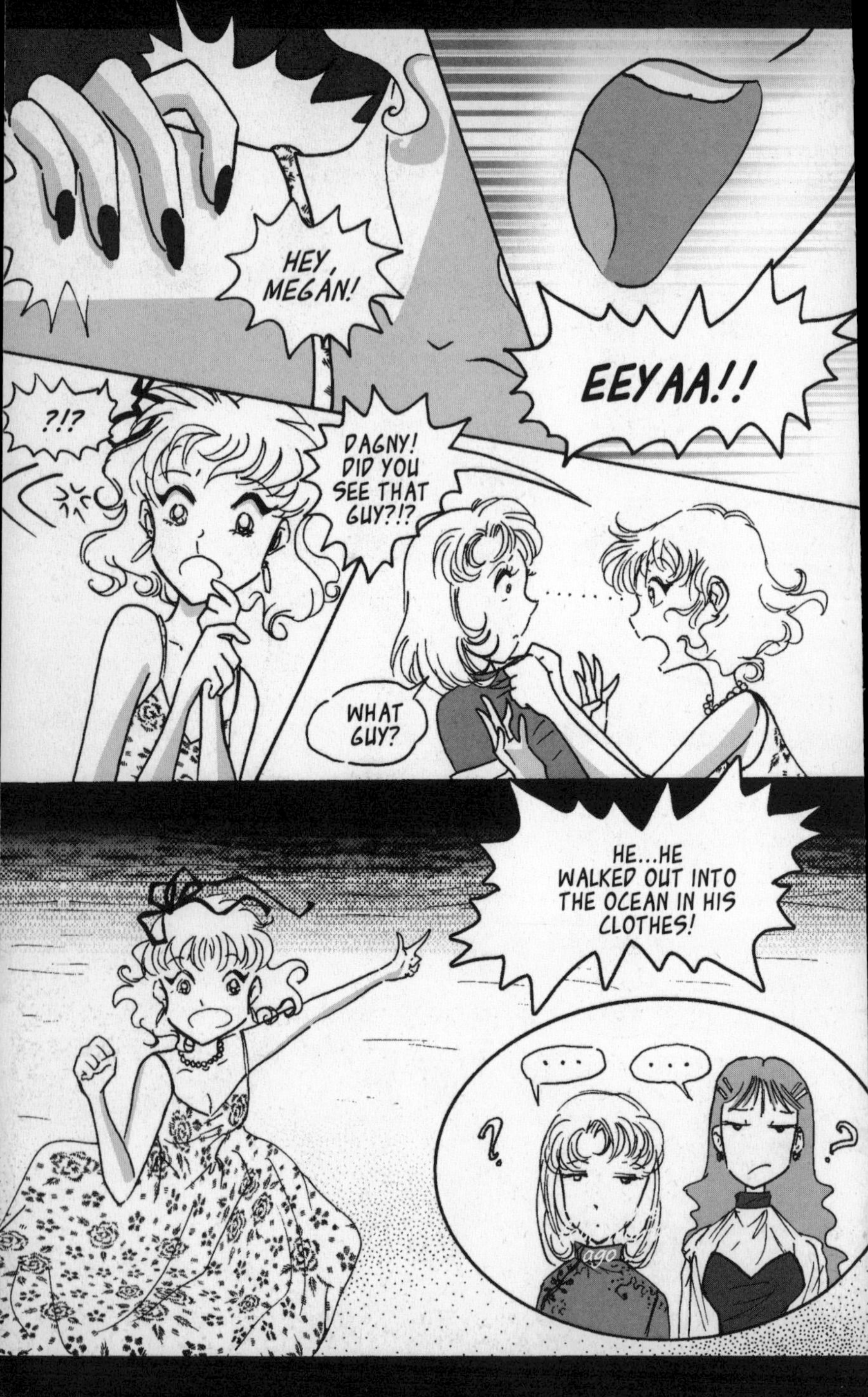
HEY, MEGAN!
EEYAA!!
?!?
DAGNY! DID YOU SEE THAT GUY?!?
......
WHAT GUY?
HE...HE WALKED OUT INTO THE OCEAN IN HIS CLOTHES!
...
...
?
?

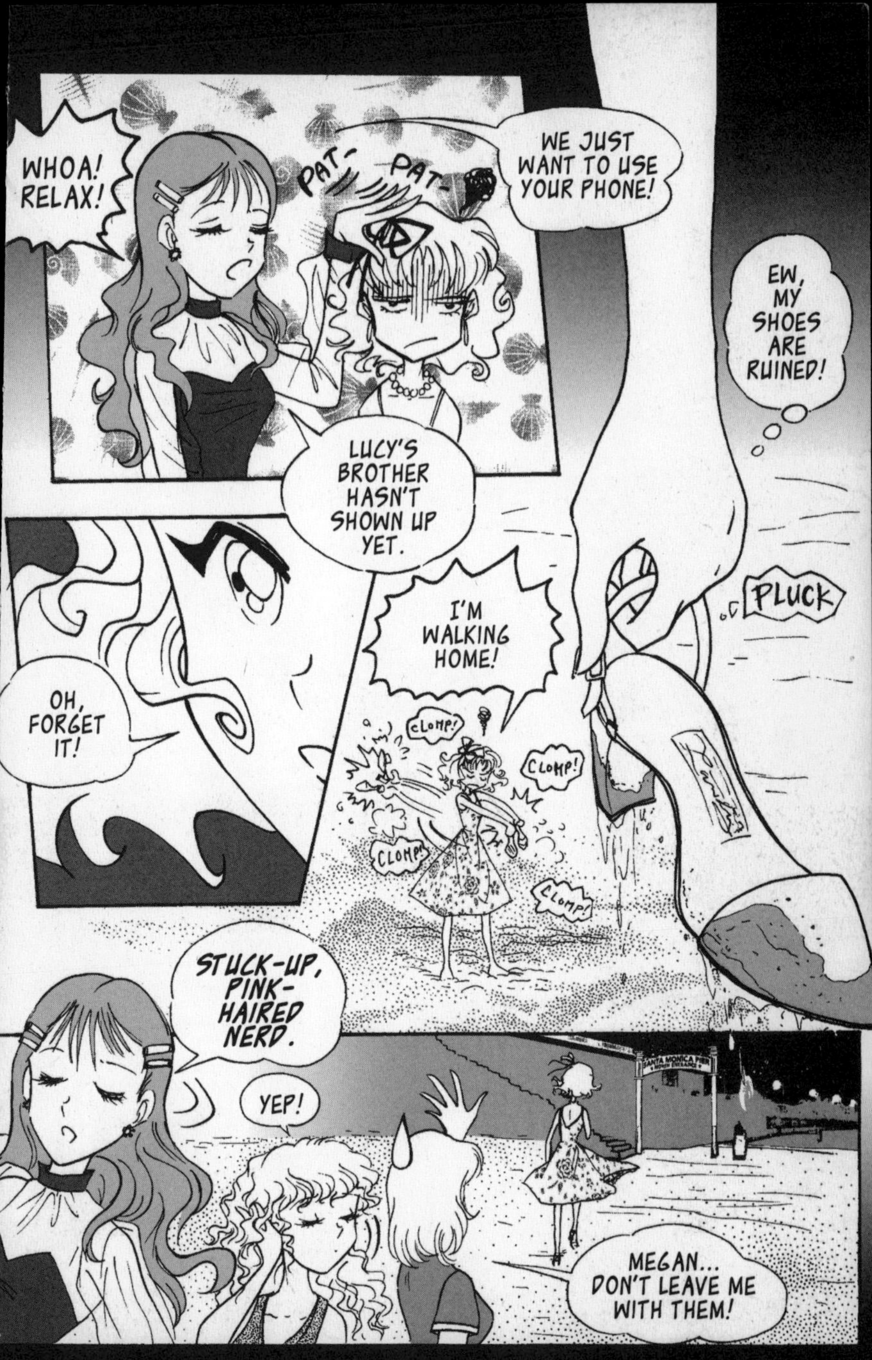
WHOA! RELAX!
PAT- PAT-
WE JUST WANT TO USE YOUR PHONE!
LUCY'S BROTHER HASN'T SHOWN UP YET.
OH, FORGET IT!
EW, MY SHOES ARE RUINED!
PLUCK
I'M WALKING HOME!
CLOMP!
CLOMP!
CLOMP!
CLOMP!
STUCK-UP, PINK-HAIRED NERD.
YEP!
SANTA MONICA PIER
MEGAN... DON'T LEAVE ME WITH THEM!

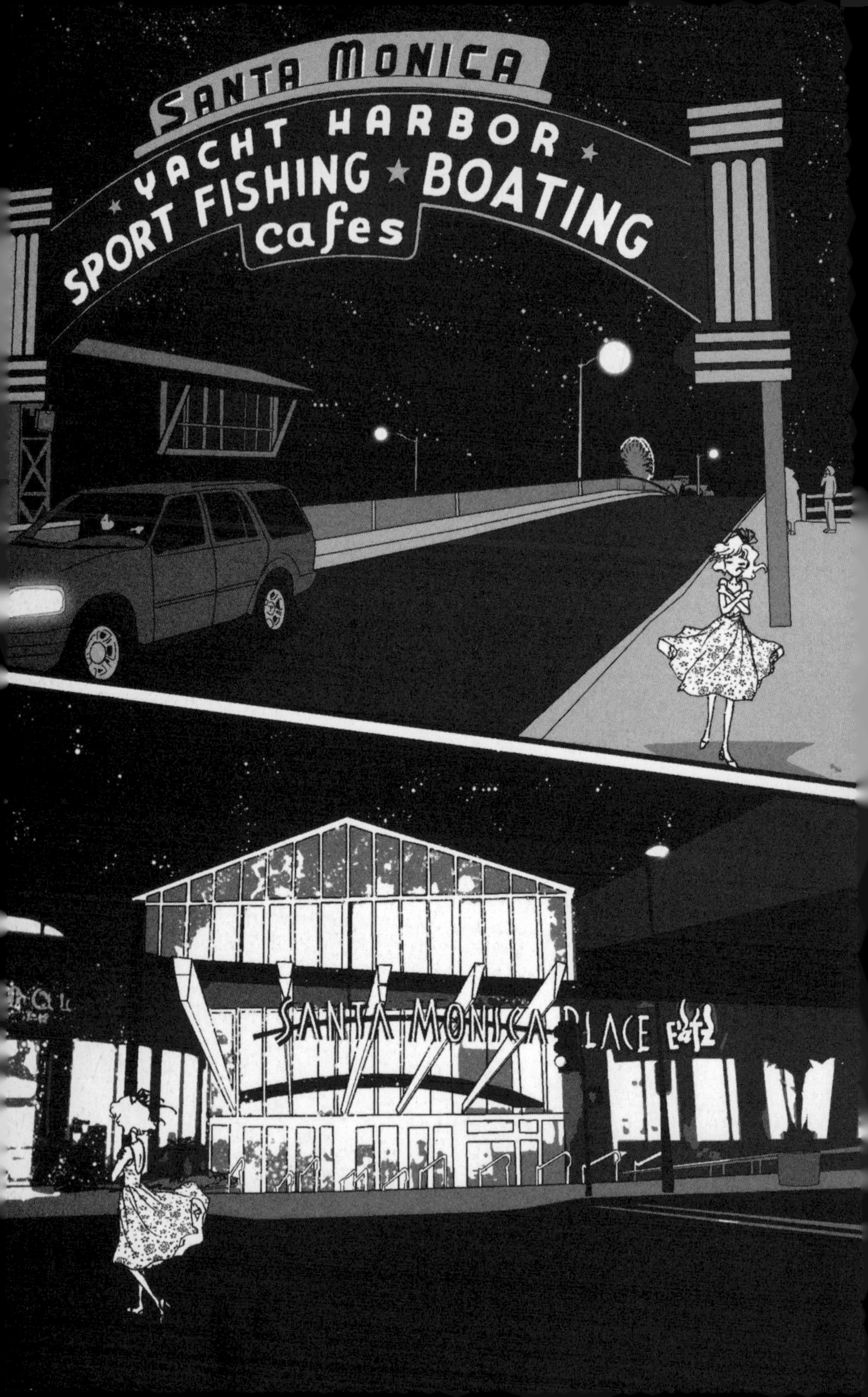
SANTA MONICA
YACHT HARBOR
SPORT FISHING
BOATING
cafes
SANTA MONICA

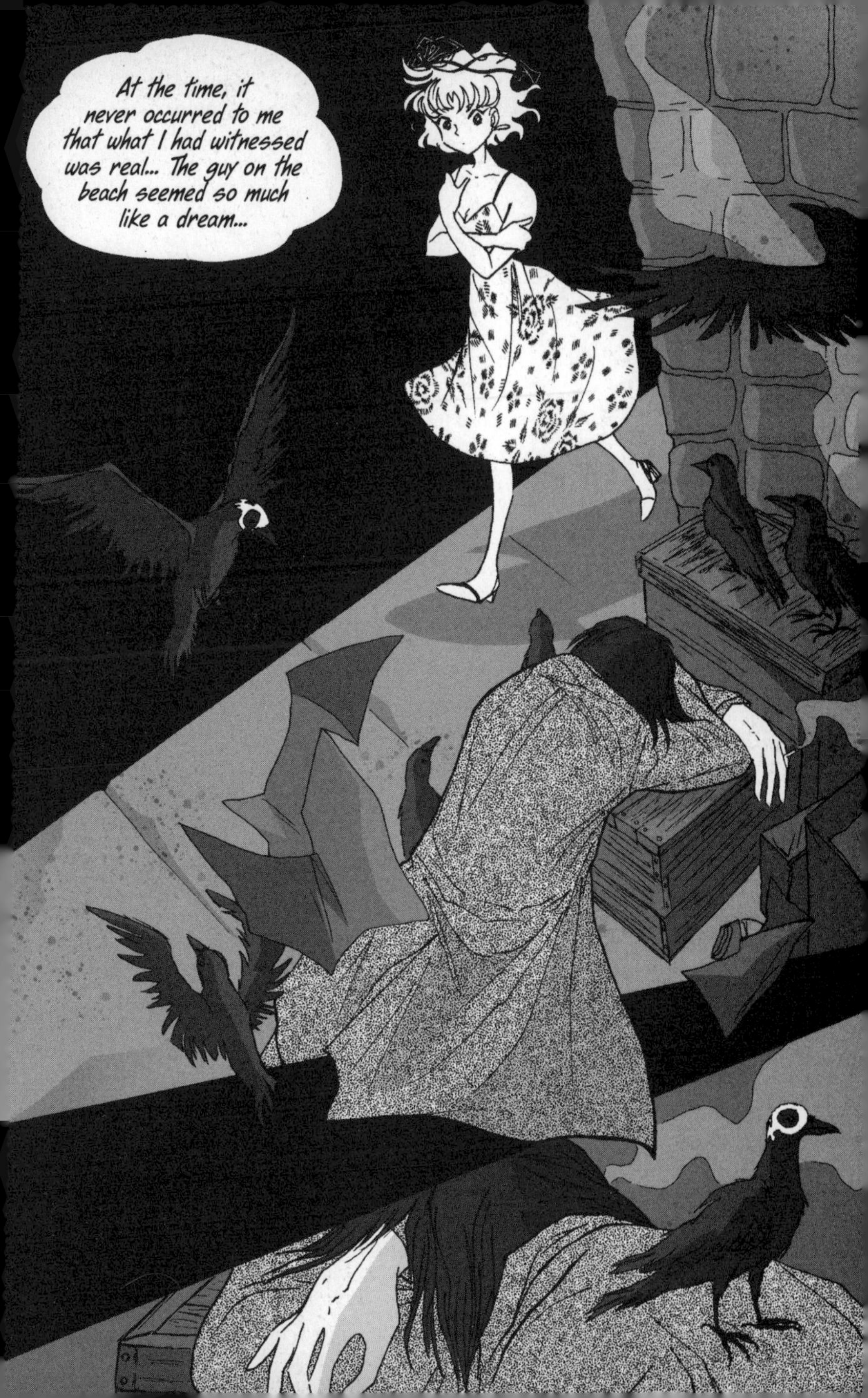
At the time, it never occurred to me that what I had witnessed was real... The guy on the beach seemed so much like a dream...

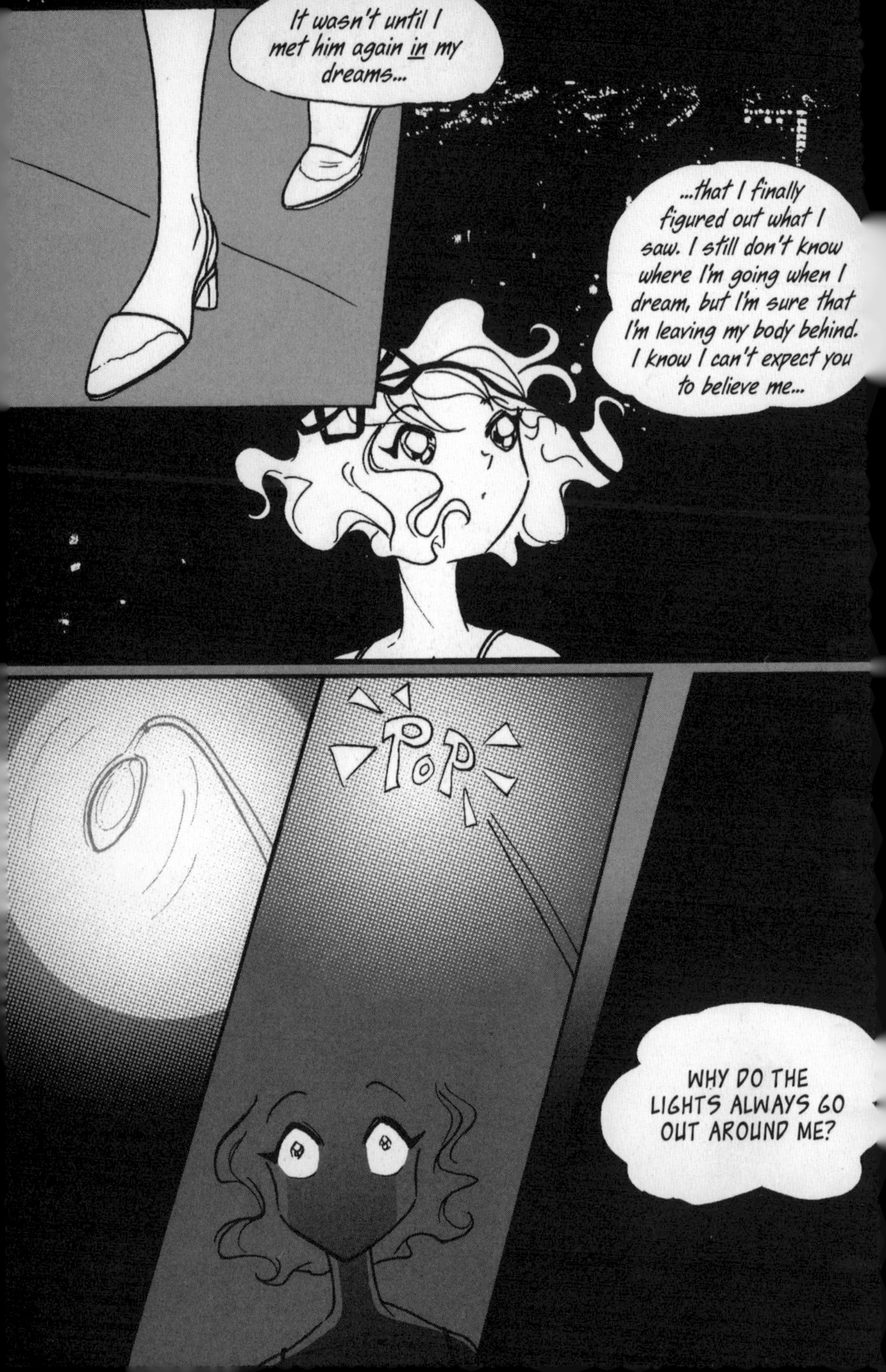
It wasn't until I met him again in my dreams...
...that I finally figured out what I saw. I still don't know where I'm going when I dream, but I'm sure that I'm leaving my body behind. I know I can't expect you to believe me...
POP
WHY DO THE LIGHTS ALWAYS GO OUT AROUND ME?

Chapter Two:

it is Quixotic

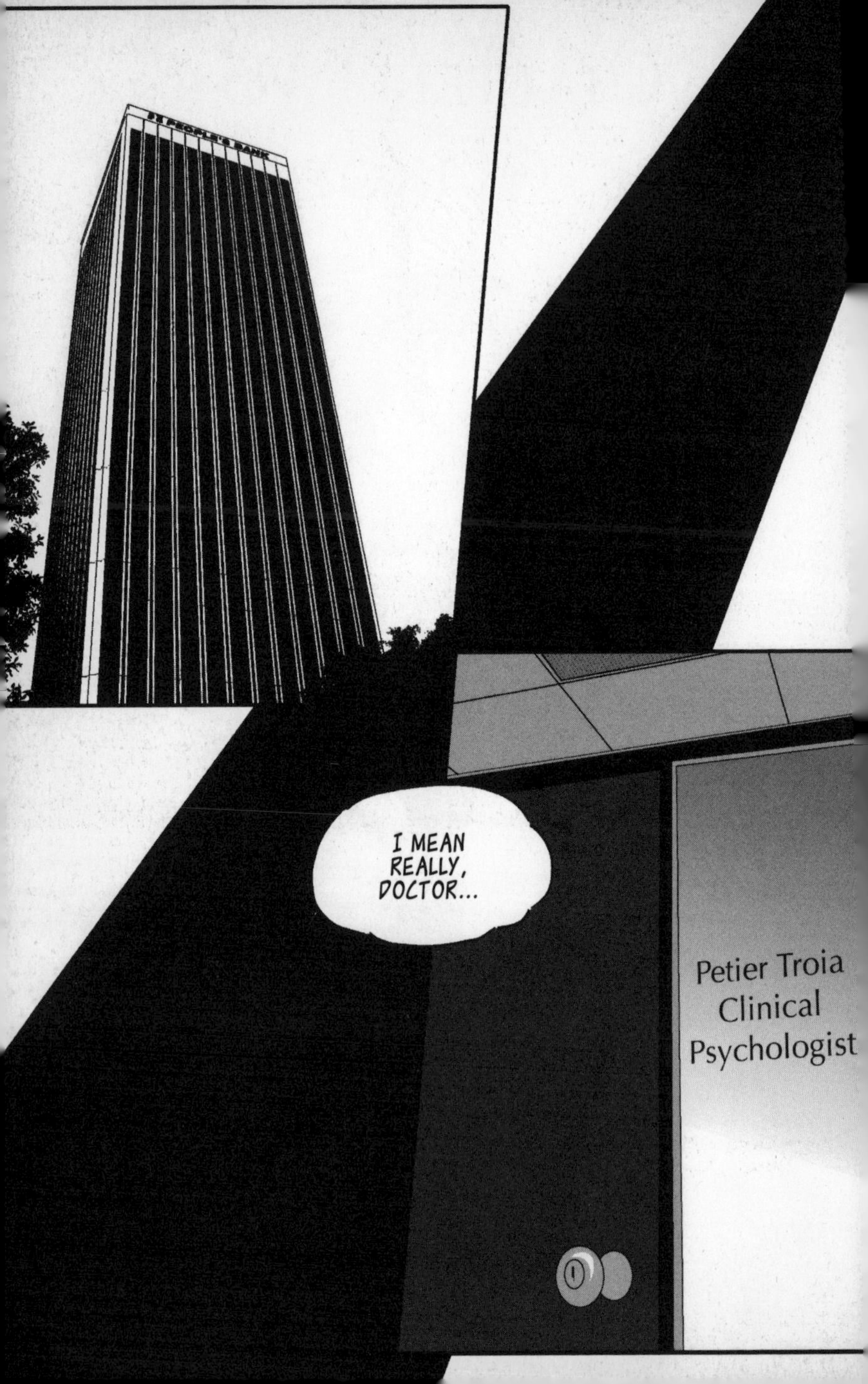
PEOPLE'S BANK
I MEAN REALLY, DOCTOR...
Petier Troia
Clinical
Psychologist

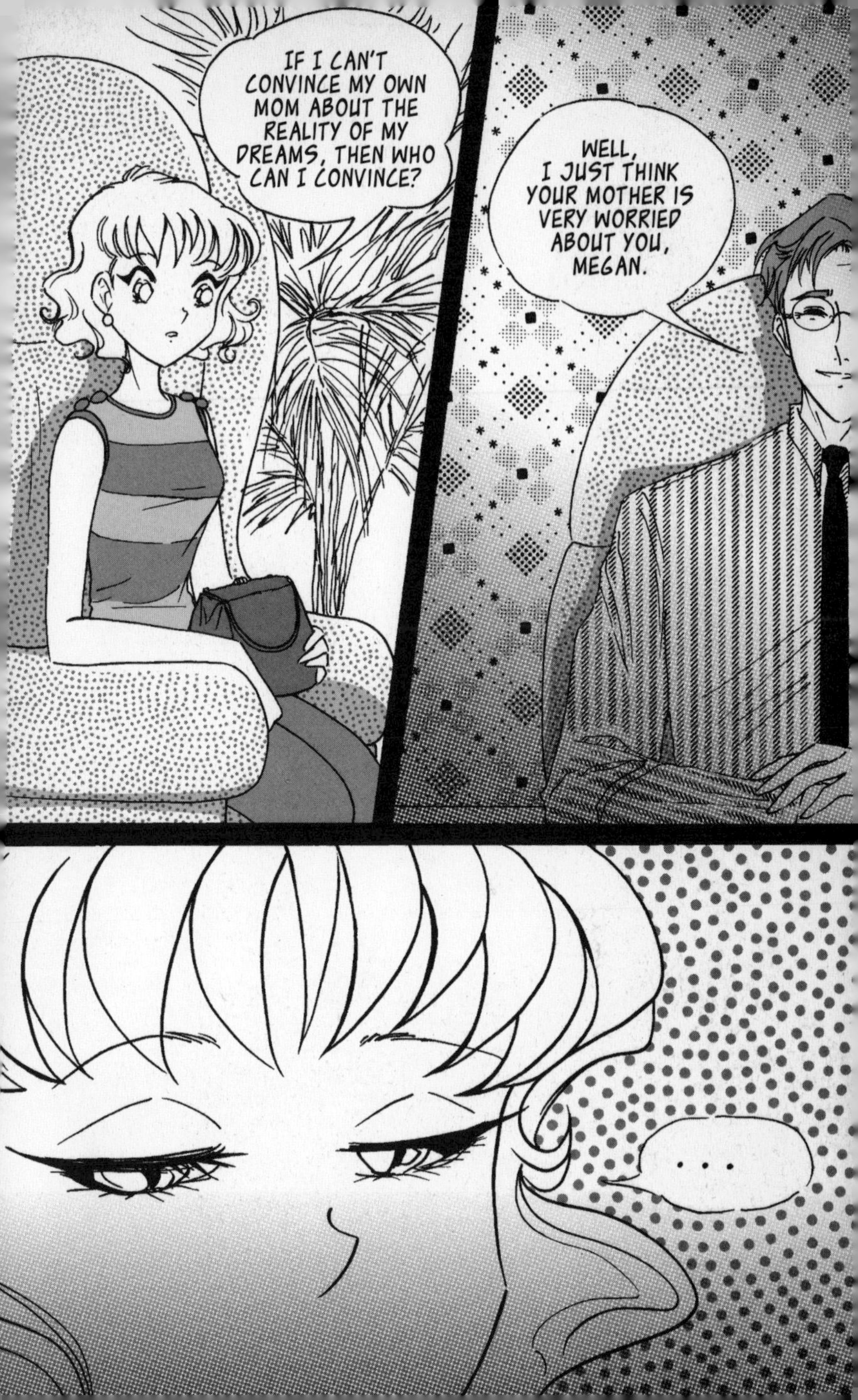
IF I CAN'T CONVINCE MY OWN MOM ABOUT THE REALITY OF MY DREAMS, THEN WHO CAN I CONVINCE?
WELL, I JUST THINK YOUR MOTHER IS VERY WORRIED ABOUT YOU, MEGAN.
...

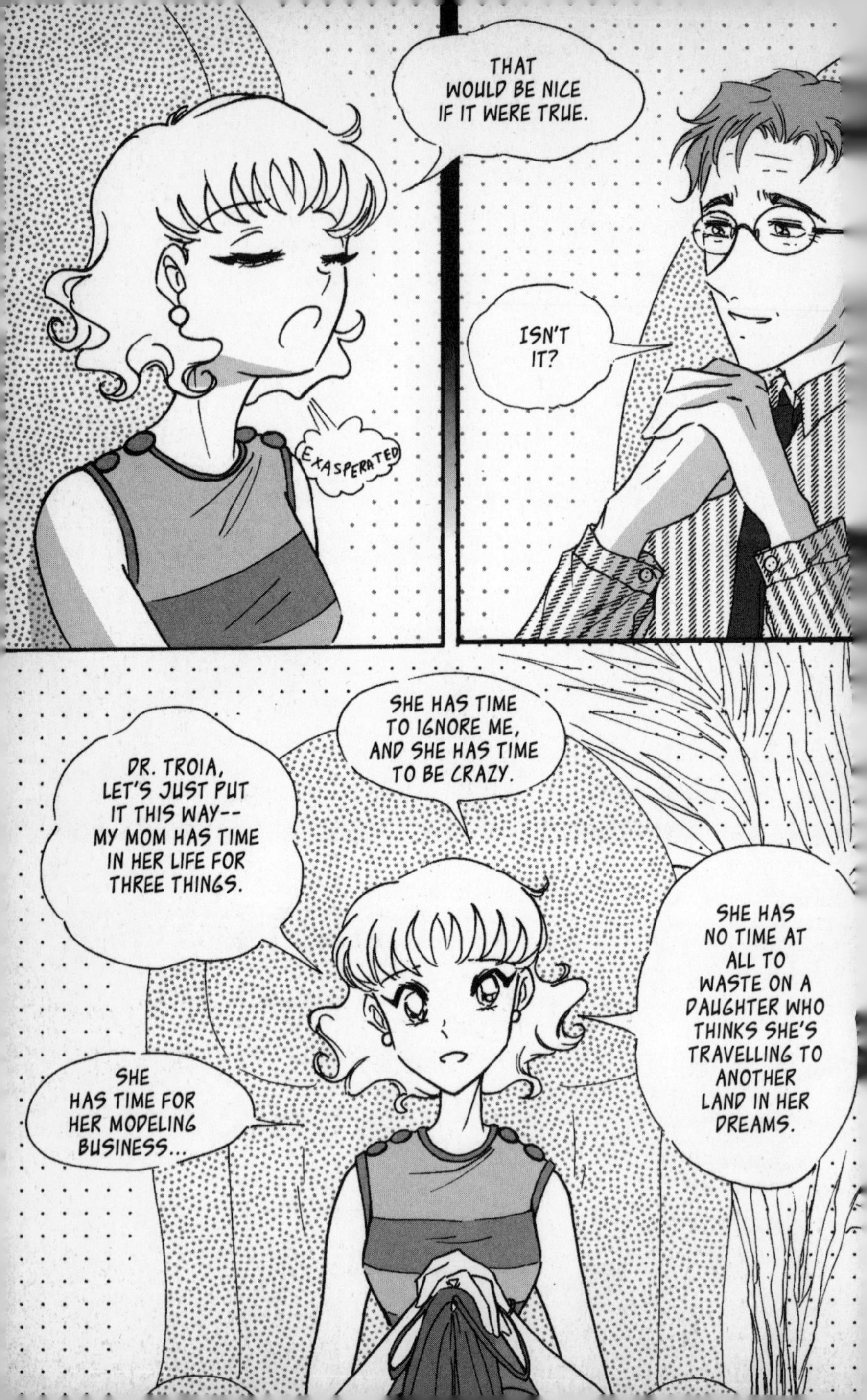
THAT WOULD BE NICE IF IT WERE TRUE.
EXASPERATED
ISN'T IT?
DR. TROIA, LET'S JUST PUT IT THIS WAY-- MY MOM HAS TIME IN HER LIFE FOR THREE THINGS.
SHE HAS TIME FOR HER MODELING BUSINESS...
SHE HAS TIME TO IGNORE ME, AND SHE HAS TIME TO BE CRAZY.
SHE HAS NO TIME AT ALL TO WASTE ON A DAUGHTER WHO THINKS SHE'S TRAVELLING TO ANOTHER LAND IN HER DREAMS.

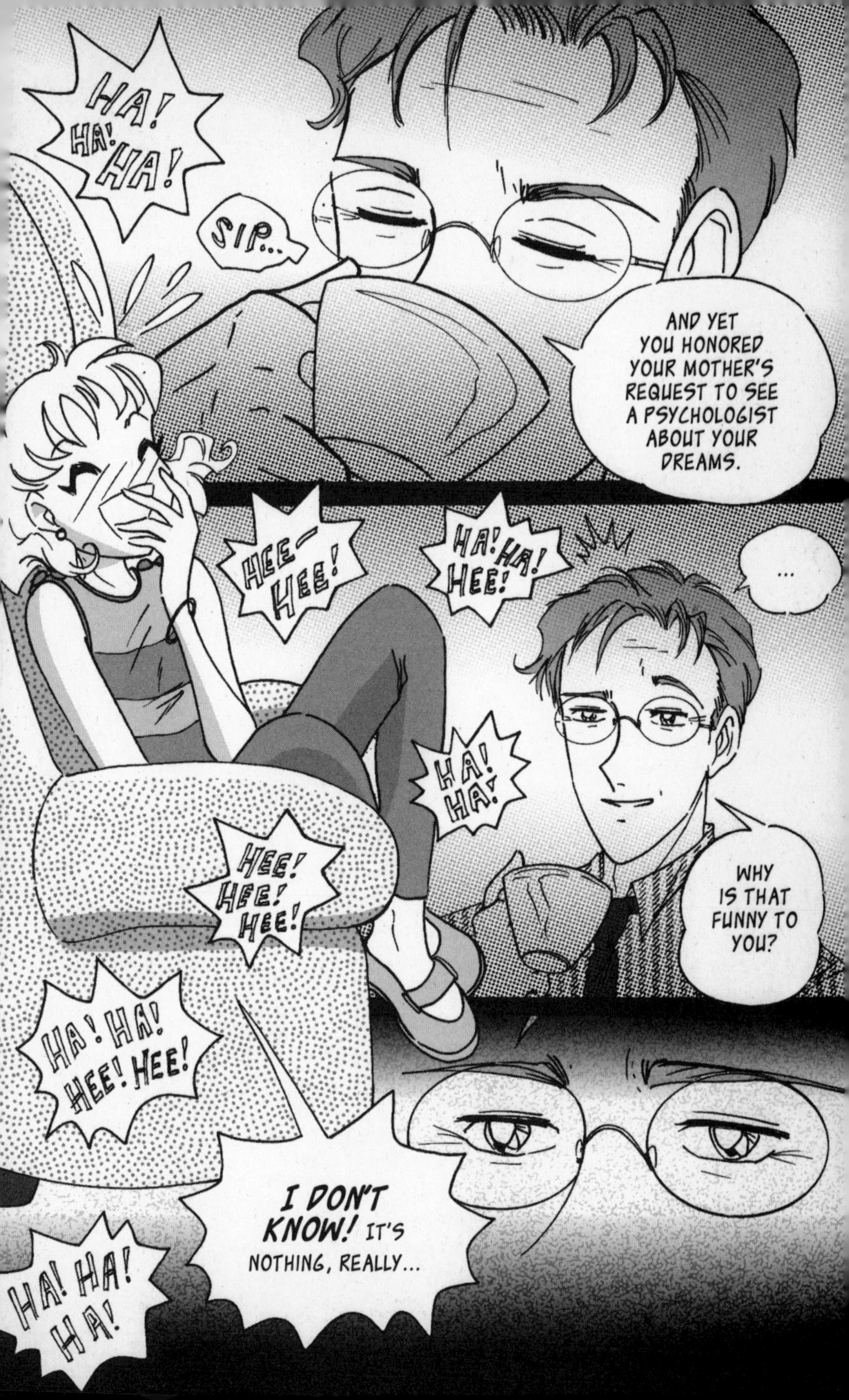
HA! HA! HA!
SIP...
AND YET YOU HONORED YOUR MOTHER'S REQUEST TO SEE A PSYCHOLOGIST ABOUT YOUR DREAMS.
HEE-HEE!
HA! HA! HEE!
...
HA! HA!
HEE! HEE! HEE!
WHY IS THAT FUNNY TO YOU?
HA! HA! HEE! HEE!
I DON'T KNOW! IT'S NOTHING, REALLY...
HA! HA! HA!

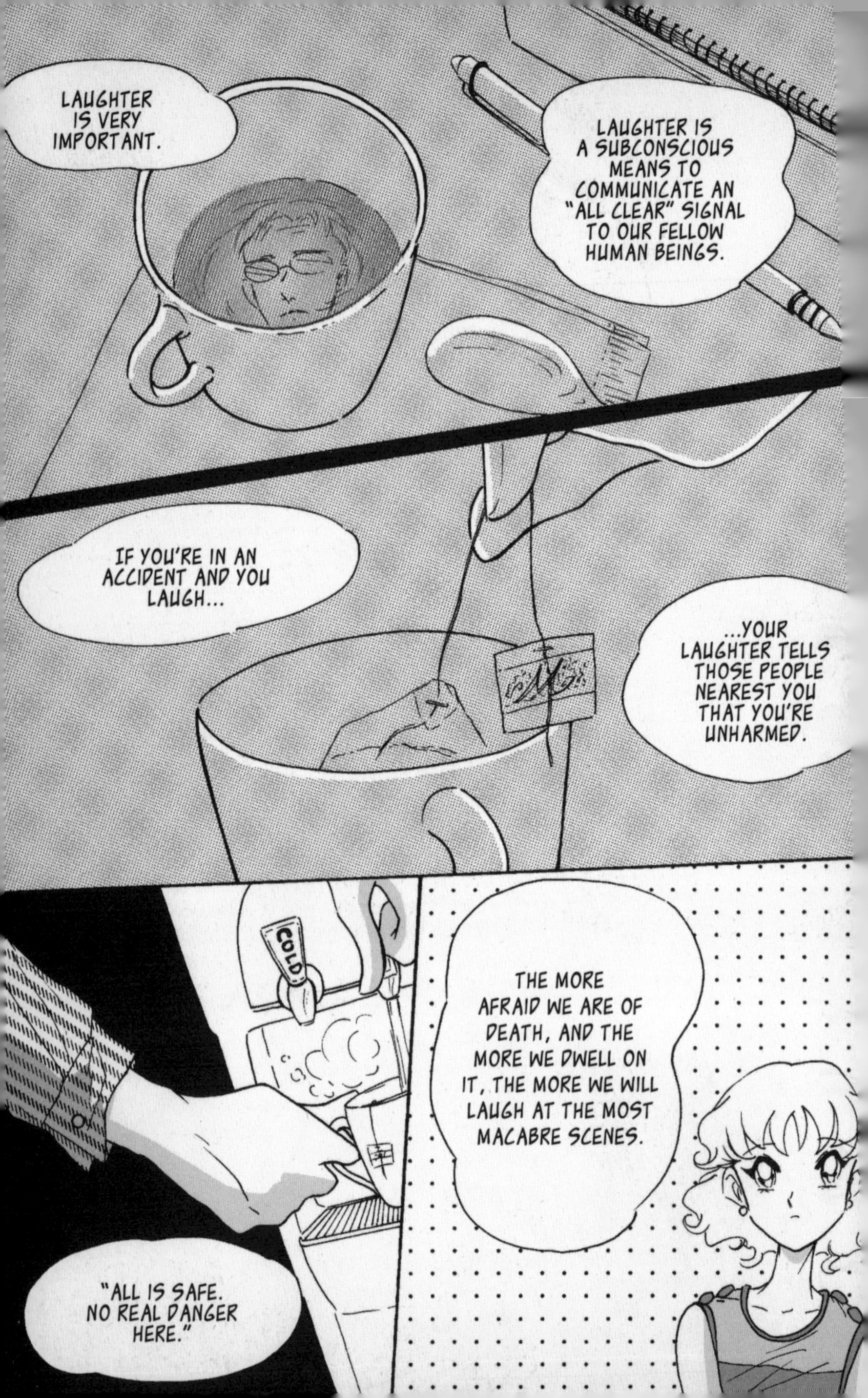
LAUGHTER IS VERY IMPORTANT.
LAUGHTER IS A SUBCONSCIOUS MEANS TO COMMUNICATE AN "ALL CLEAR" SIGNAL TO OUR FELLOW HUMAN BEINGS.
IF YOU'RE IN AN ACCIDENT AND YOU LAUGH...
...YOUR LAUGHTER TELLS THOSE PEOPLE NEAREST YOU THAT YOU'RE UNHARMED.
COLD
"ALL IS SAFE. NO REAL DANGER HERE."
THE MORE AFRAID WE ARE OF DEATH, AND THE MORE WE DWELL ON IT, THE MORE WE WILL LAUGH AT THE MOST MACABRE SCENES.

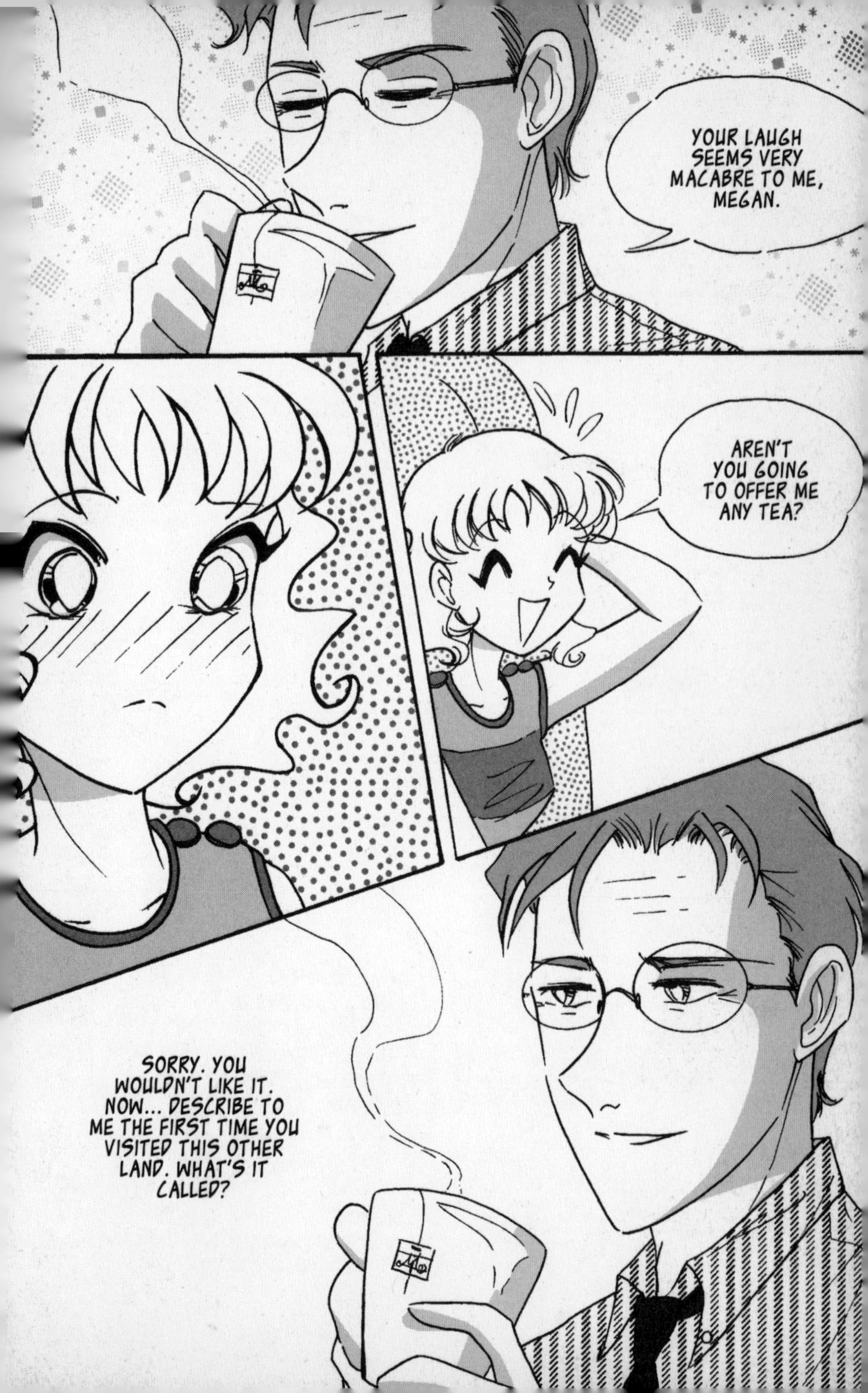
YOUR LAUGH SEEMS VERY MACABRE TO ME, MEGAN.
AREN'T YOU GOING TO OFFER ME ANY TEA?
SORRY. YOU WOULDN'T LIKE IT. NOW... DESCRIBE TO ME THE FIRST TIME YOU VISITED THIS OTHER LAND. WHAT'S IT CALLED?

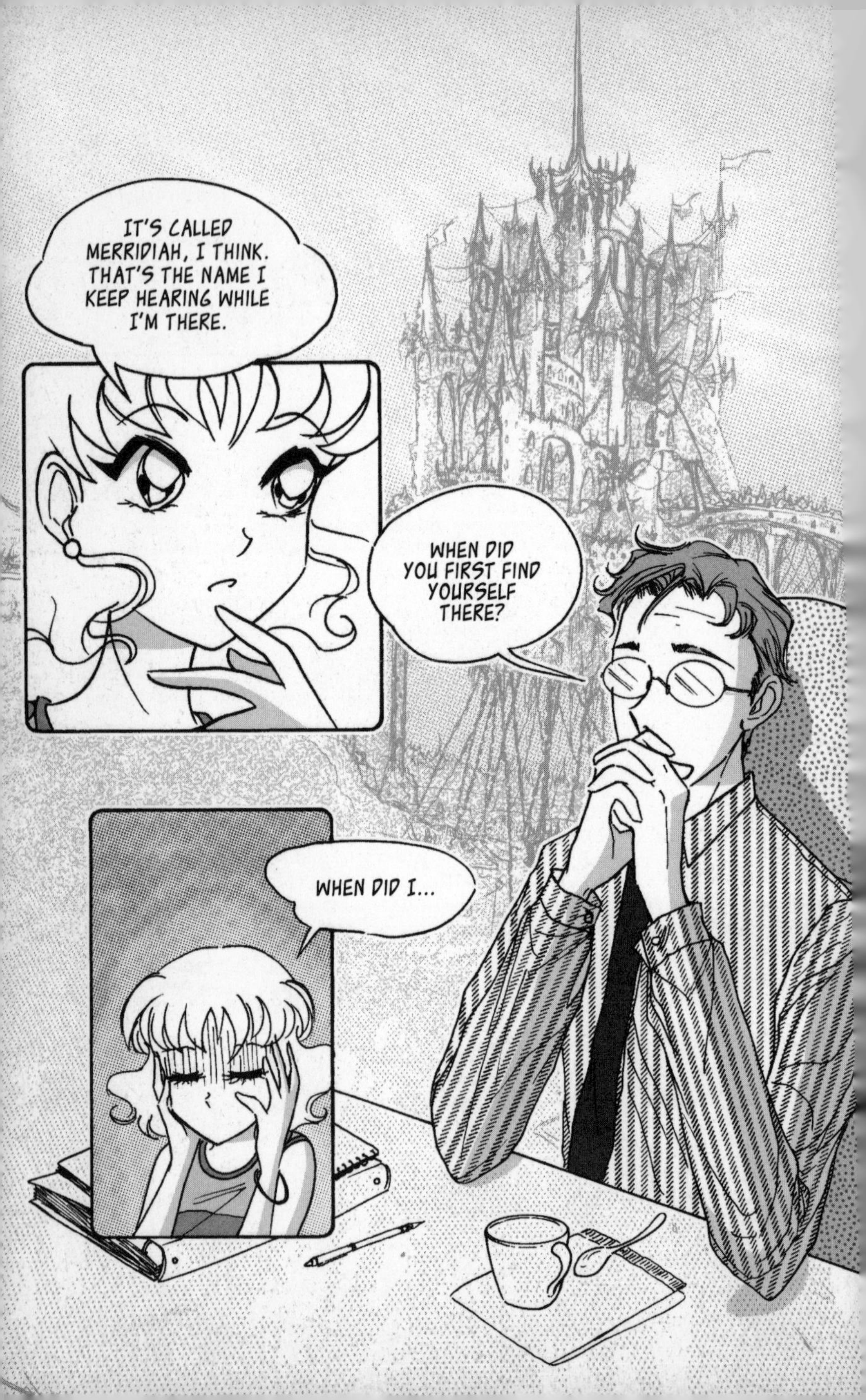
IT'S CALLED MERRIDIAH, I THINK. THAT'S THE NAME I KEEP HEARING WHILE I'M THERE.
WHEN DID YOU FIRST FIND YOURSELF THERE?
WHEN DID I...

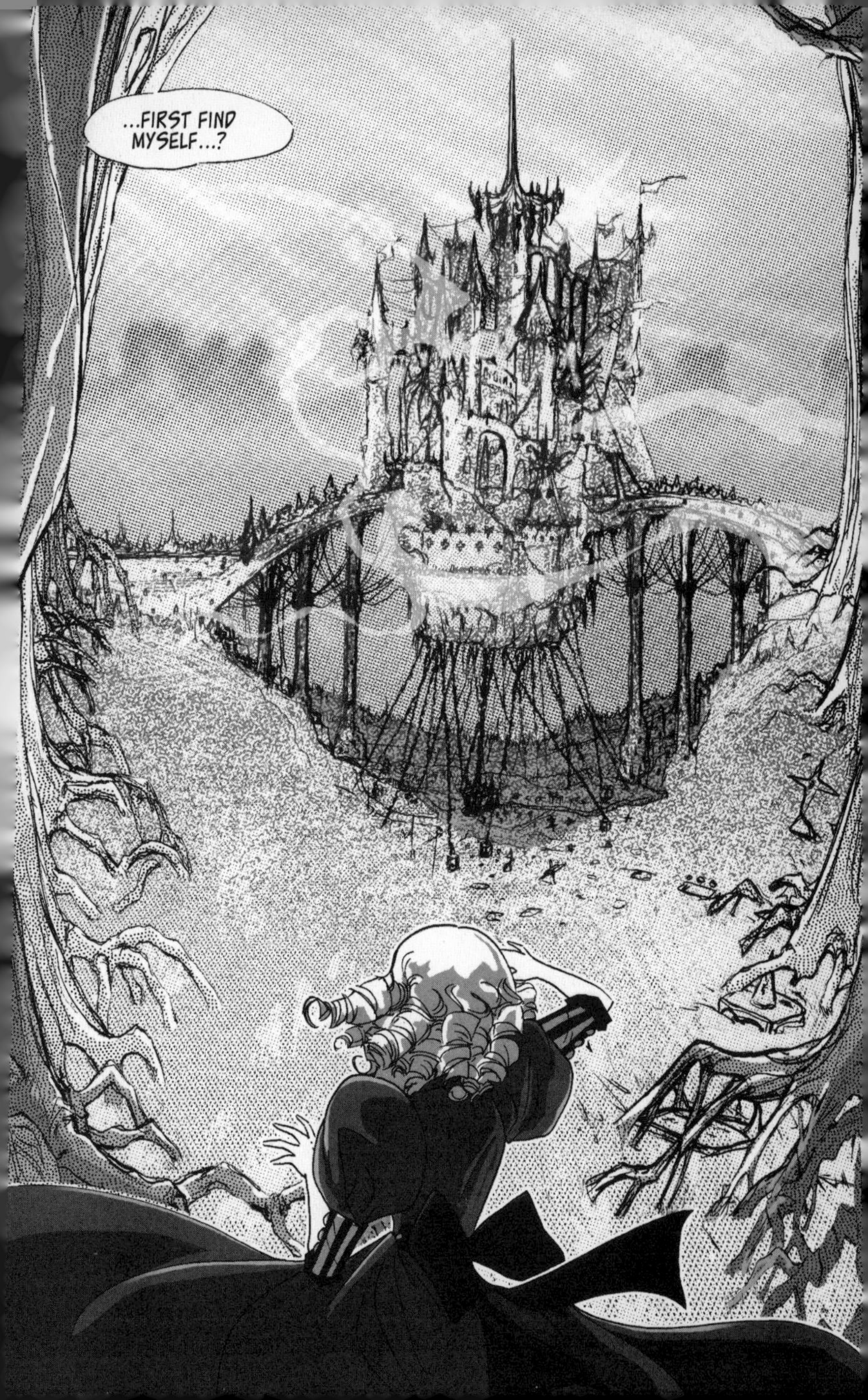
...FIRST FIND MYSELF...?

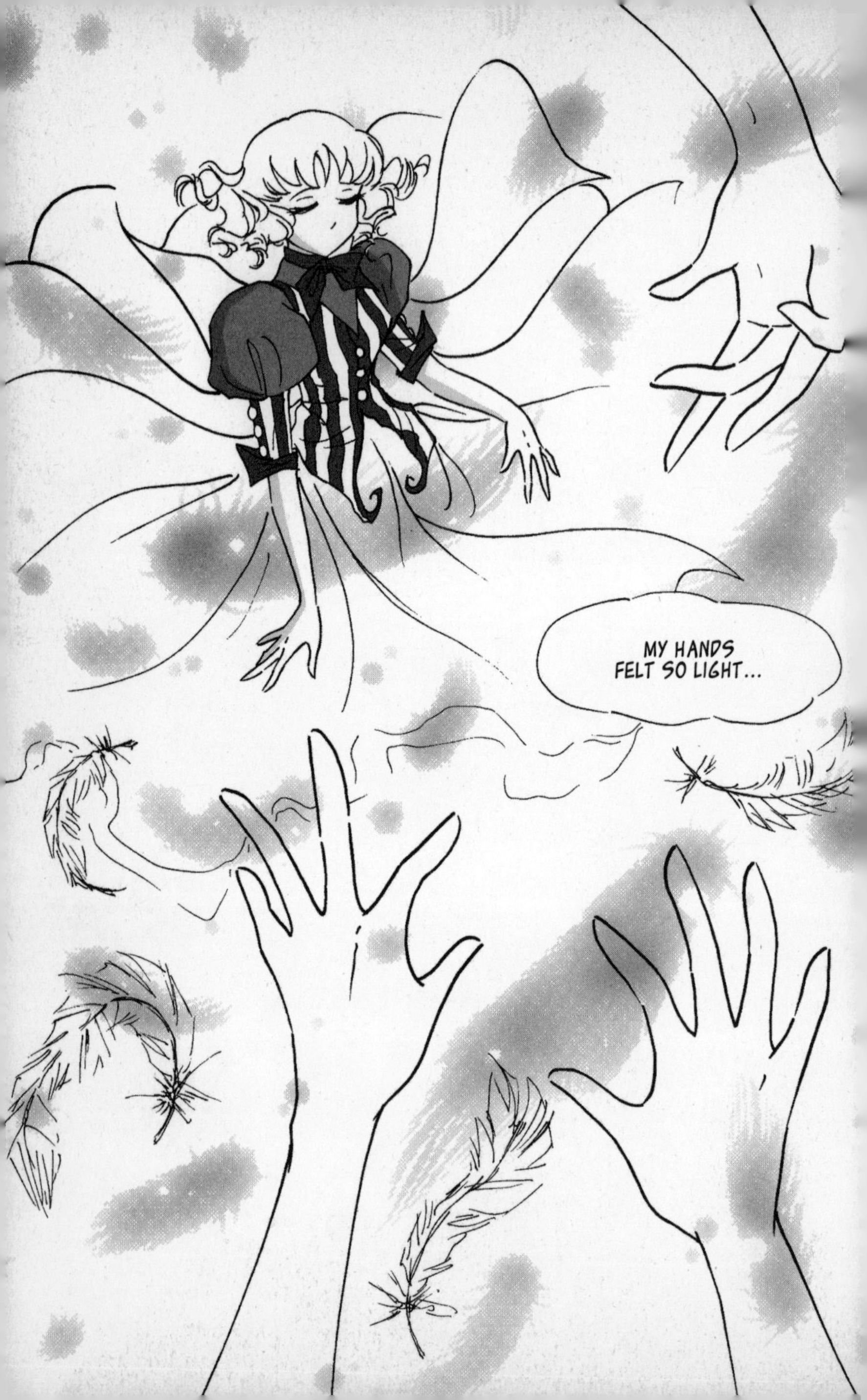
MY HANDS FELT SO LIGHT...

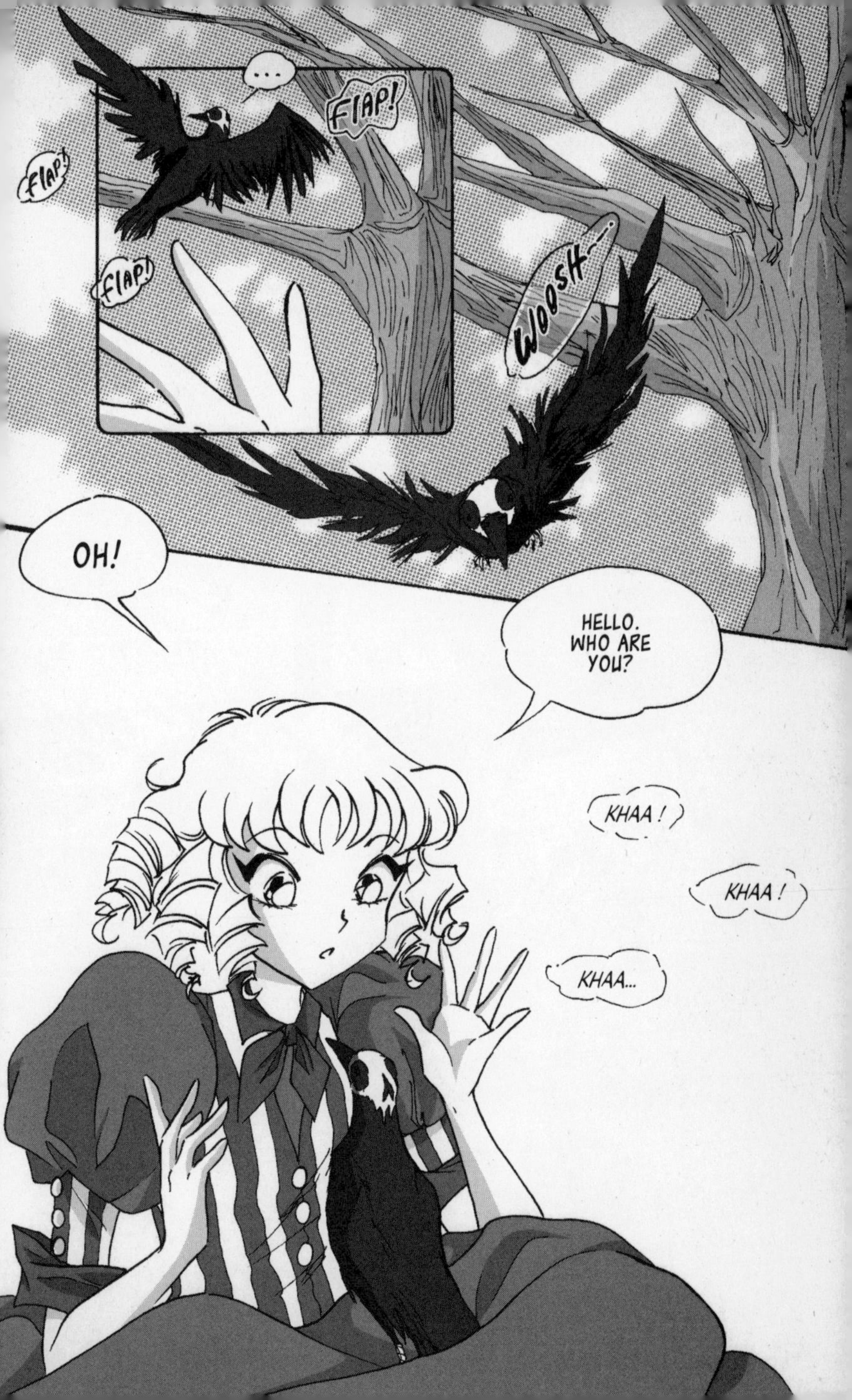
...
FLAP!
FLAP!
FLAP!
WOOSH
OH!
HELLO. WHO ARE YOU?
KHAA!
KHAA!
KHAA...

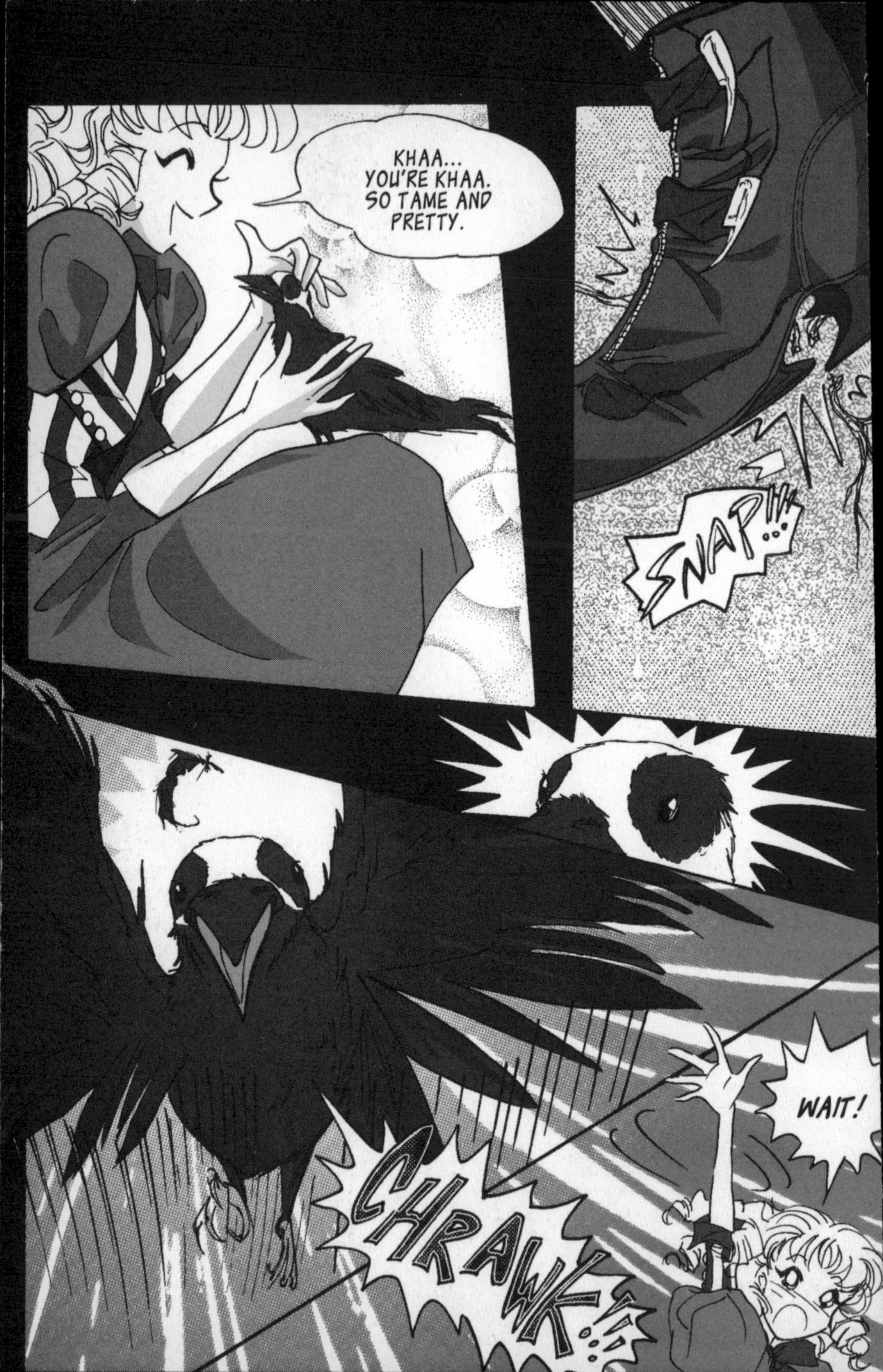
KHAA... YOU'RE KHAA. SO TAME AND PRETTY.
SNAP!!...
WAIT!
CHRAWK!!...

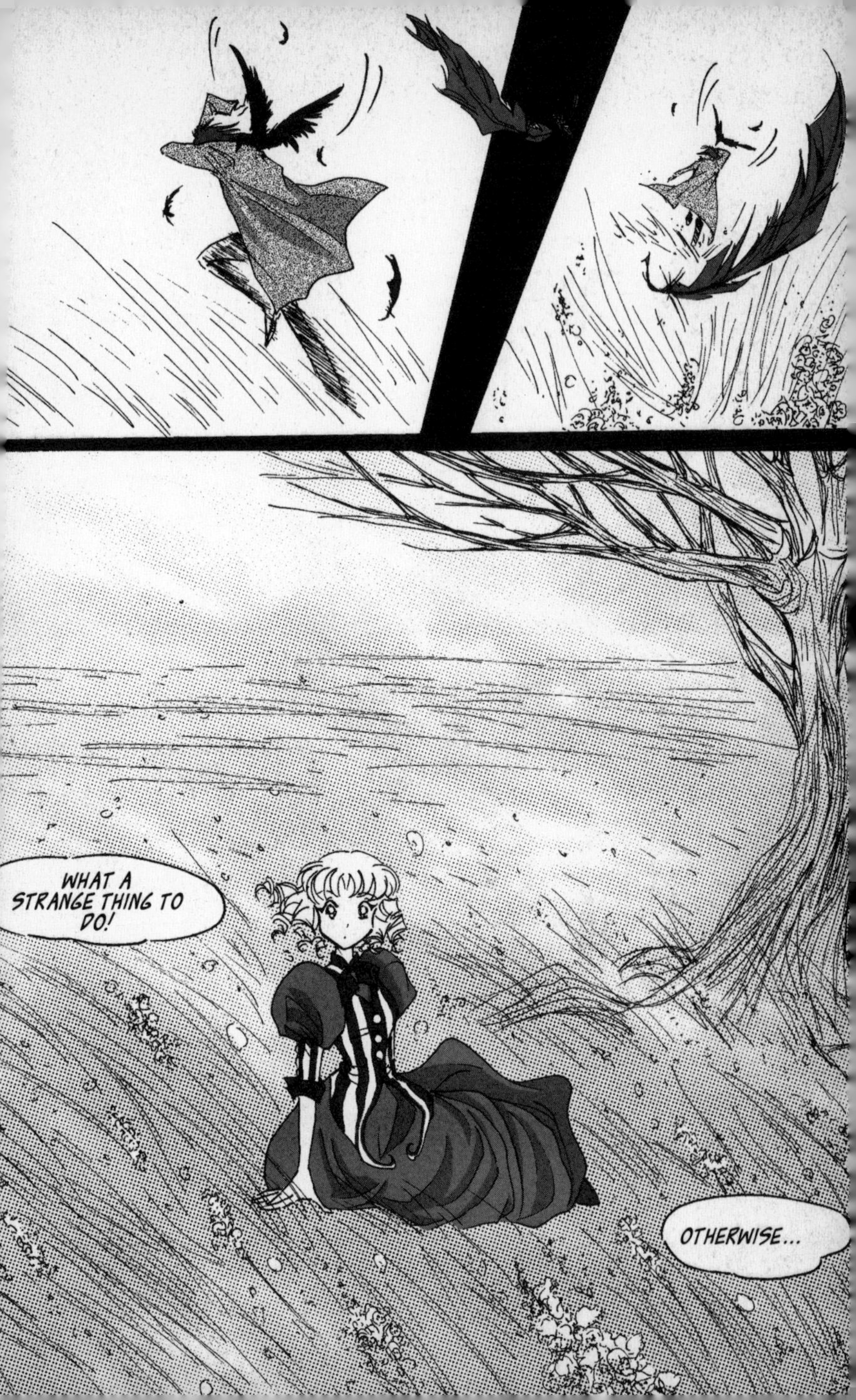
WHAT A STRANGE THING TO DO!
OTHERWISE...

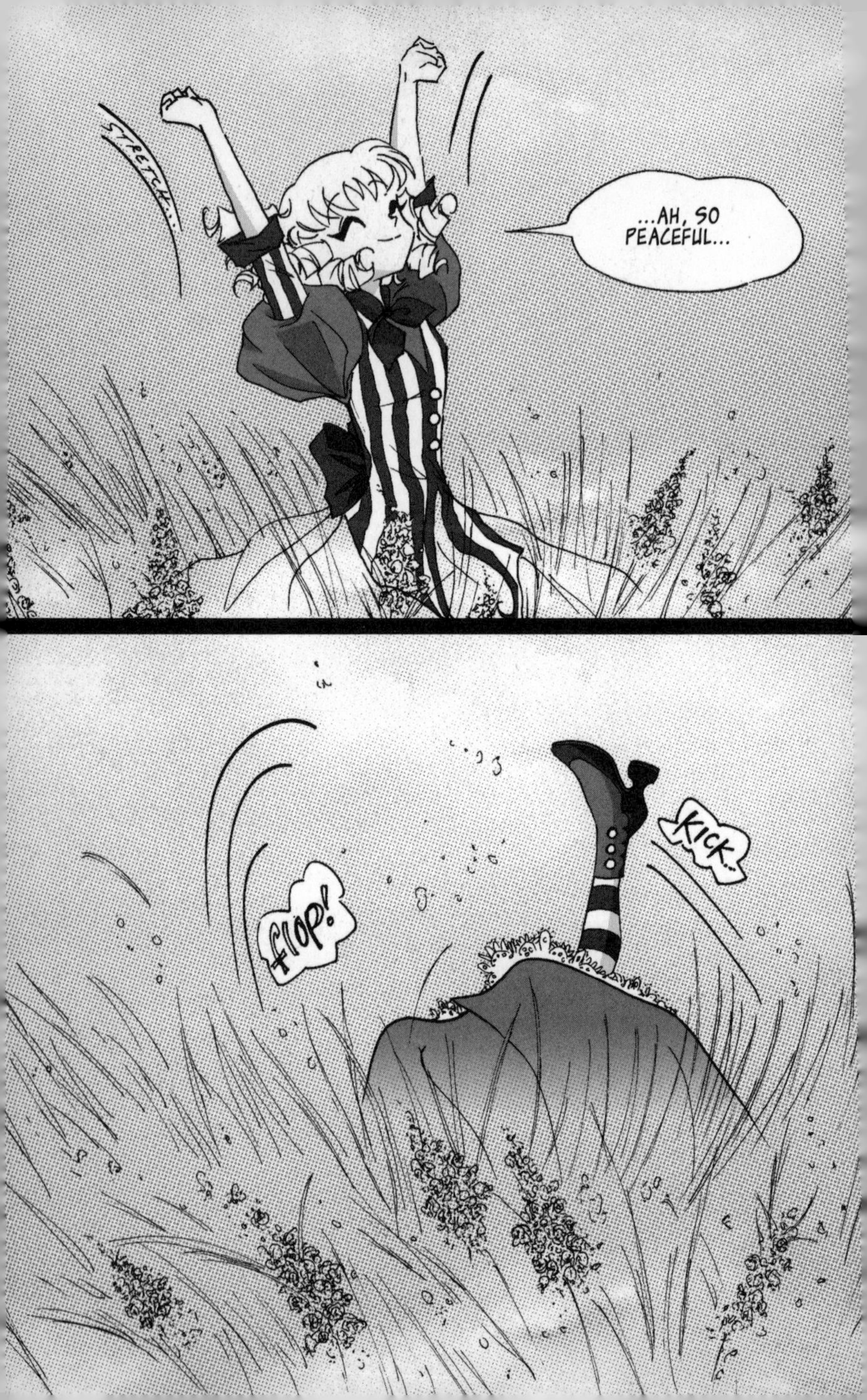
STRETCH...
...AH, SO PEACEFUL...
FLOP!
KICK...

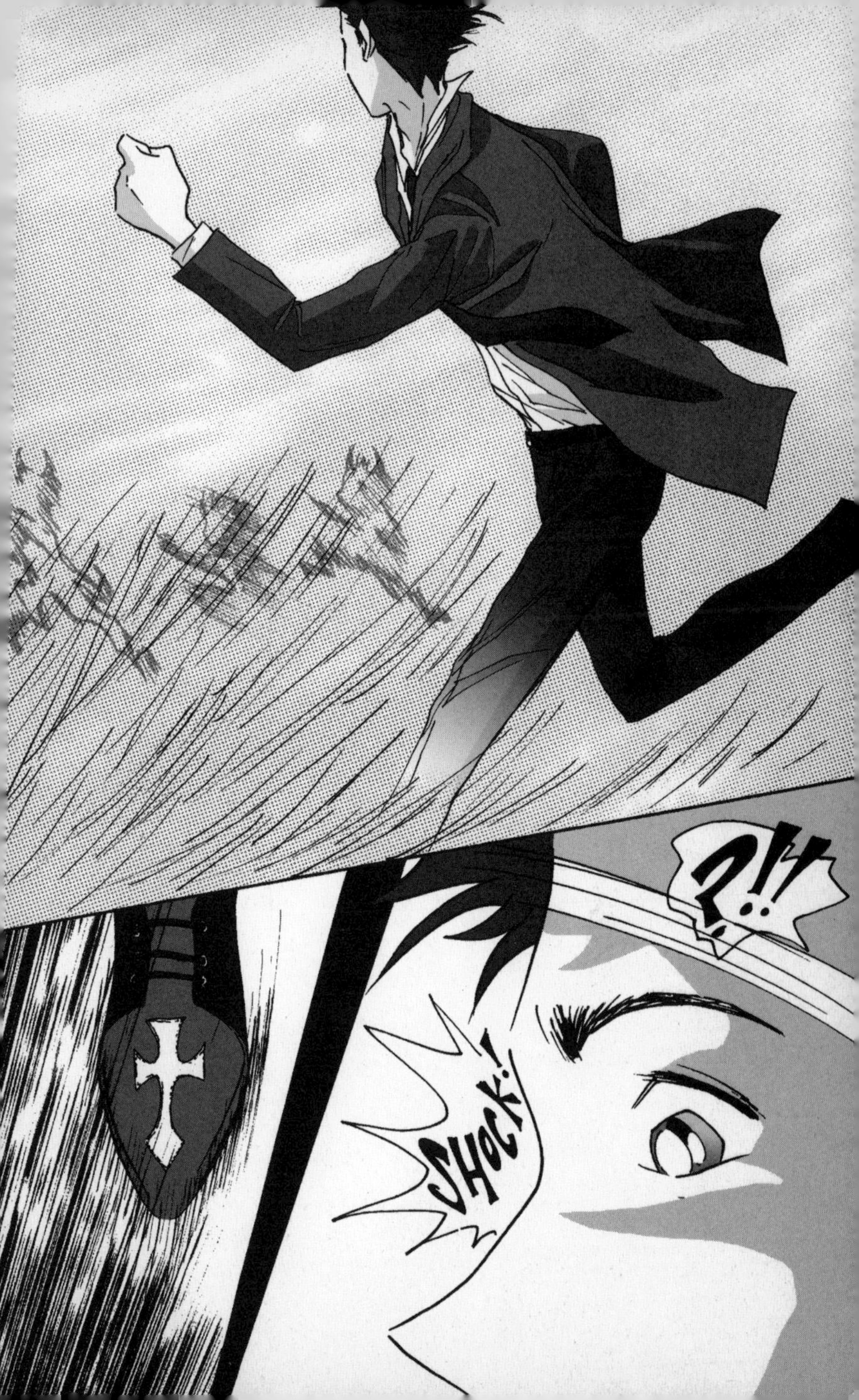
?!!
SHOCK!

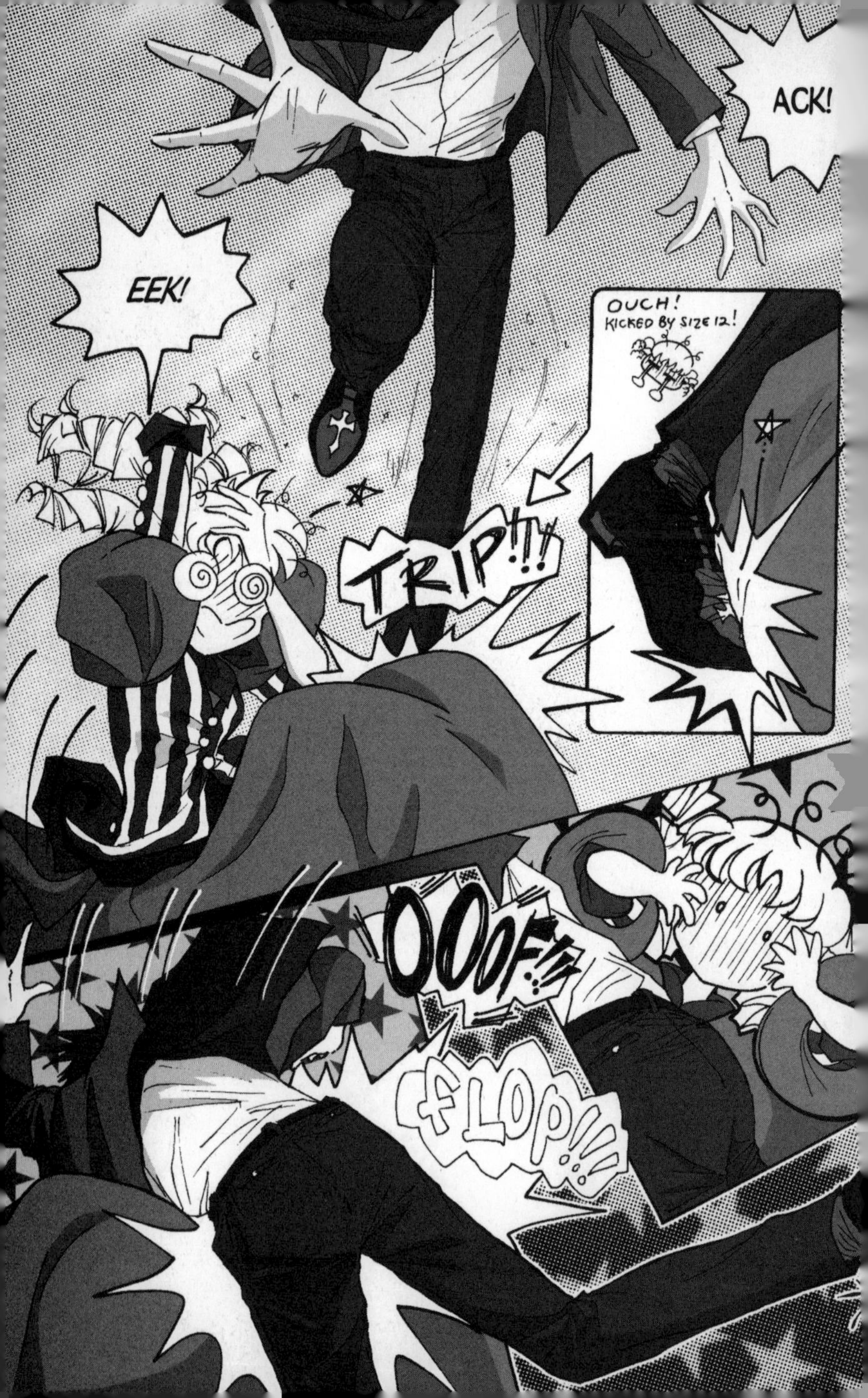
ACK!
EEK!
OUCH!
KICKED BY SIZE 12!
TRIP!!!
OOOF!!!
FLOP!!!

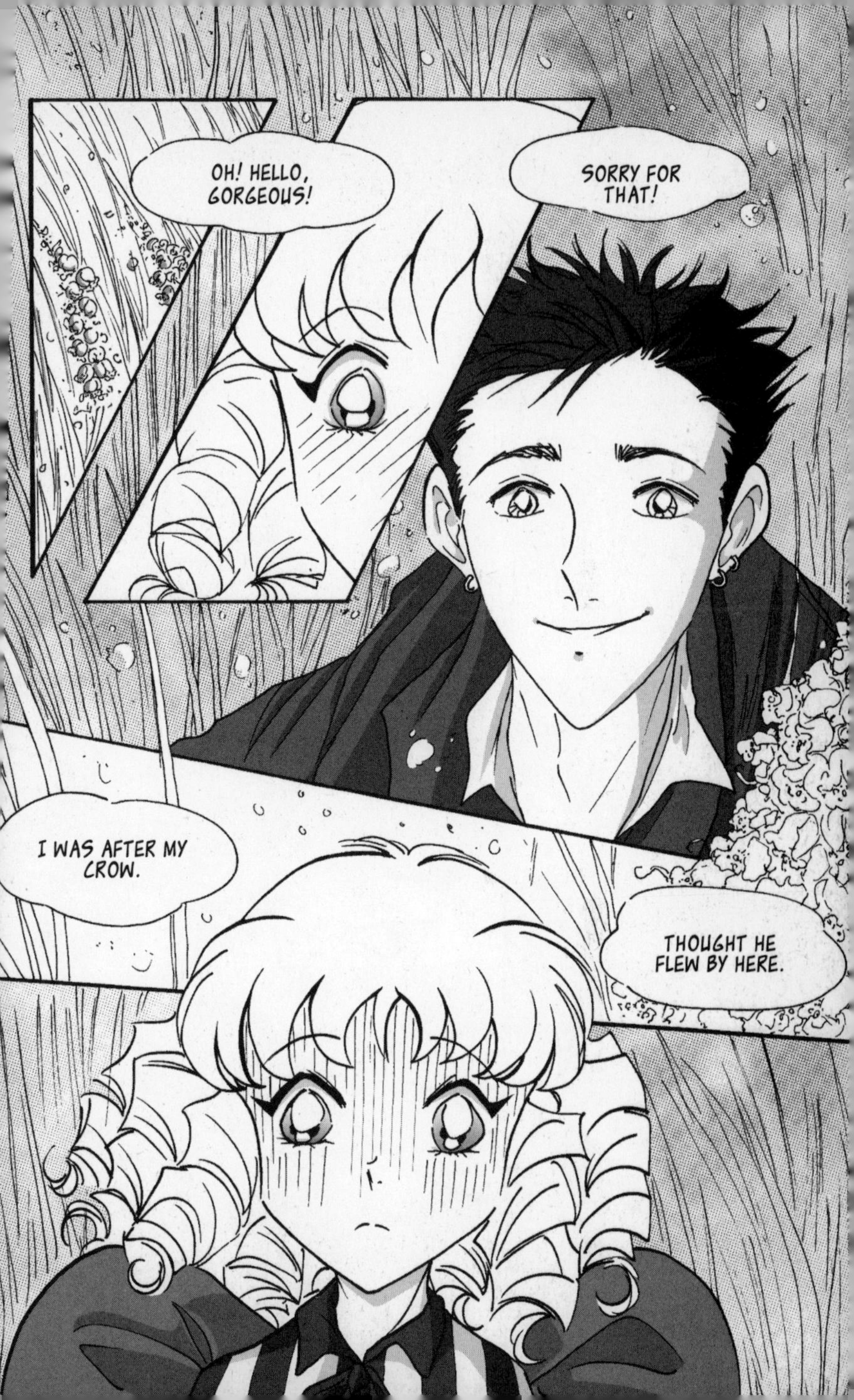
OH! HELLO, GORGEOUS!
SORRY FOR THAT!
I WAS AFTER MY CROW.
THOUGHT HE FLEW BY HERE.

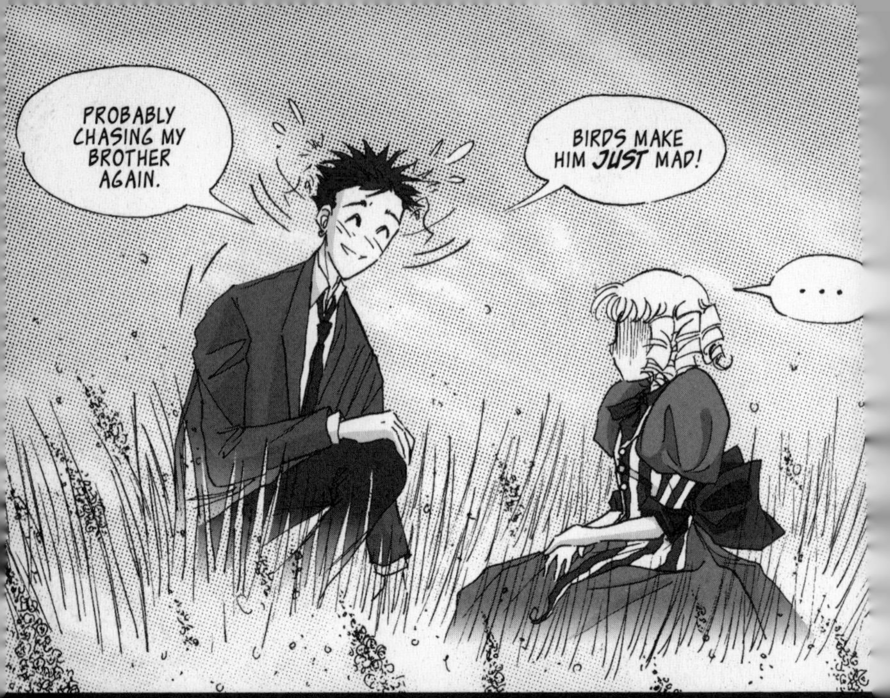
PROBABLY CHASING MY BROTHER AGAIN.
BIRDS MAKE HIM *JUST* MAD!
...
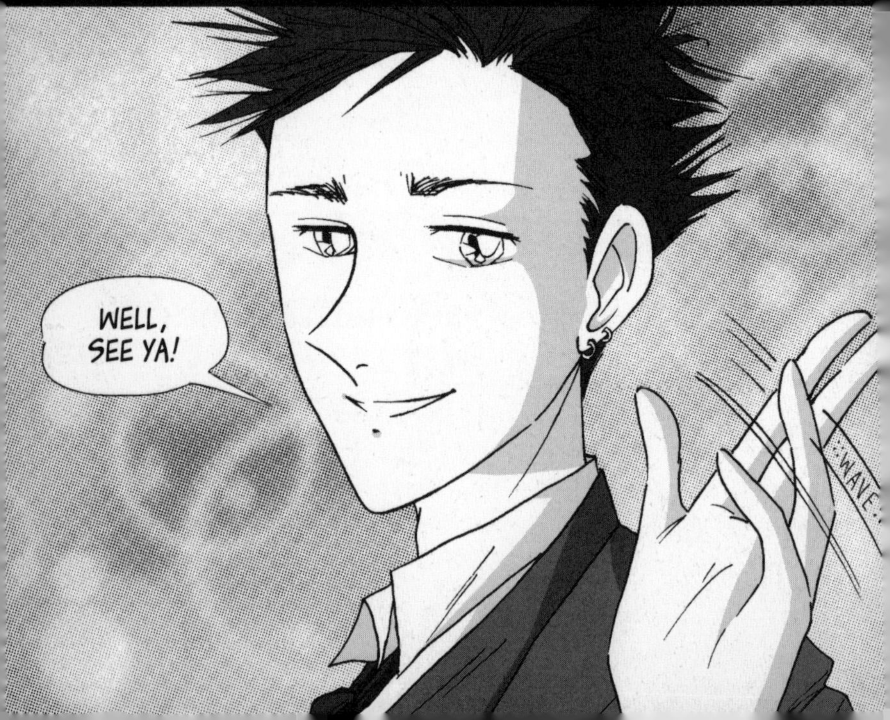
WELL, SEE YA!
::WAVE::

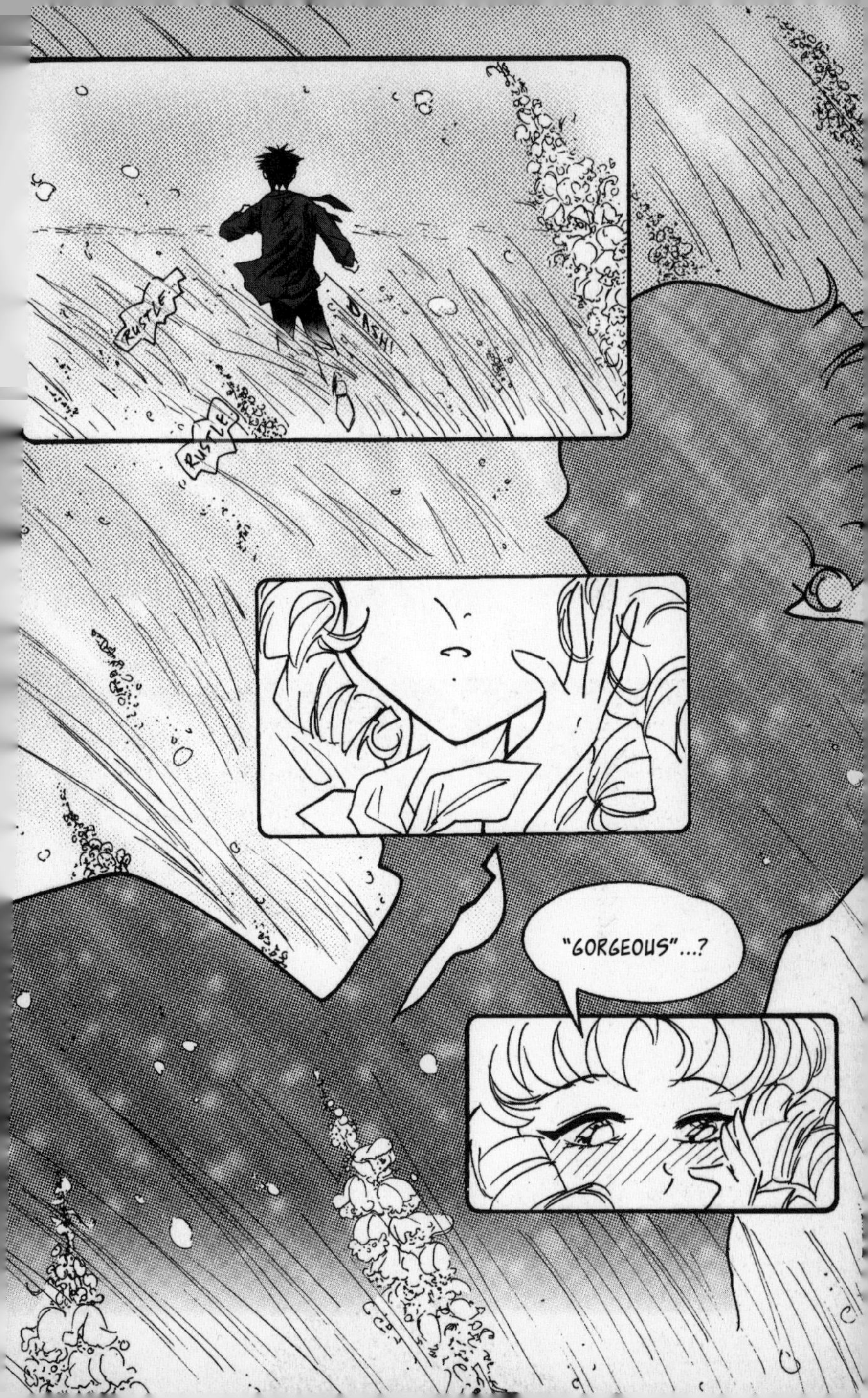
RUSTLE
DASH!
RUSTLE
"GORGEOUS"...?

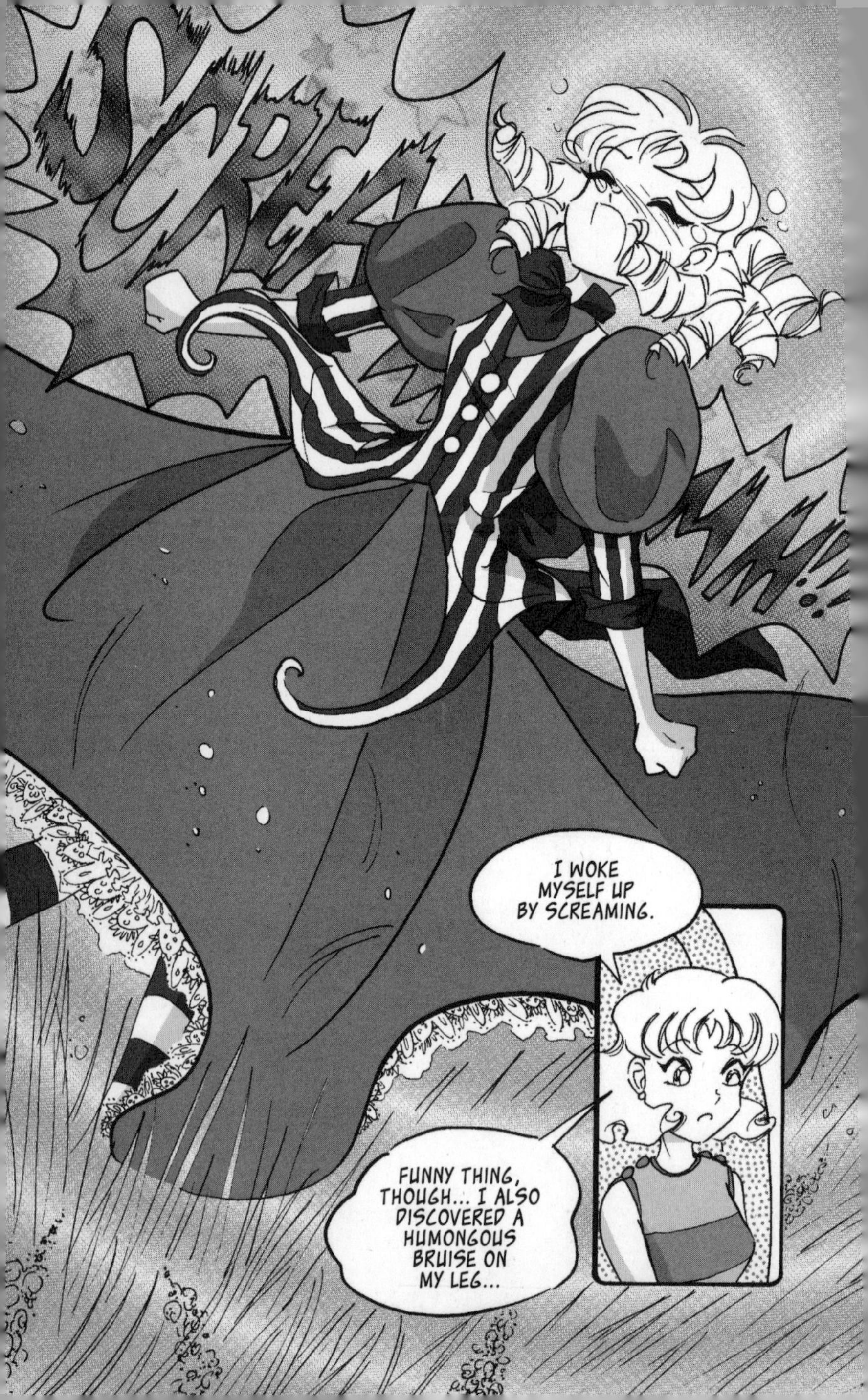
SCREAM!!
I WOKE MYSELF UP BY SCREAMING.
FUNNY THING, THOUGH... I ALSO DISCOVERED A HUMONGOUS BRUISE ON MY LEG...

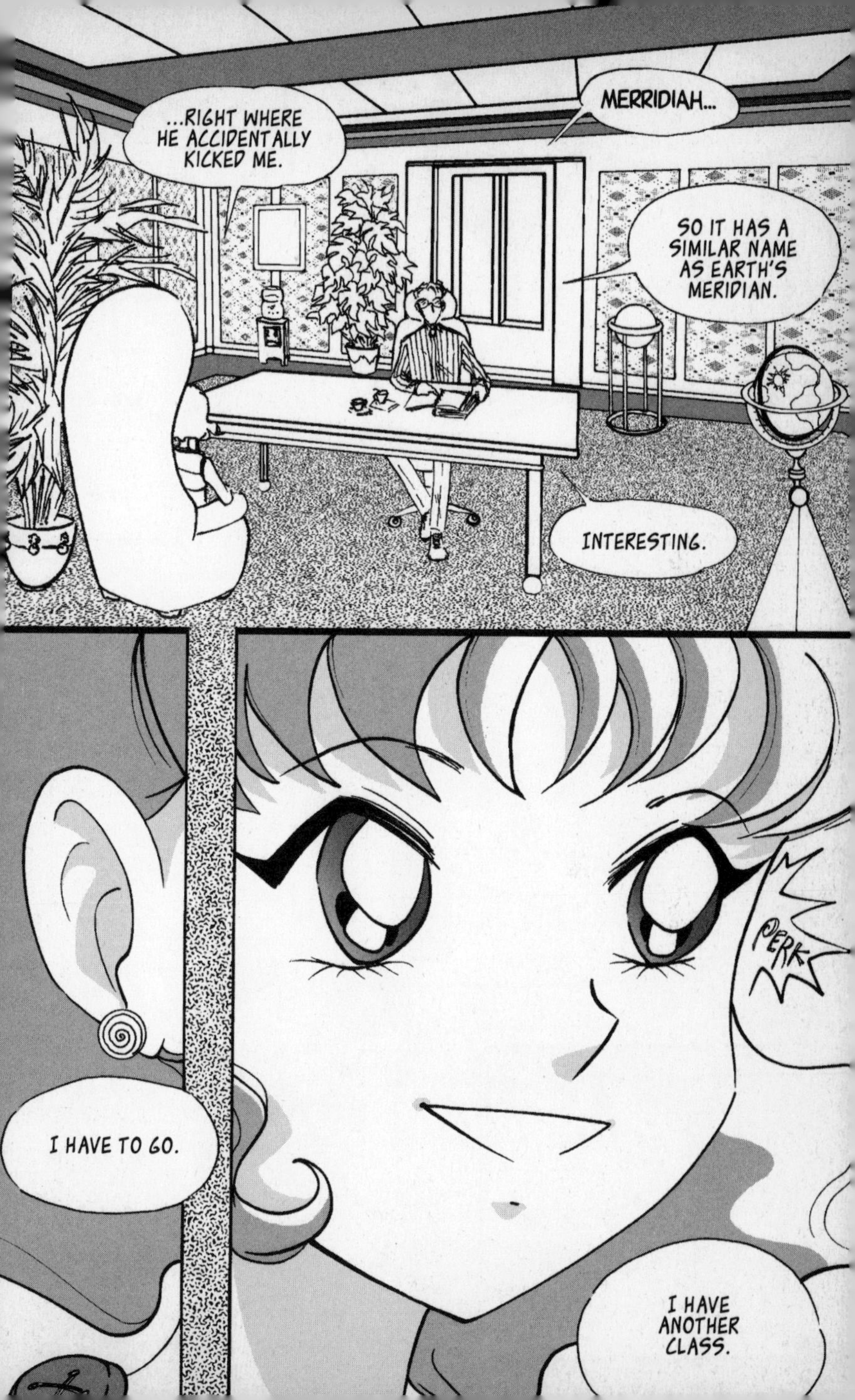
...RIGHT WHERE HE ACCIDENTALLY KICKED ME.
MERRIDIAH...
SO IT HAS A SIMILAR NAME AS EARTH'S MERIDIAN.
INTERESTING.
I HAVE TO GO.
PERK
I HAVE ANOTHER CLASS.

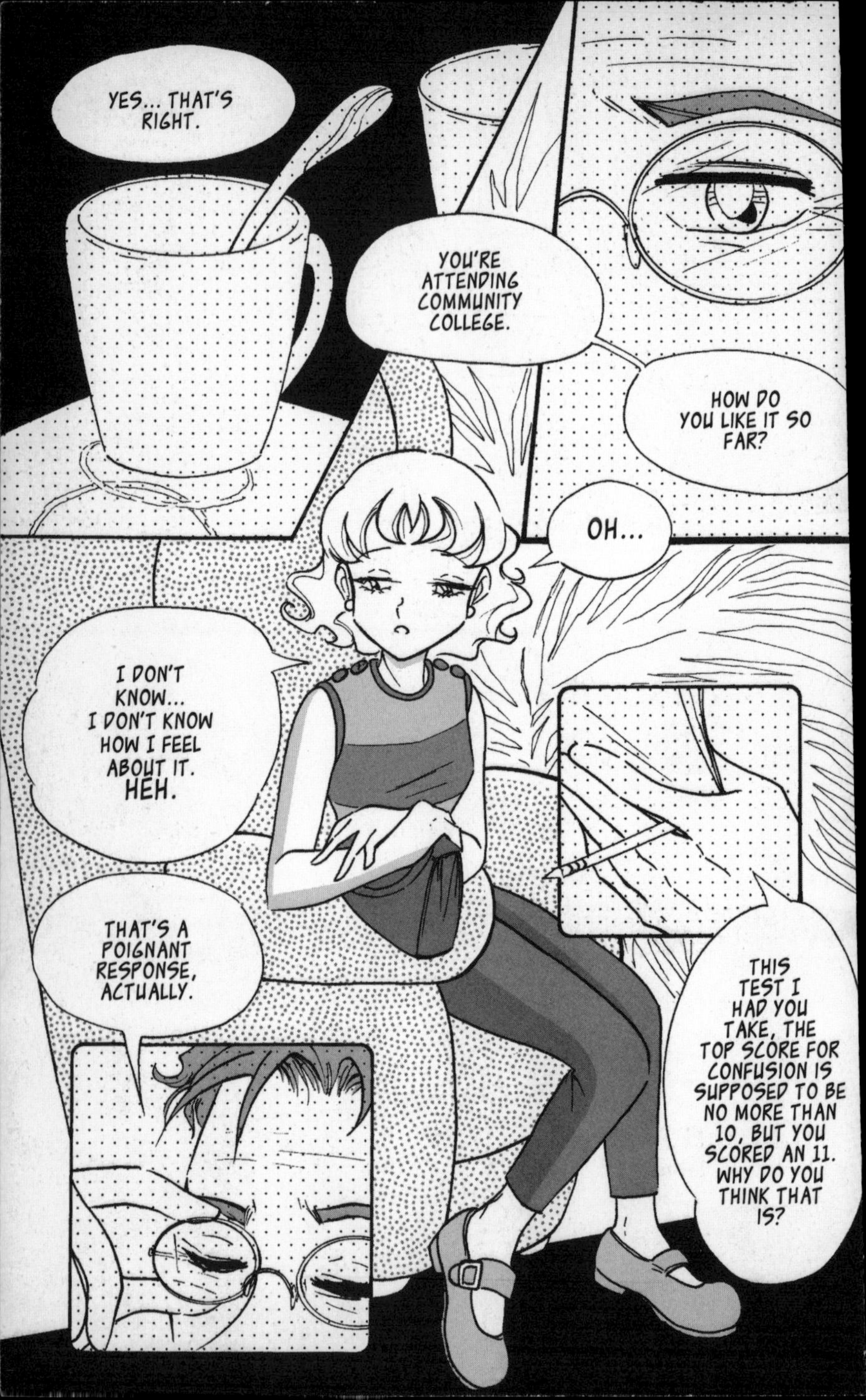
YES... THAT'S RIGHT.
YOU'RE ATTENDING COMMUNITY COLLEGE.
HOW DO YOU LIKE IT SO FAR?
OH...
I DON'T KNOW... I DON'T KNOW HOW I FEEL ABOUT IT. HEH.
THAT'S A POIGNANT RESPONSE, ACTUALLY.
THIS TEST I HAD YOU TAKE, THE TOP SCORE FOR CONFUSION IS SUPPOSED TO BE NO MORE THAN 10, BUT YOU SCORED AN 11. WHY DO YOU THINK THAT IS?

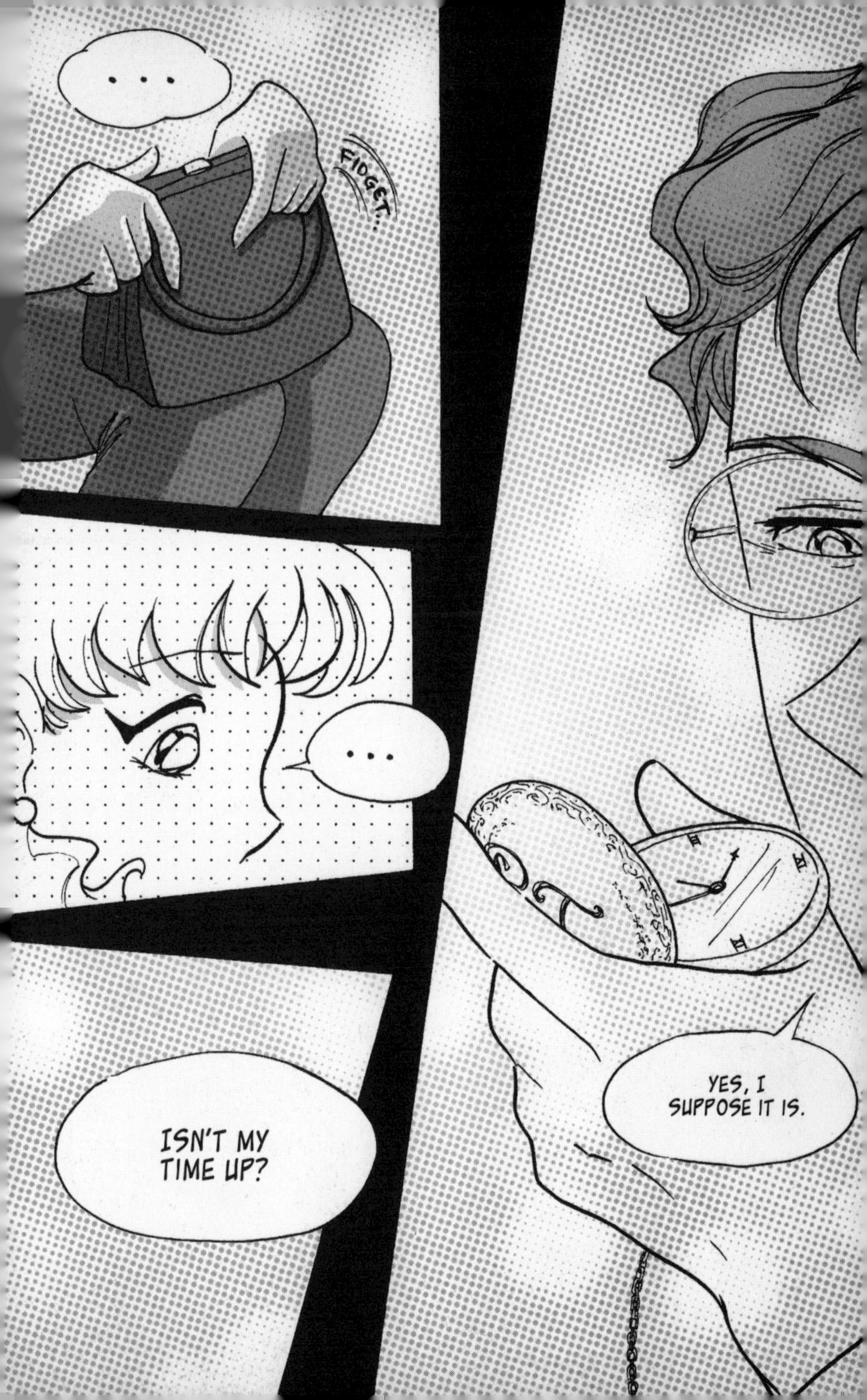
...
FIDGET...
...
ISN'T MY TIME UP?
YES, I SUPPOSE IT IS.

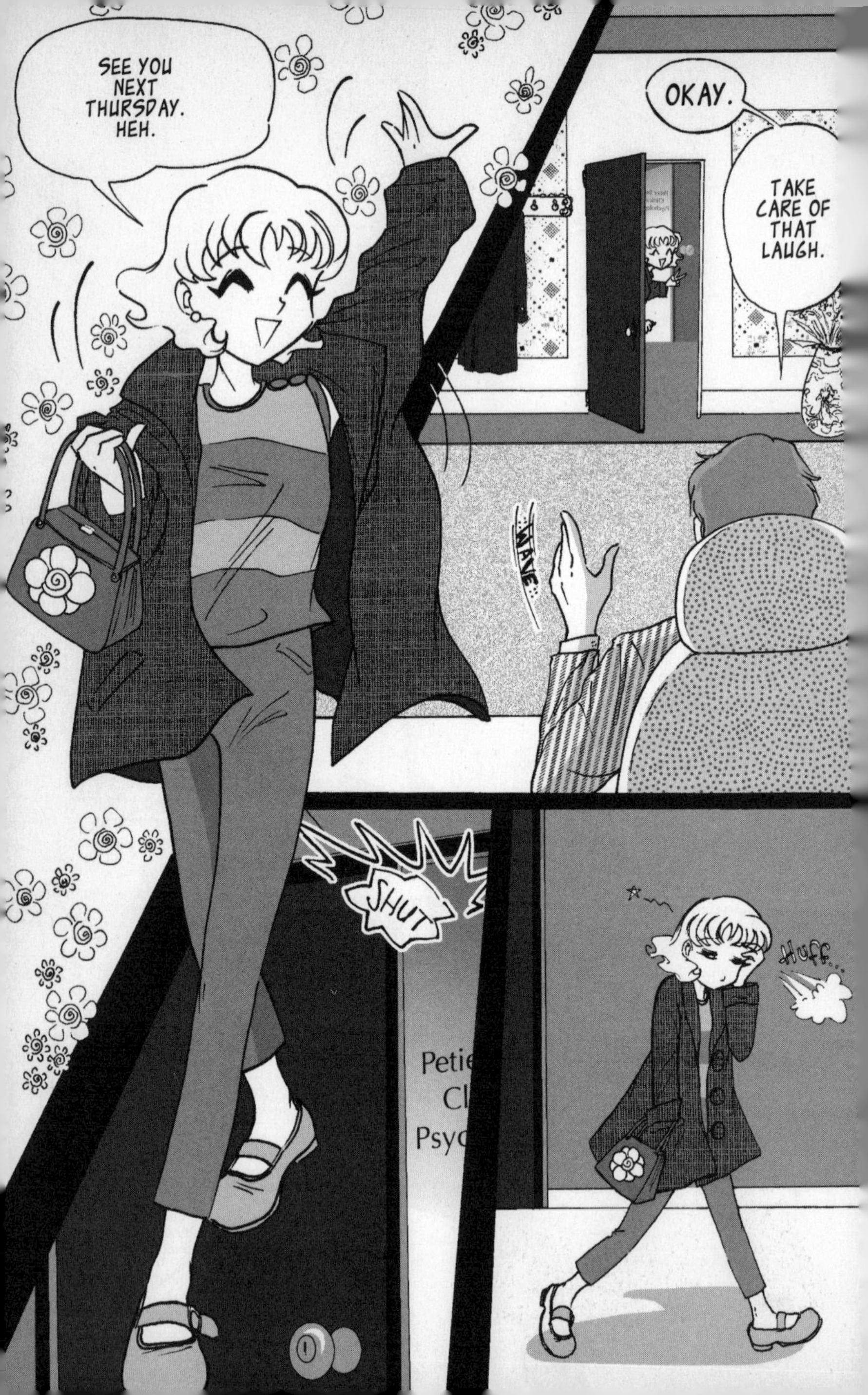
SEE YOU NEXT THURSDAY. HEH.
OKAY.
TAKE CARE OF THAT LAUGH.
WAVE
SHUT
Petie
Cl
Psyc
Huff...

CHAPTER THREE: IT IS TREASURABLE

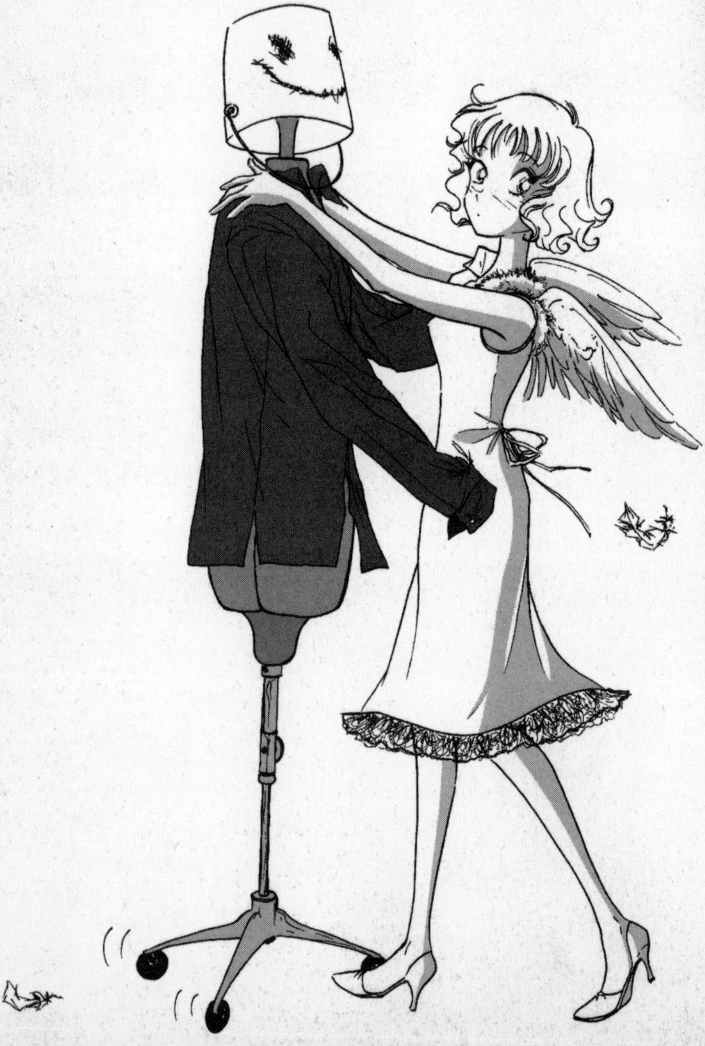

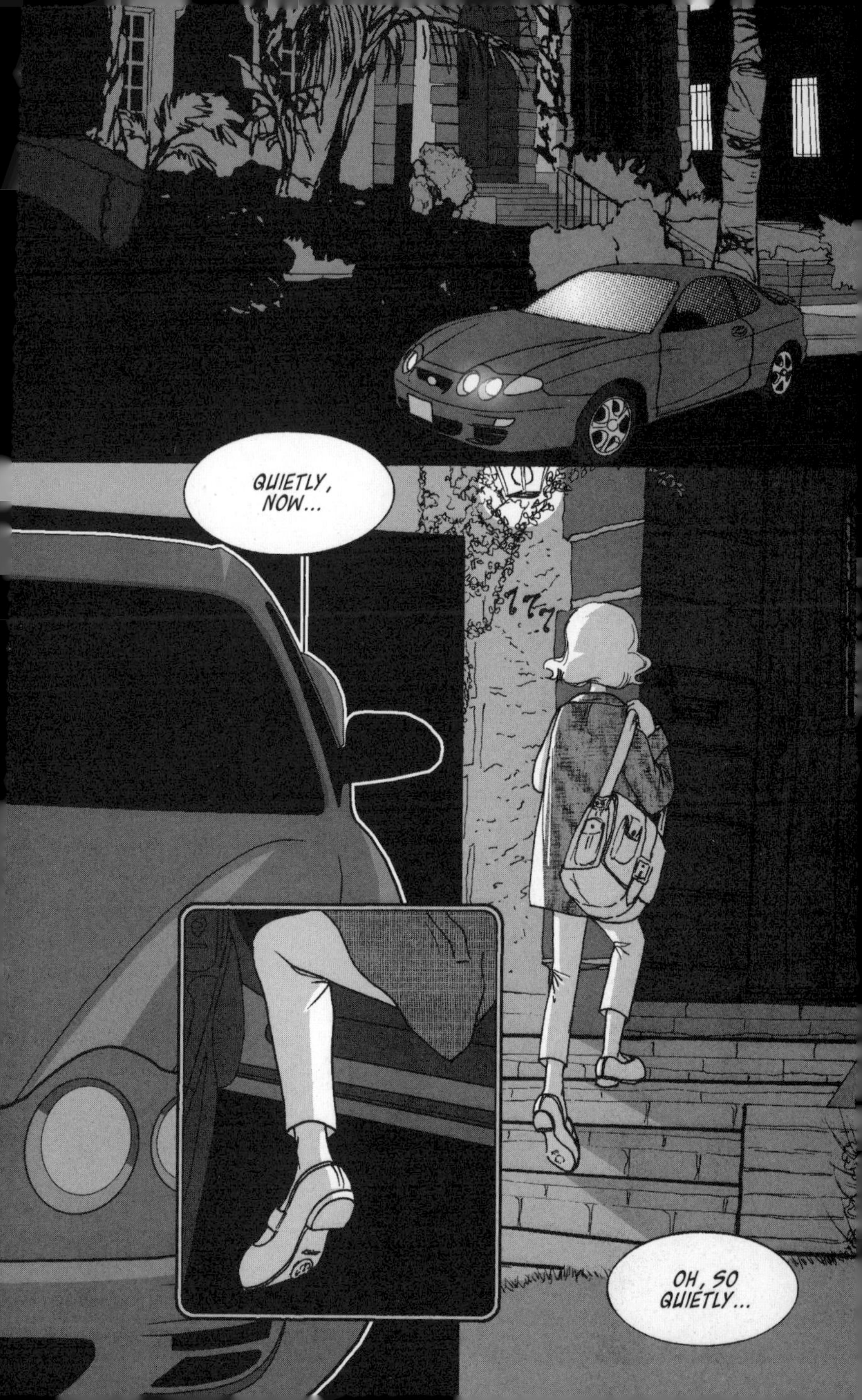
QUIETLY, NOW...
OH, SO QUIETLY...

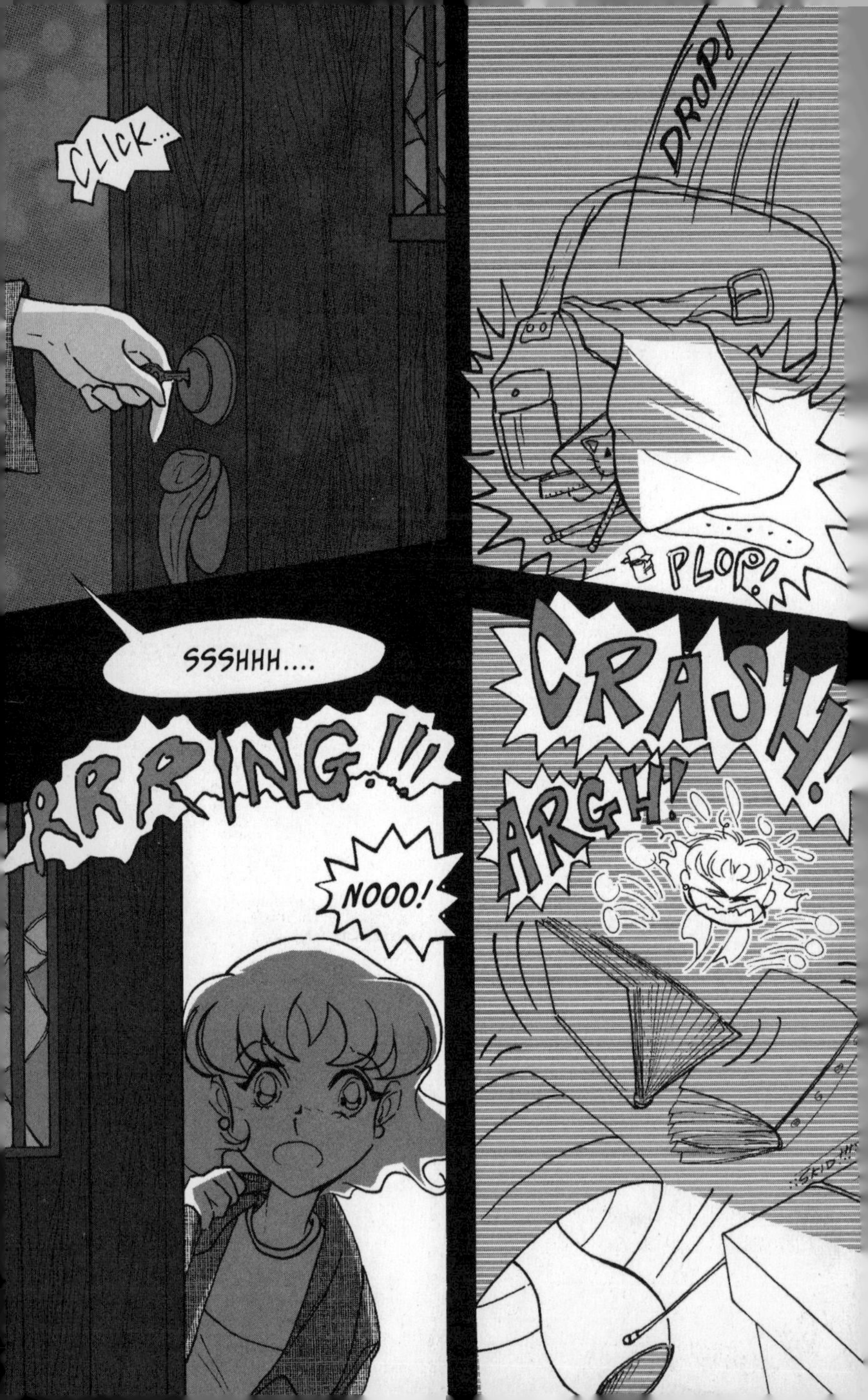
CLICK...
DROP!
PLOP!
SSSHHH....
RRRING!!!
NOOO!
CRASH!
ARGH!
SKID!!!

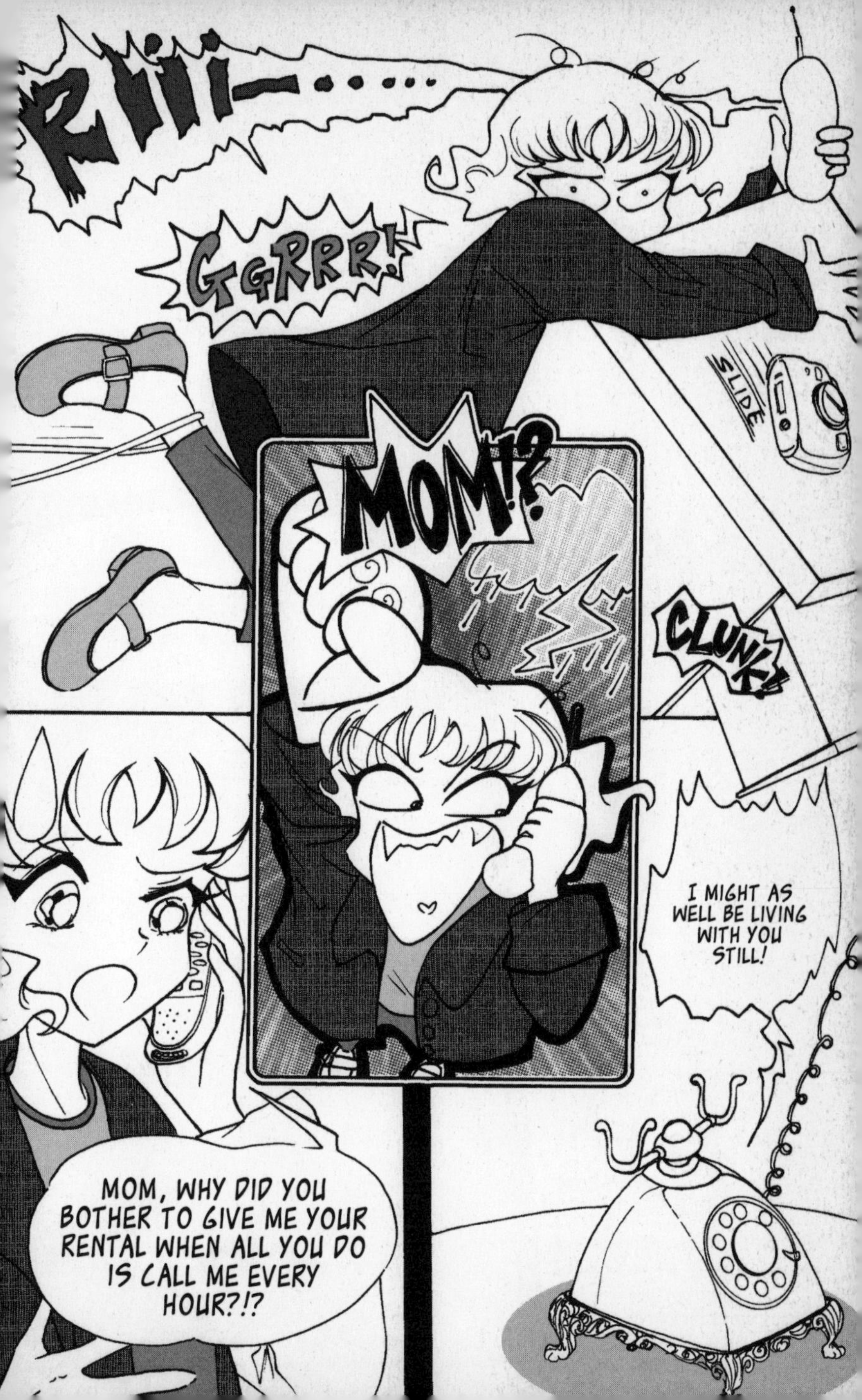
RIII-.......
GGRRR!
SLIDE
MOM!?
CLUNK!
I MIGHT AS WELL BE LIVING WITH YOU STILL!
MOM, WHY DID YOU BOTHER TO GIVE ME YOUR RENTAL WHEN ALL YOU DO IS CALL ME EVERY HOUR?!?

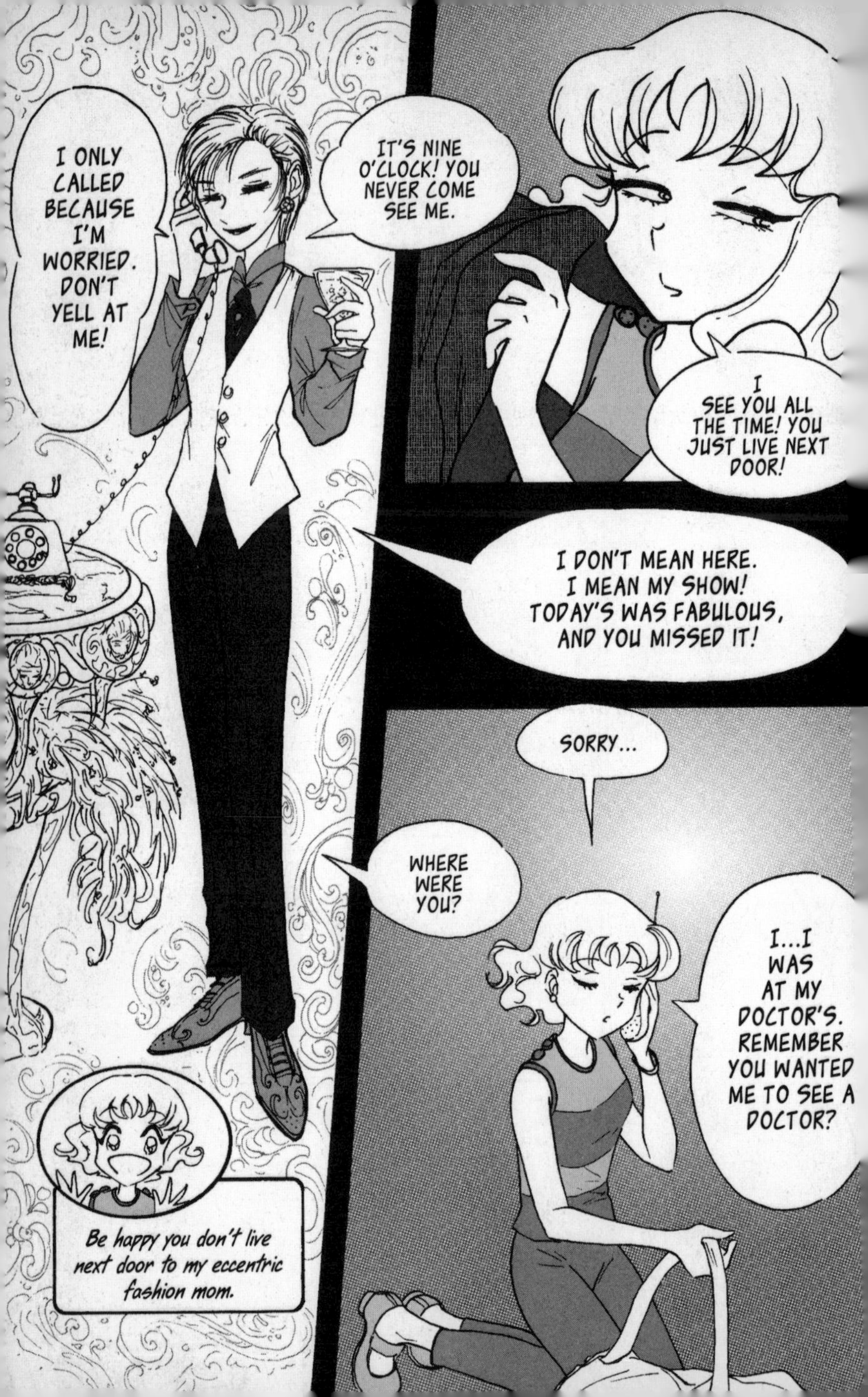
I ONLY CALLED BECAUSE I'M WORRIED. DON'T YELL AT ME!
IT'S NINE O'CLOCK! YOU NEVER COME SEE ME.
I DON'T MEAN HERE. I MEAN MY SHOW! TODAY'S WAS FABULOUS, AND YOU MISSED IT!
WHERE WERE YOU?
Be happy you don't live next door to my eccentric fashion mom.
I SEE YOU ALL THE TIME! YOU JUST LIVE NEXT DOOR!
SORRY...
I...I WAS AT MY DOCTOR'S. REMEMBER YOU WANTED ME TO SEE A DOCTOR?

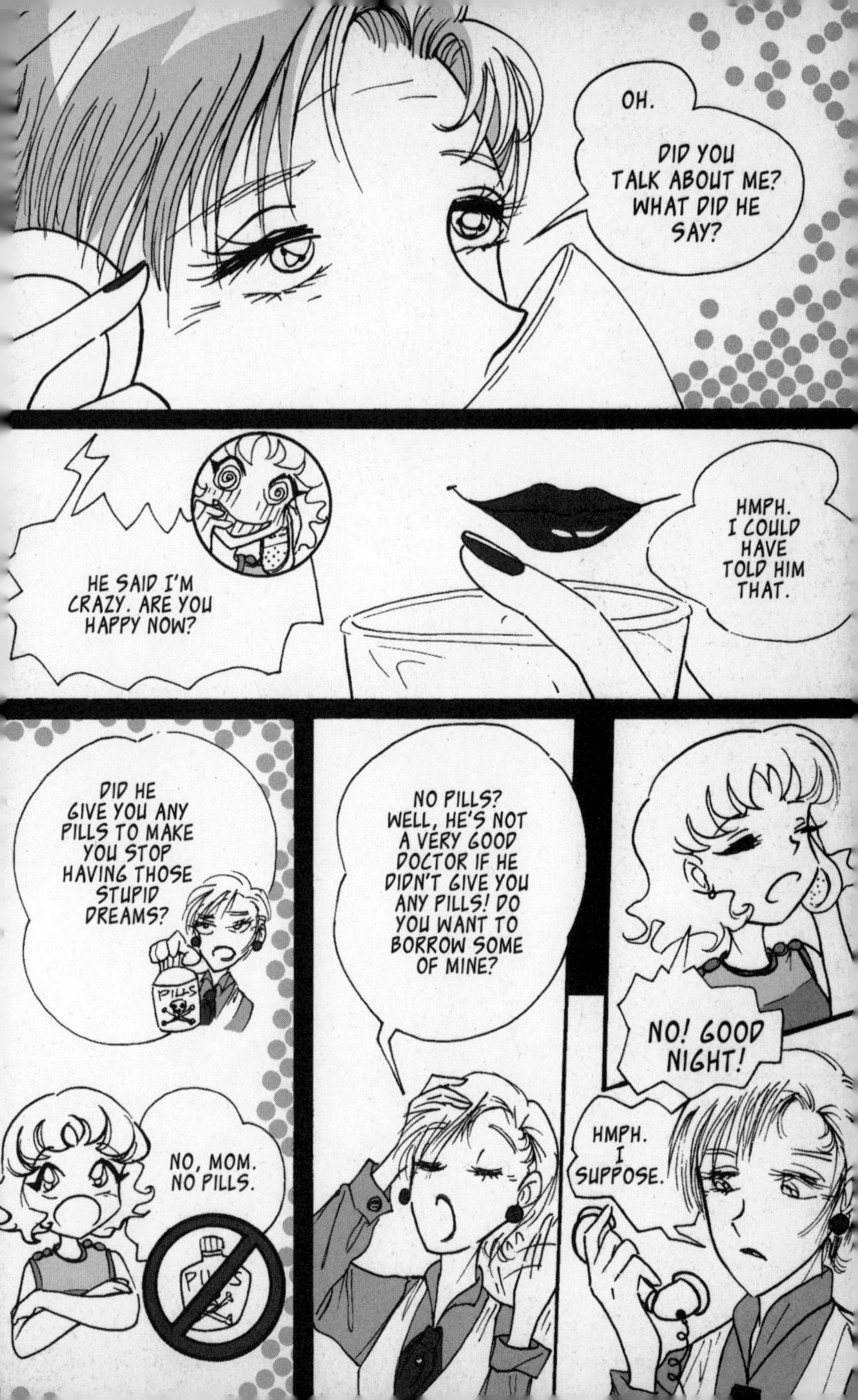
OH.
DID YOU TALK ABOUT ME? WHAT DID HE SAY?
HE SAID I'M CRAZY. ARE YOU HAPPY NOW?
HMPH. I COULD HAVE TOLD HIM THAT.
DID HE GIVE YOU ANY PILLS TO MAKE YOU STOP HAVING THOSE STUPID DREAMS?
PILLS
NO, MOM. NO PILLS.
NO PILLS? WELL, HE'S NOT A VERY GOOD DOCTOR IF HE DIDN'T GIVE YOU ANY PILLS! DO YOU WANT TO BORROW SOME OF MINE?
NO! GOOD NIGHT!
HMPH. I SUPPOSE.

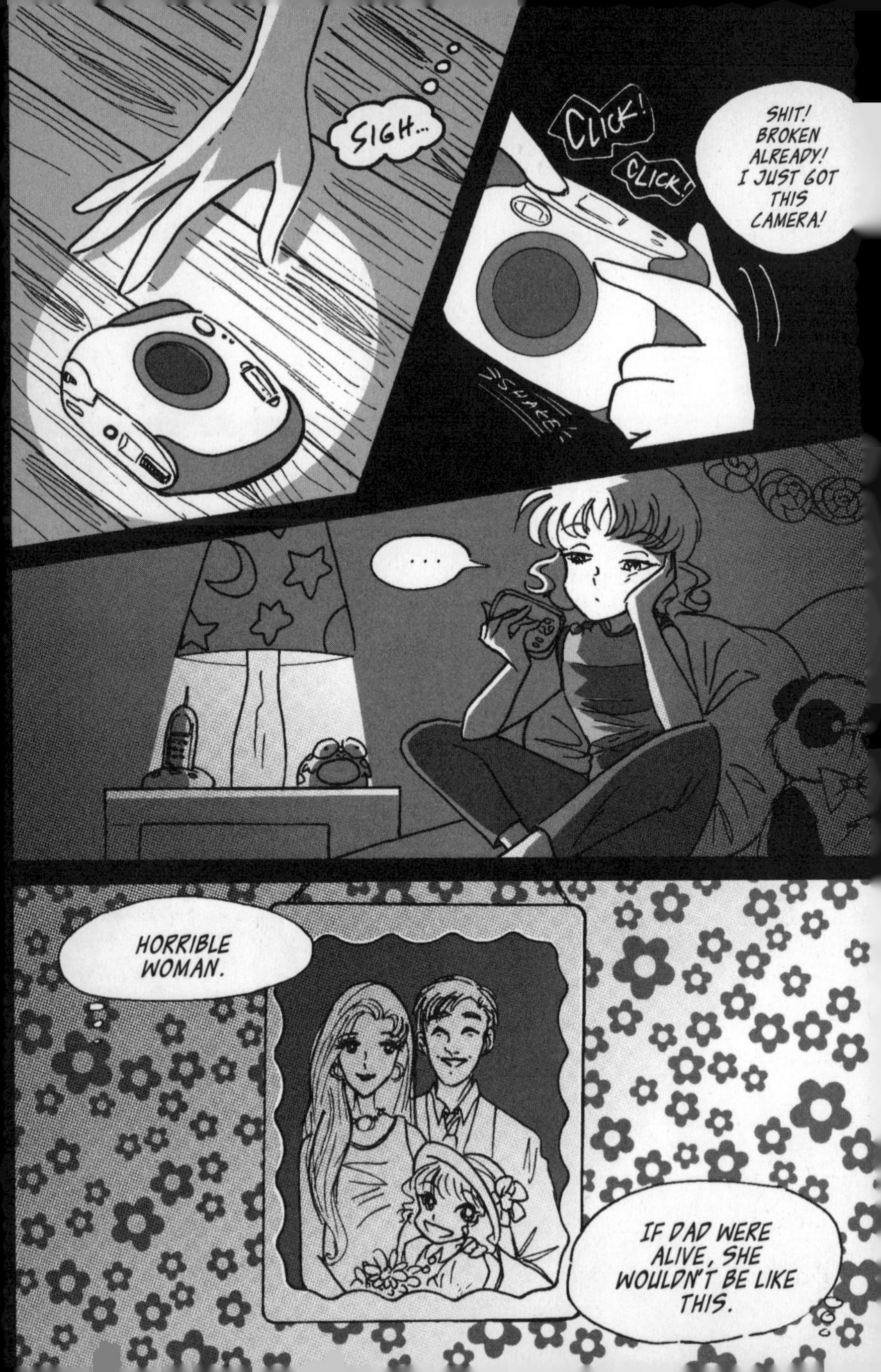
SIGH...
CLICK!
CLICK!
SHIT! BROKEN ALREADY! I JUST GOT THIS CAMERA!
SHAKE
...
HORRIBLE WOMAN.
IF DAD WERE ALIVE, SHE WOULDN'T BE LIKE THIS.

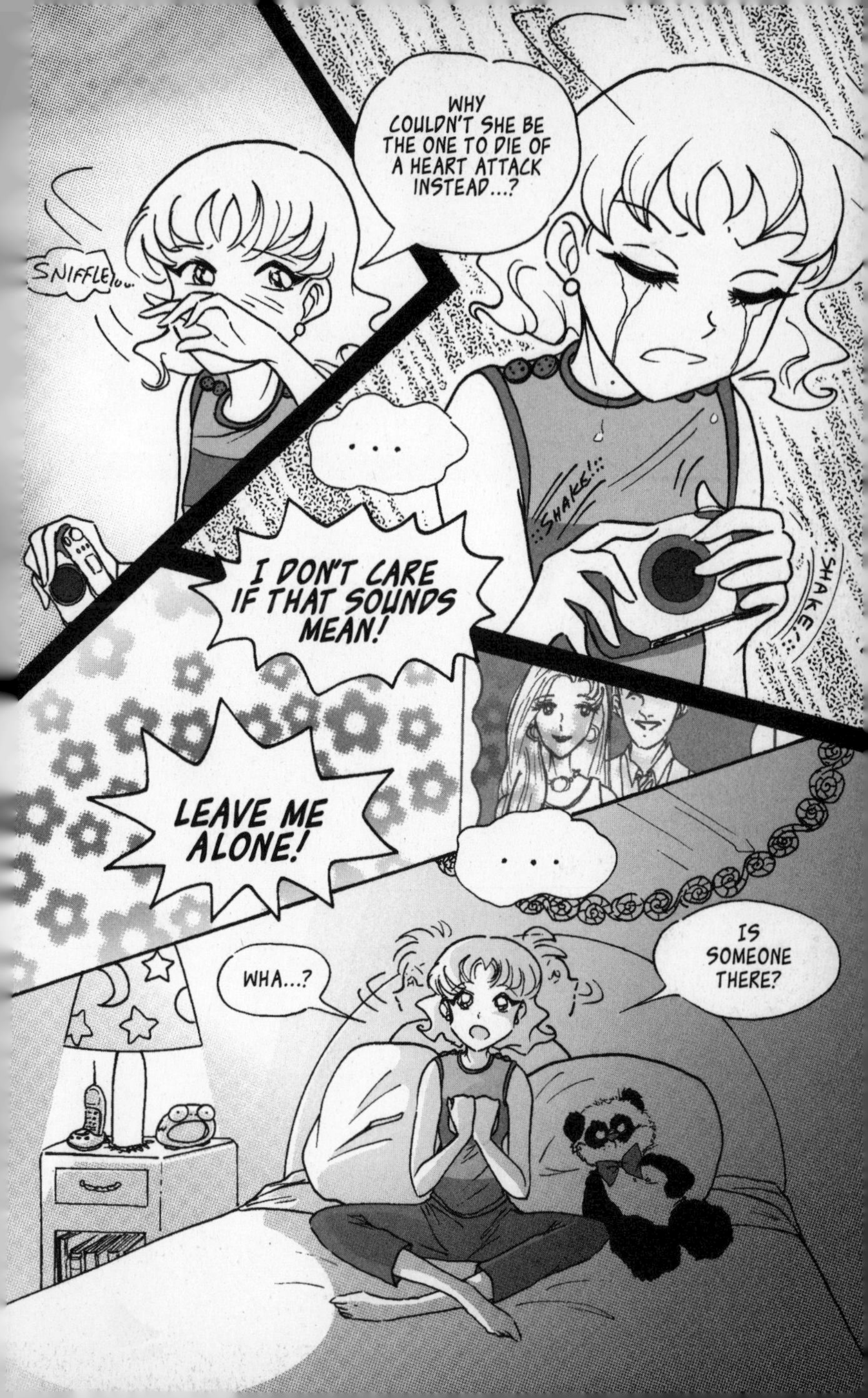
SNIFFLE...
WHY COULDN'T SHE BE THE ONE TO DIE OF A HEART ATTACK INSTEAD...?
...
SHAKE!!
SHAKE!!
I DON'T CARE IF THAT SOUNDS MEAN!
LEAVE ME ALONE!
...
WHA...?
IS SOMEONE THERE?

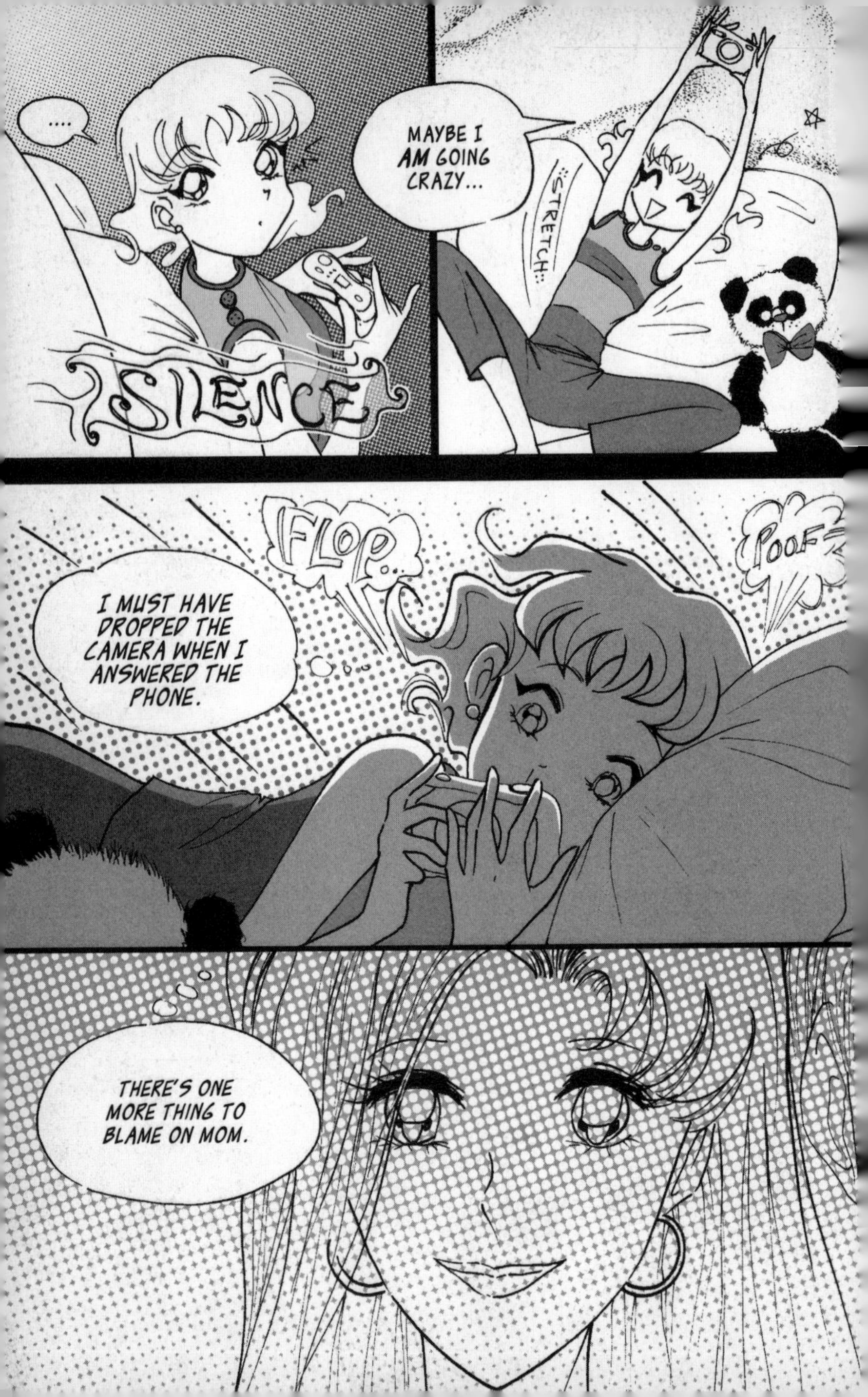
.....
SILENCE
MAYBE I AM GOING CRAZY...
::STRETCH::
I MUST HAVE DROPPED THE CAMERA WHEN I ANSWERED THE PHONE.
FLOP...
POOF
THERE'S ONE MORE THING TO BLAME ON MOM.

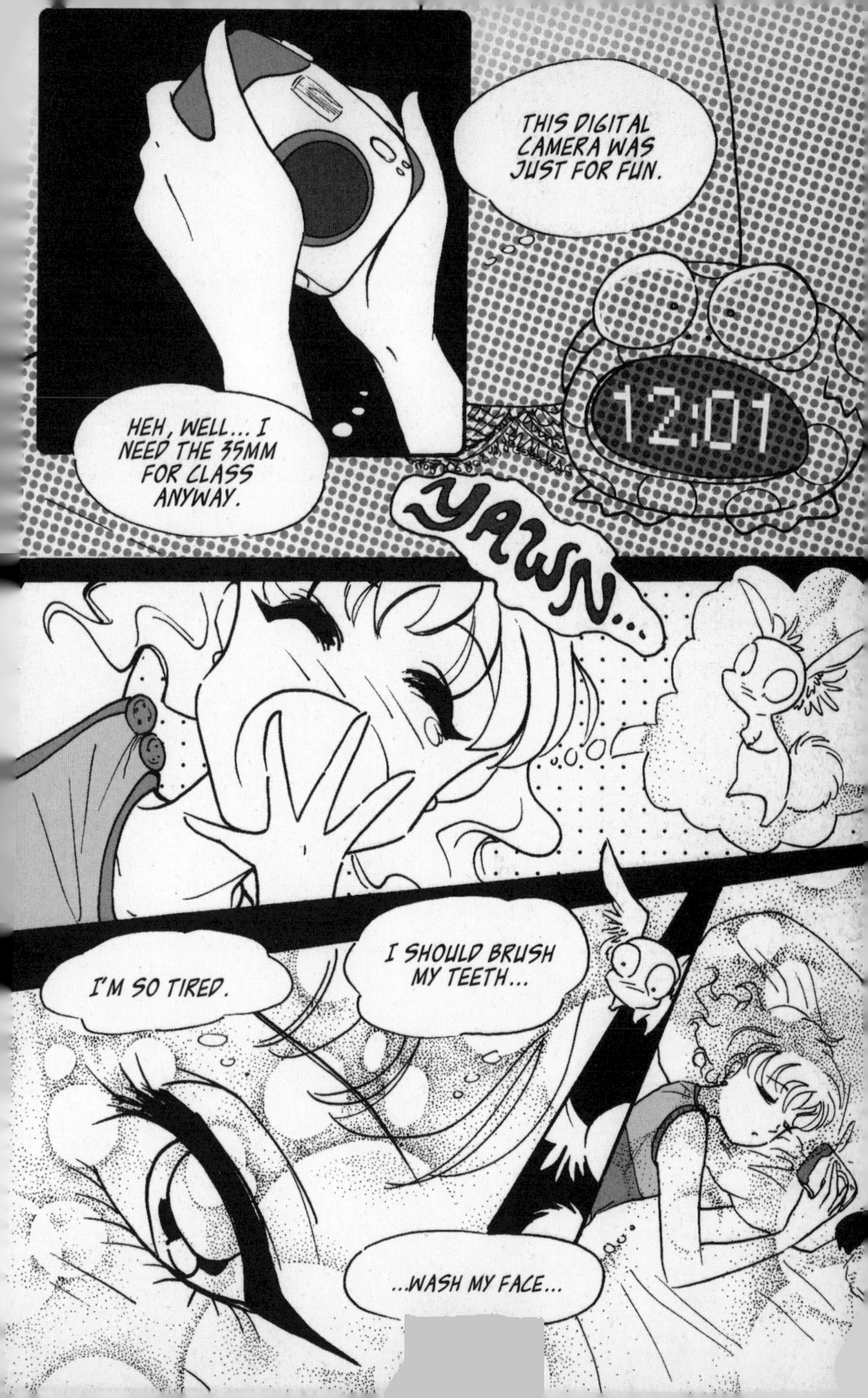
THIS DIGITAL CAMERA WAS JUST FOR FUN.
HEH, WELL... I NEED THE 35MM FOR CLASS ANYWAY.
12:01
YAWN...
I'M SO TIRED.
I SHOULD BRUSH MY TEETH...
...WASH MY FACE...

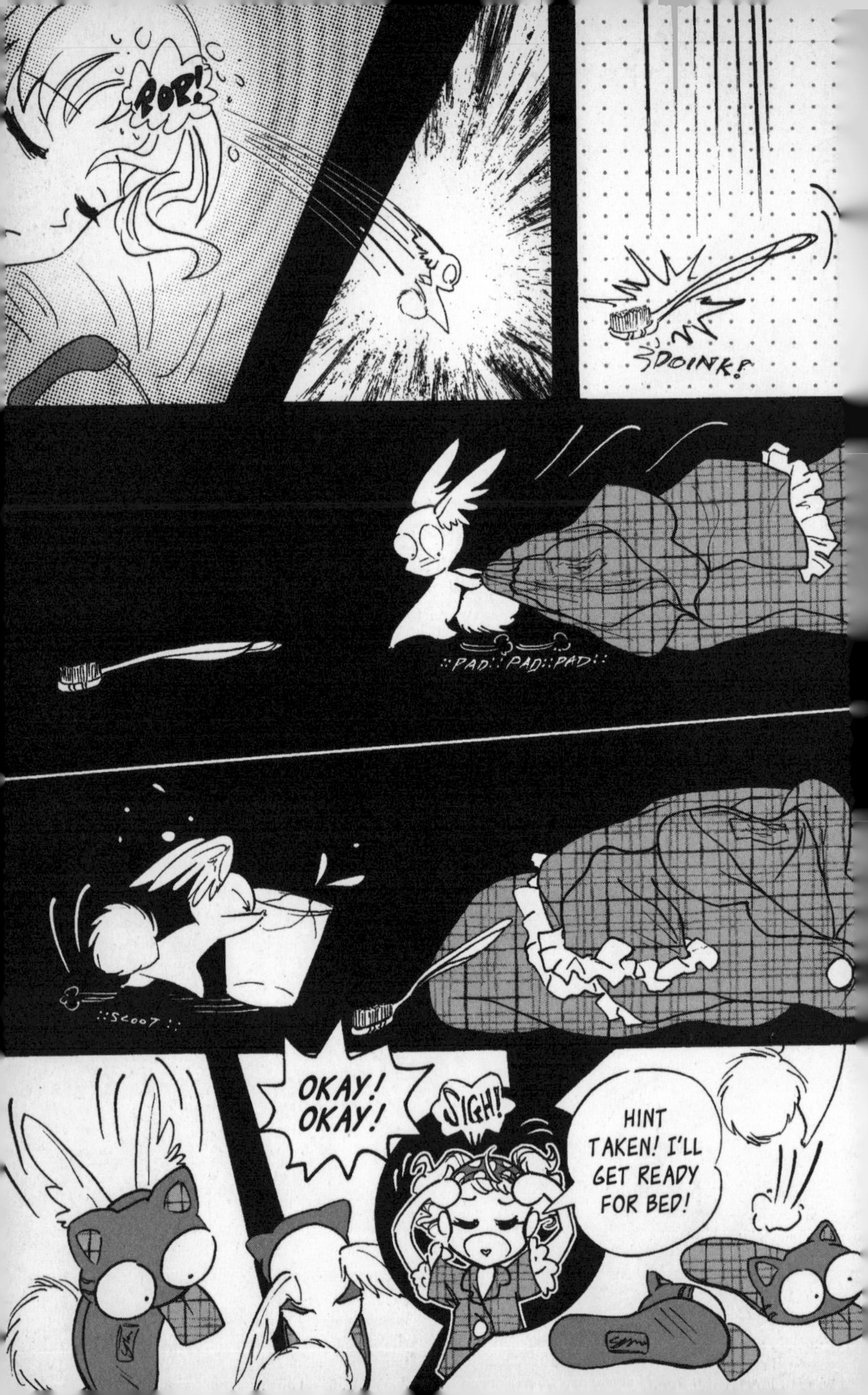
POP!
DOINK!
::PAD::PAD::PAD::
::SCOOT::
OKAY! OKAY!
SIGH!
HINT TAKEN! I'LL GET READY FOR BED!

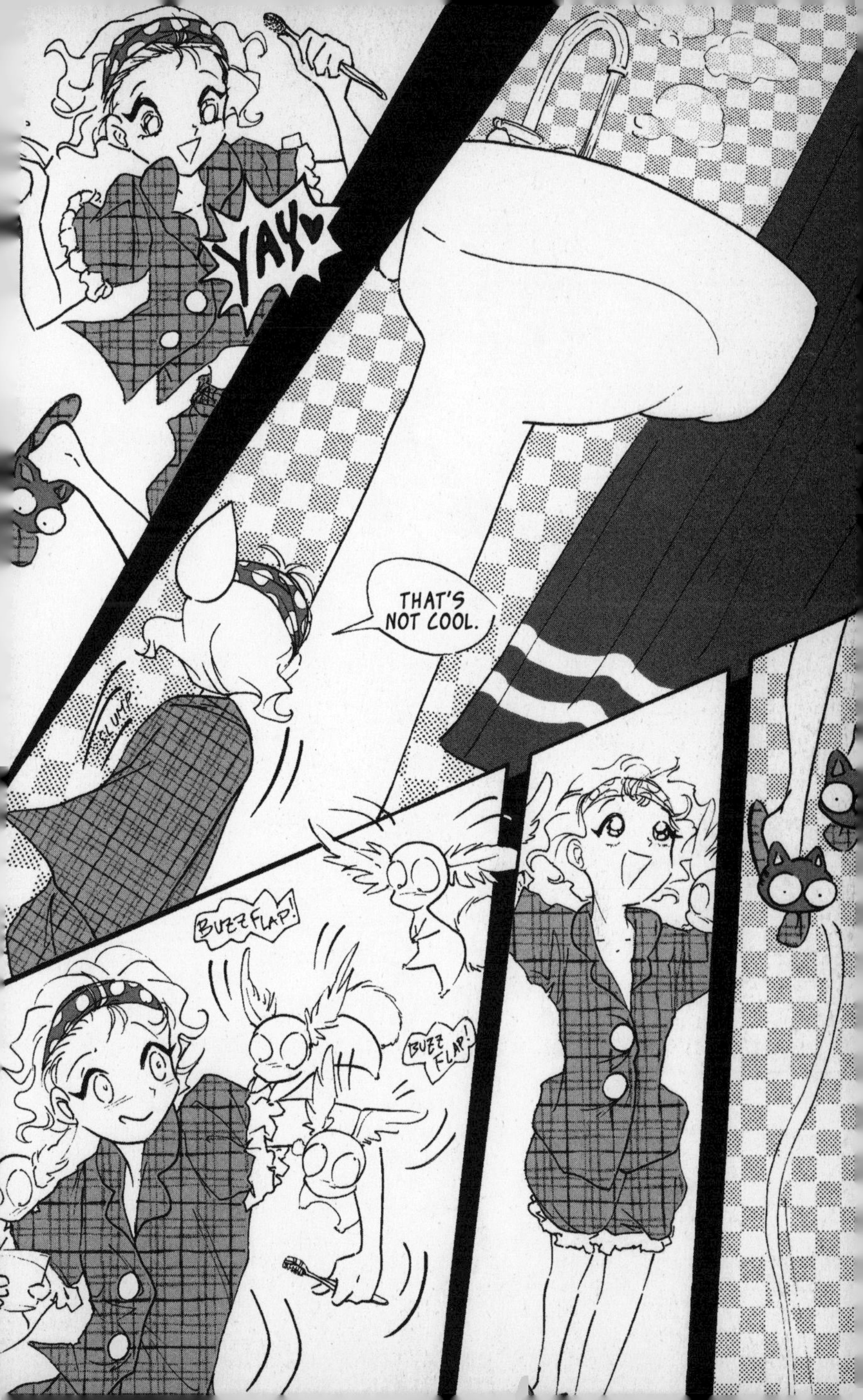
YAY♥
SLUMP
THAT'S NOT COOL.
BUZZ FLAP!
BUZZ FLAP!

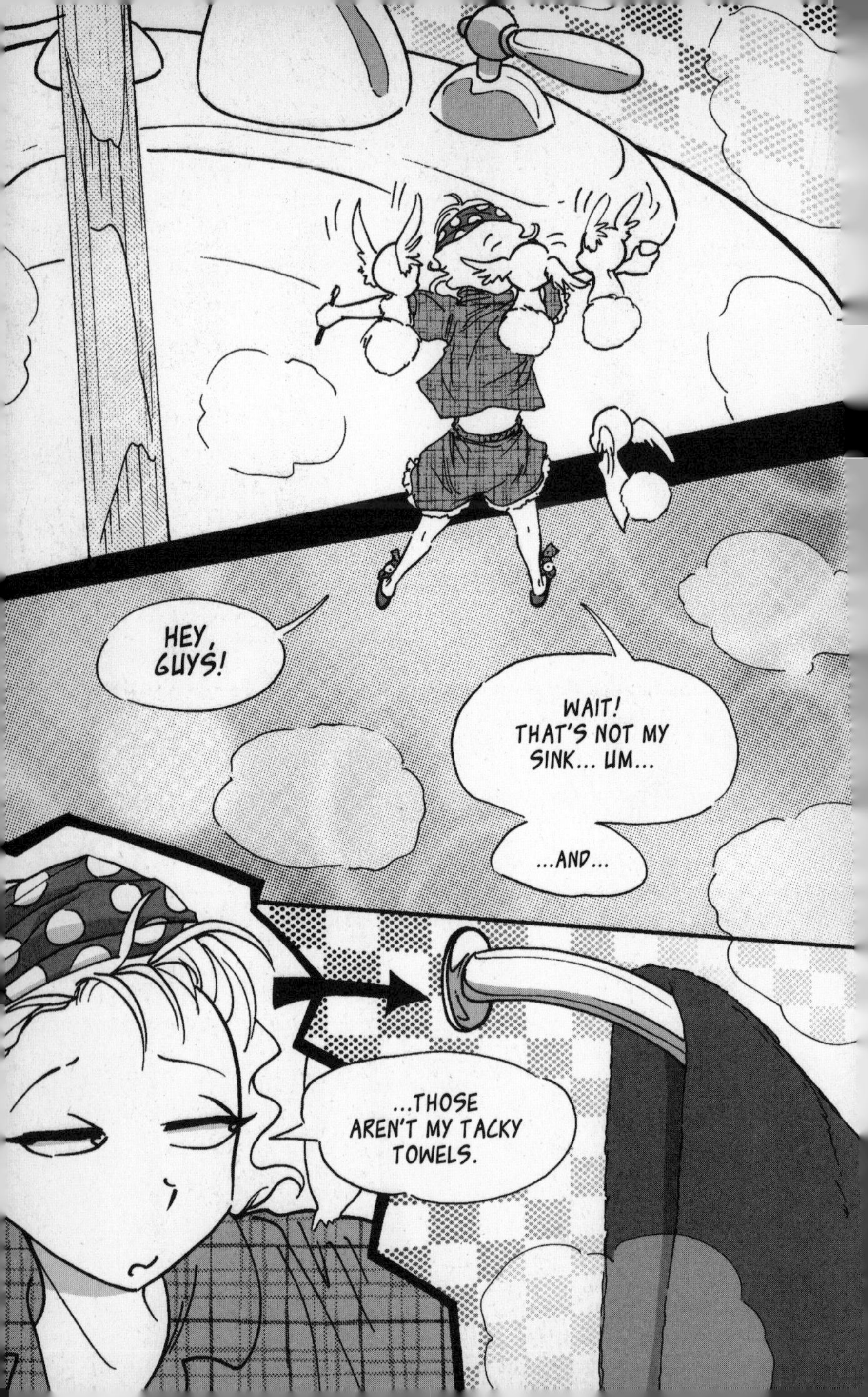
HEY, GUYS!
WAIT! THAT'S NOT MY SINK... UM...
...AND...
...THOSE AREN'T MY TACKY TOWELS.

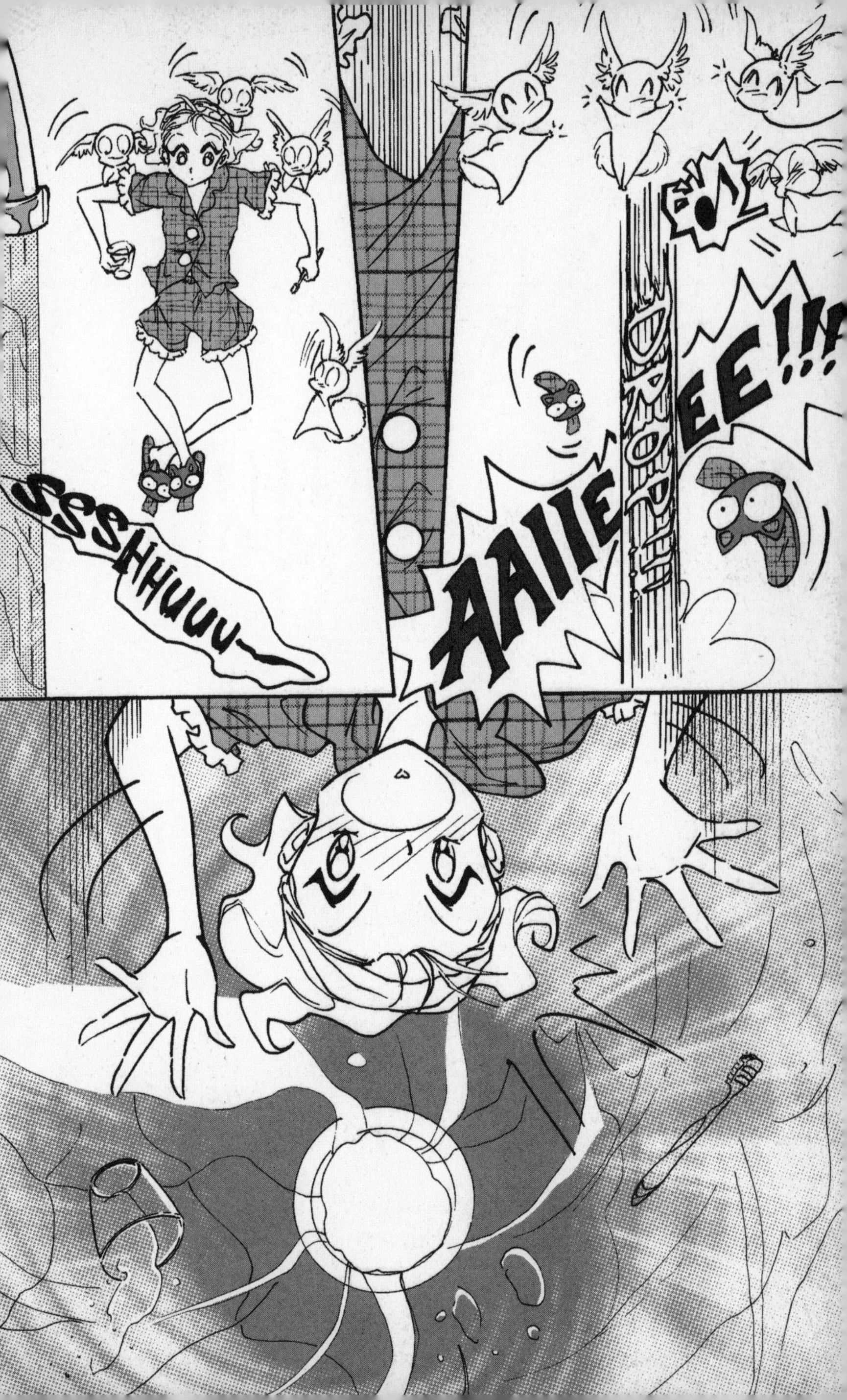
SSSHHUUUU~
AAIIEEE!!!

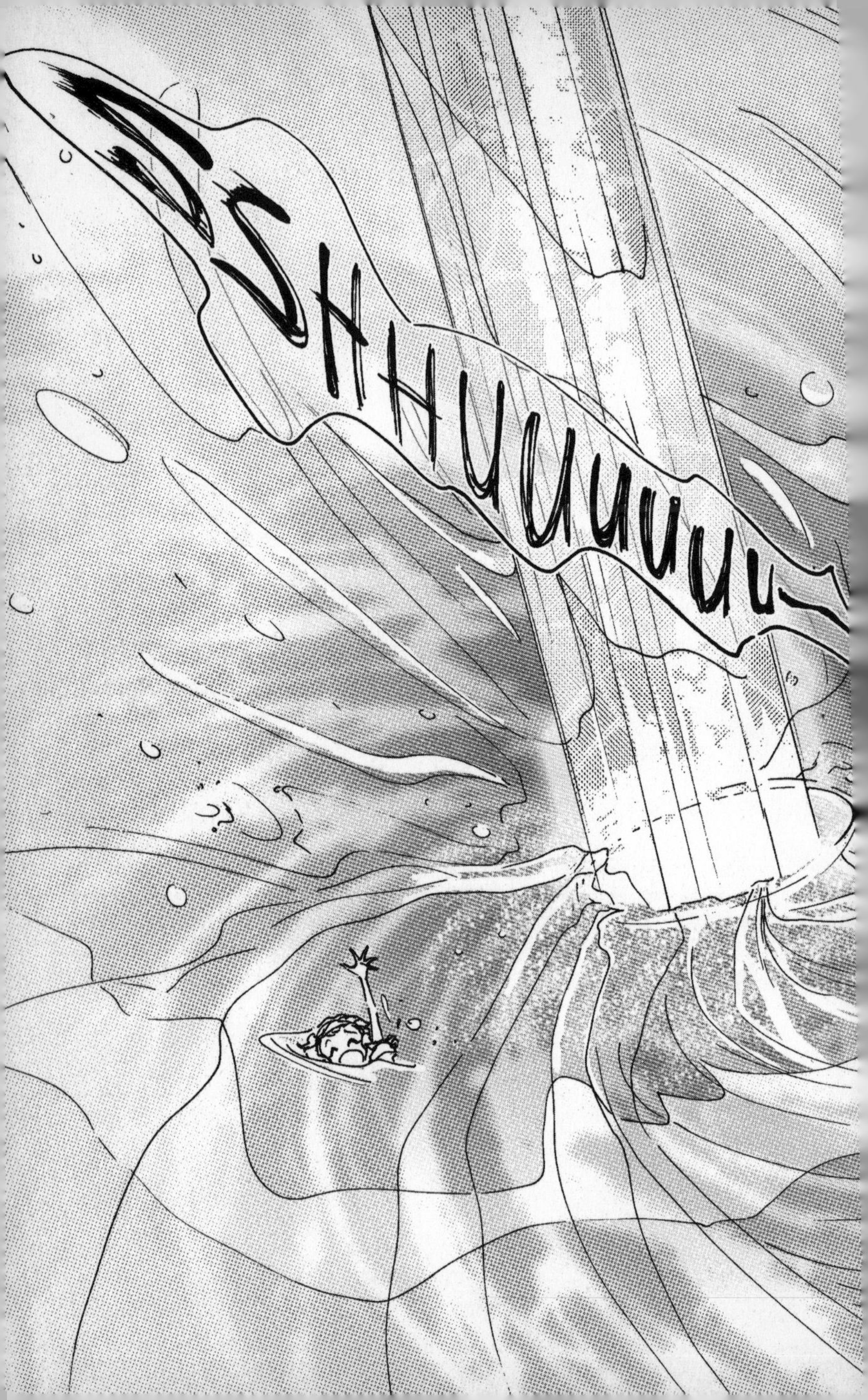
SHHUUUUUU

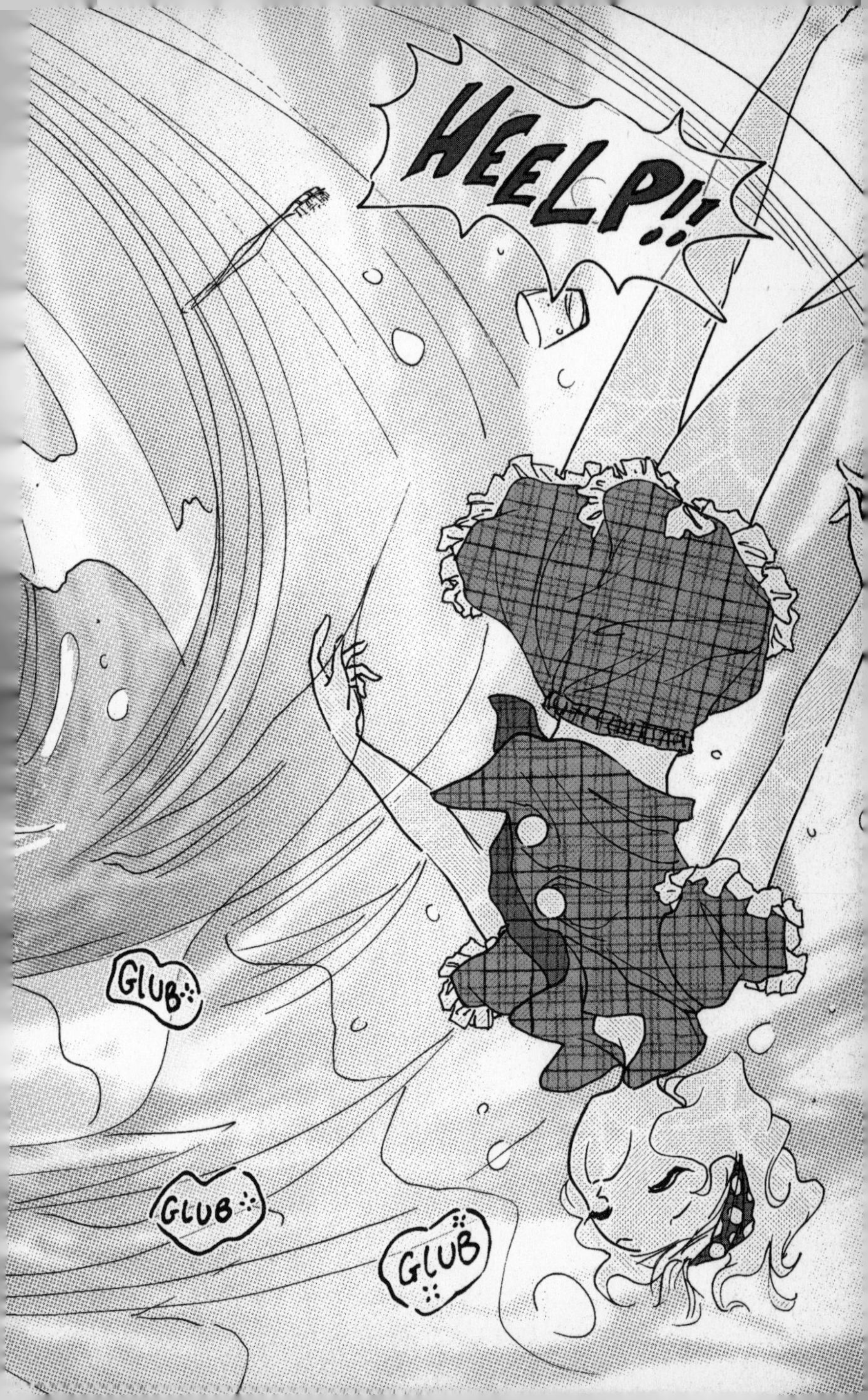
HEELP!!
GLUB
GLUB
GLUB

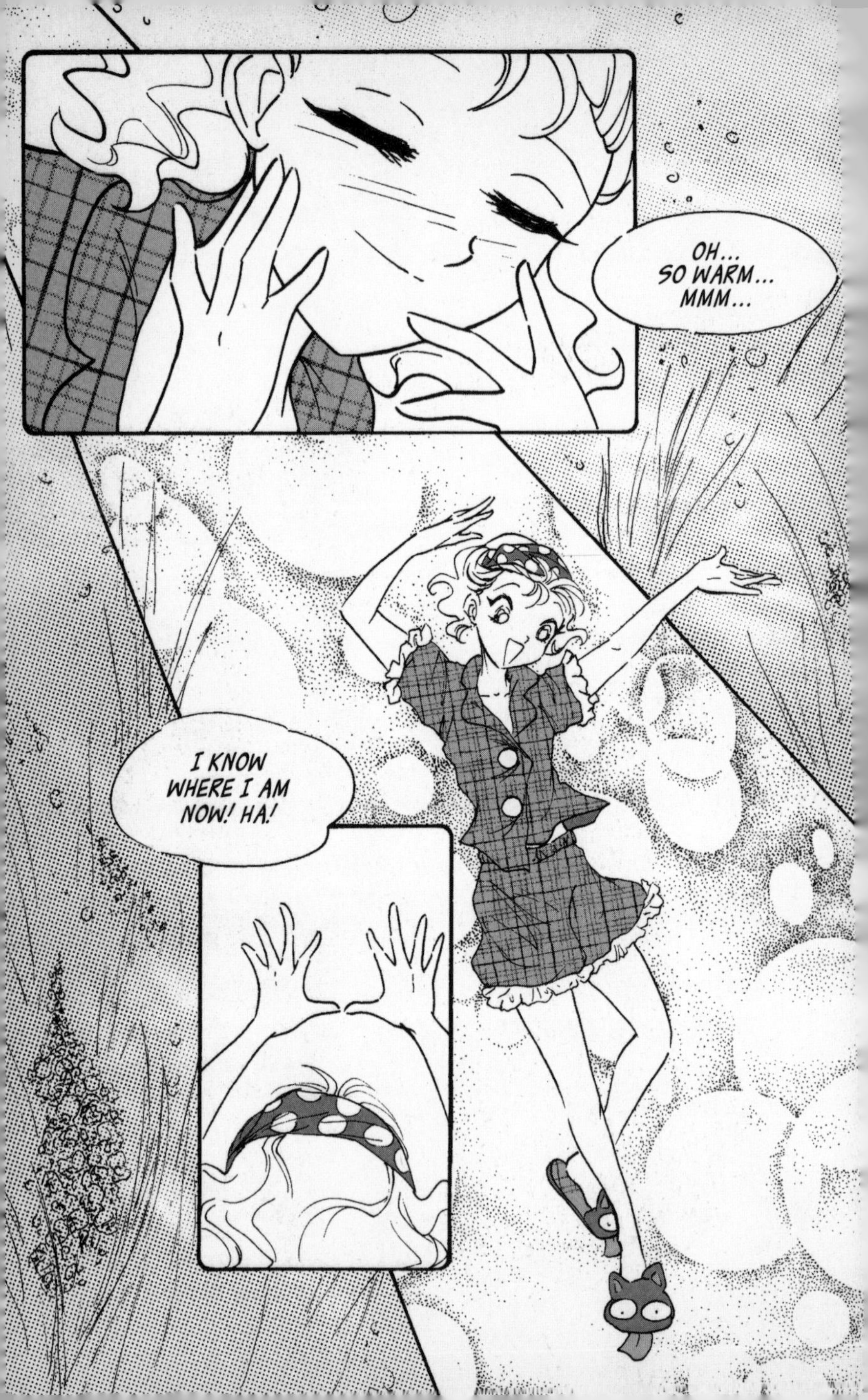
OH... SO WARM... MMM...
I KNOW WHERE I AM NOW! HA!

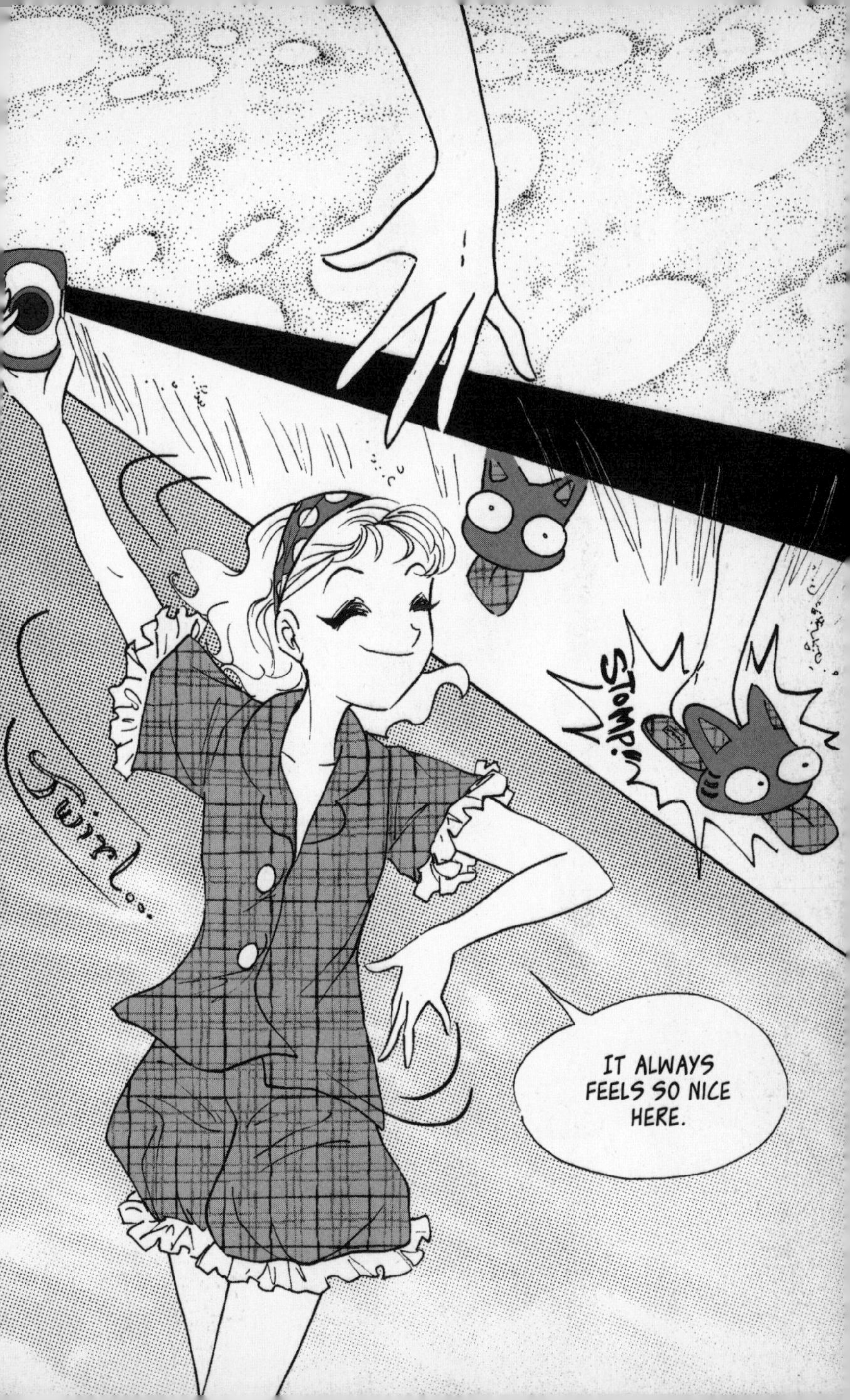
STOMP!!
Twirl...
IT ALWAYS FEELS SO NICE HERE.

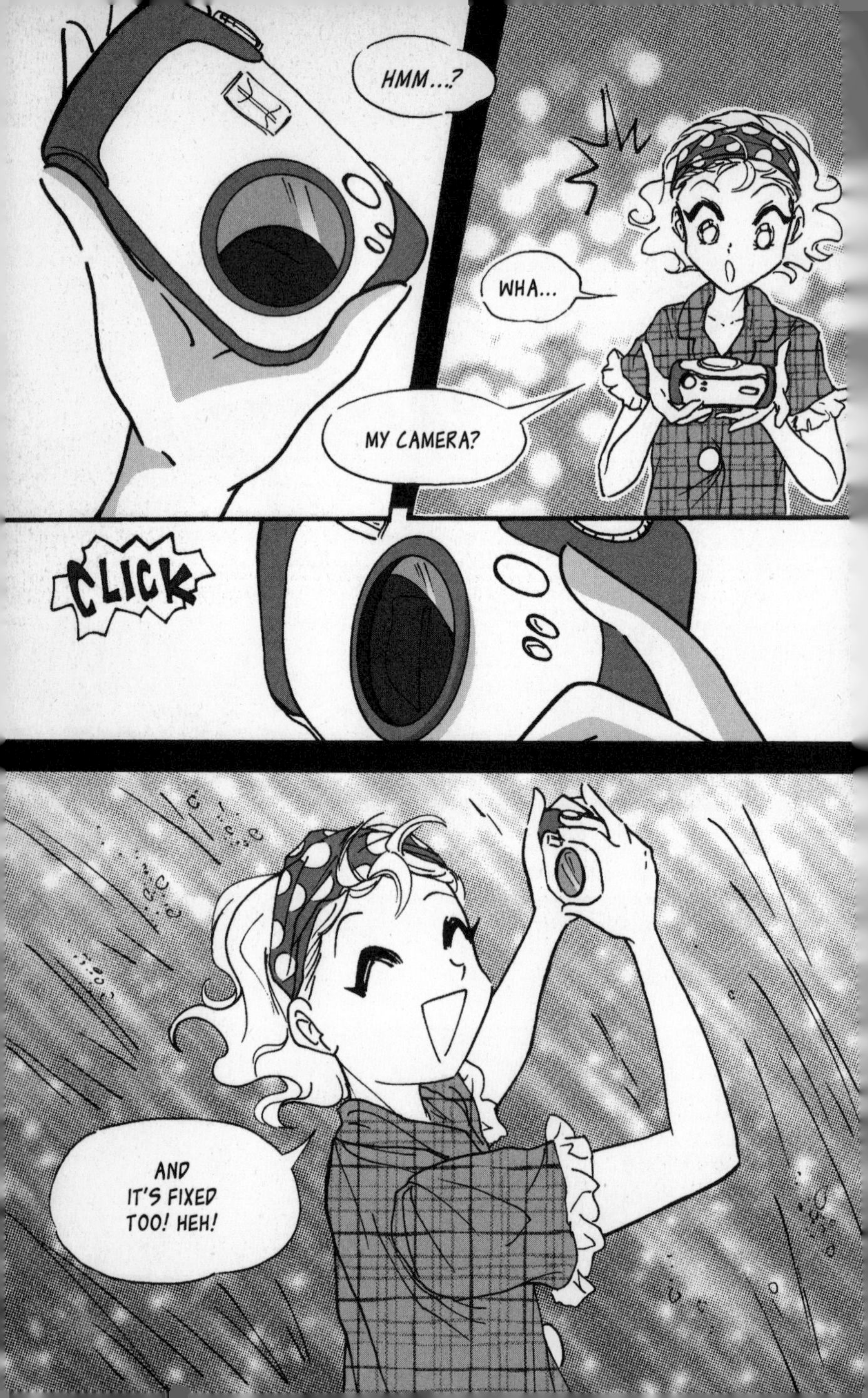
HMM...?
WHA...
MY CAMERA?
CLICK
AND IT'S FIXED TOO! HEH!

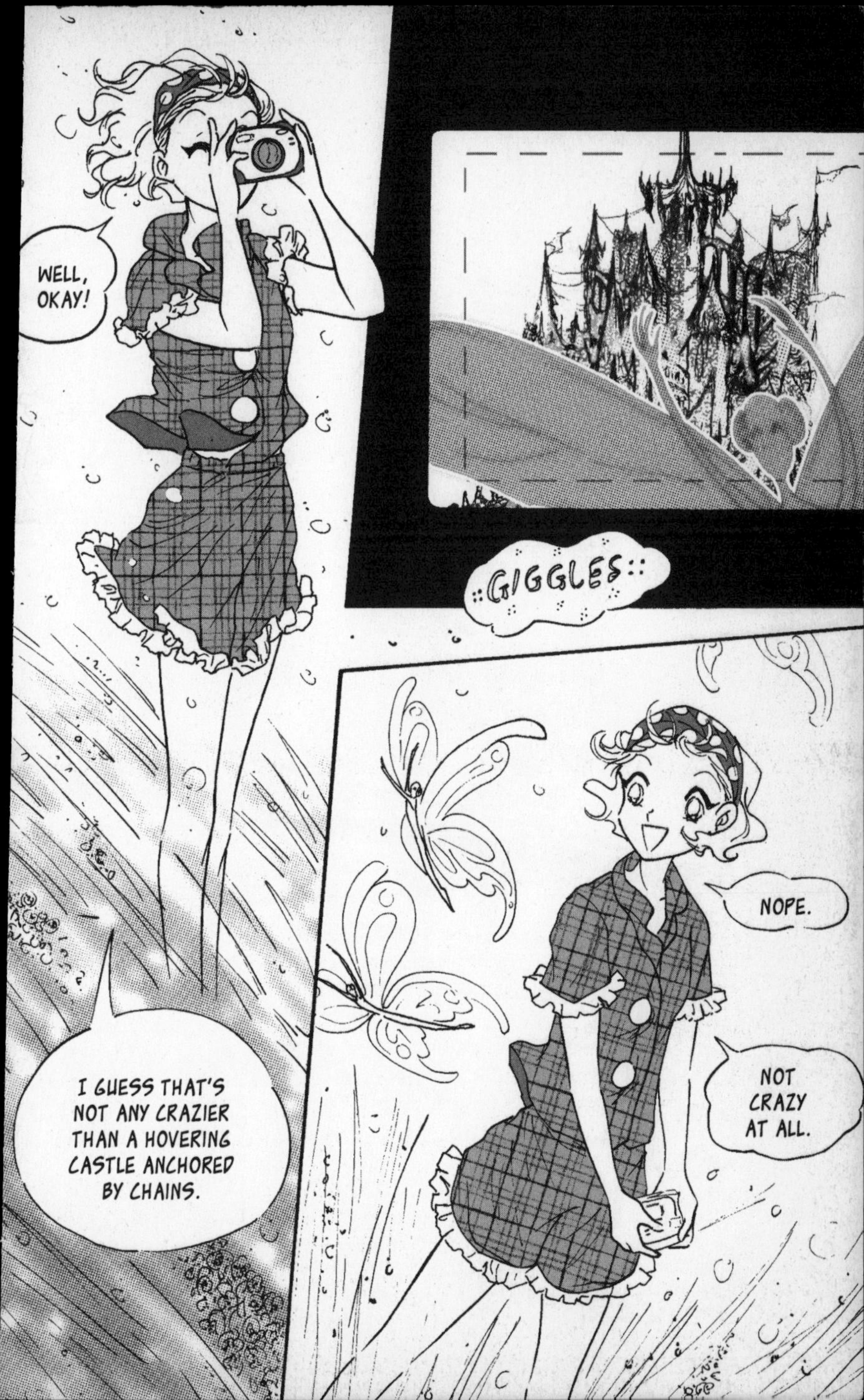
WELL, OKAY!
GIGGLES
I GUESS THAT'S NOT ANY CRAZIER THAN A HOVERING CASTLE ANCHORED BY CHAINS.
NOPE.
NOT CRAZY AT ALL.

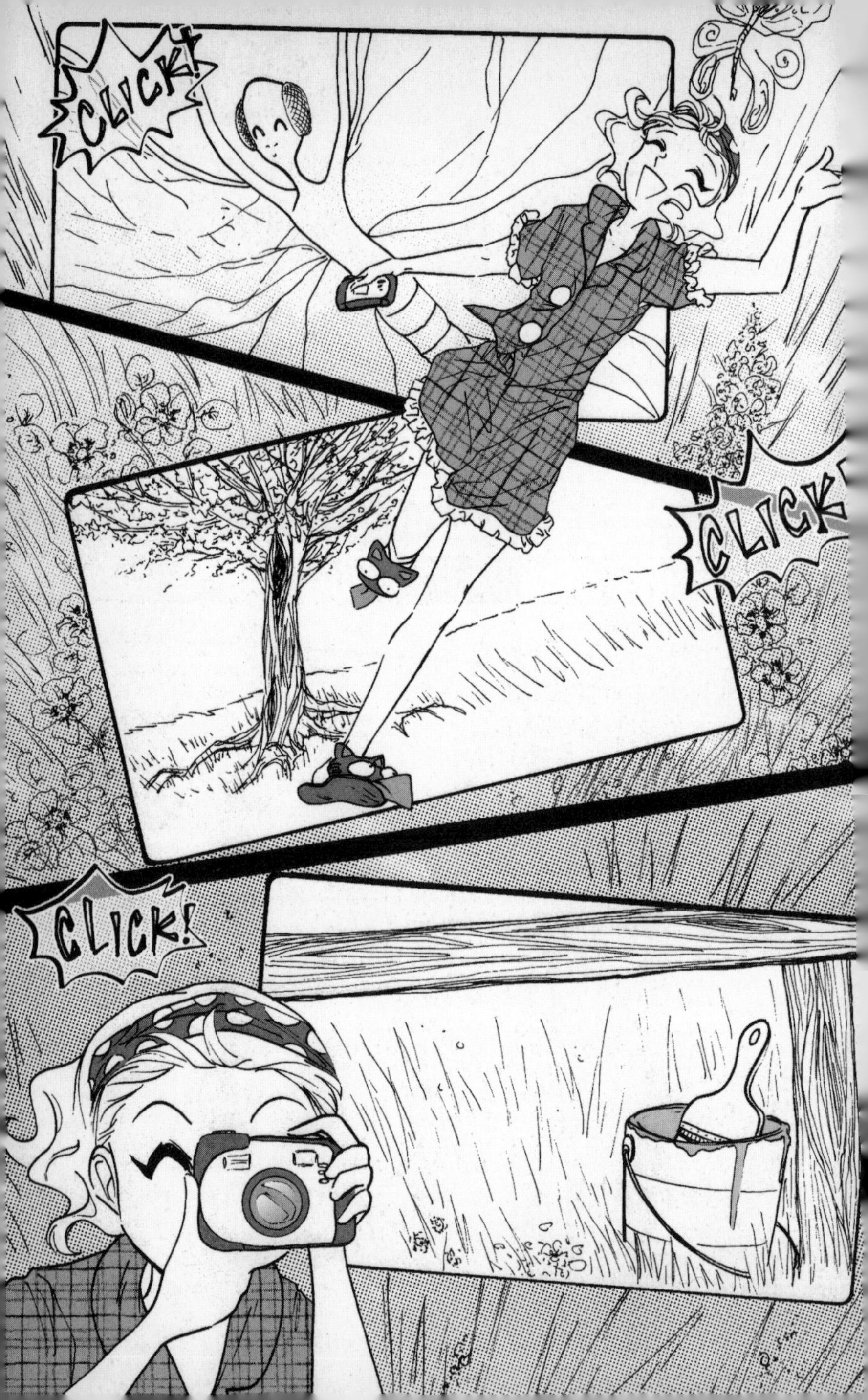
CLICK!
CLICK!
CLICK!

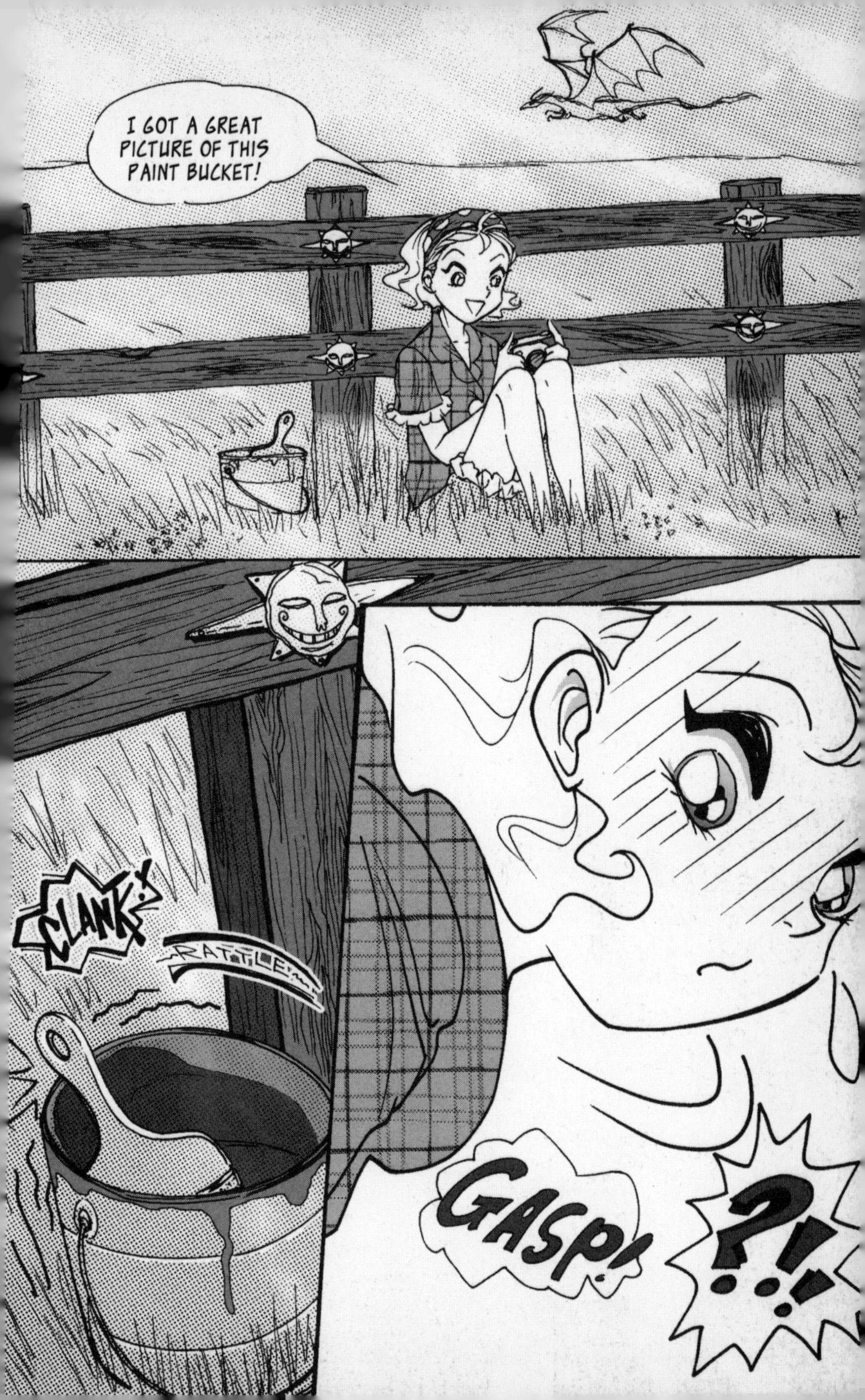
I GOT A GREAT PICTURE OF THIS PAINT BUCKET!
CLANK!
RATTLE
GASP!
?!!

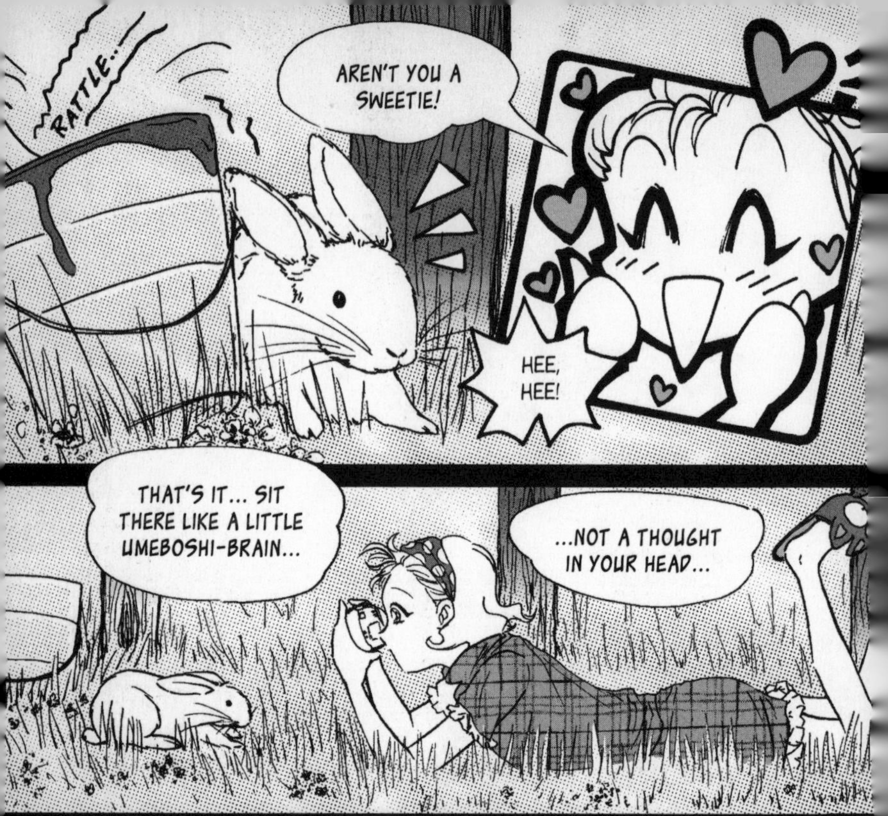
RATTLE...
AREN'T YOU A SWEETIE!
HEE, HEE!
THAT'S IT... SIT THERE LIKE A LITTLE UMEBOSHI-BRAIN...
...NOT A THOUGHT IN YOUR HEAD...

AN UMEBOSHI IS A SMALL, SHRIVELED JAPANESE PICKLED PLUM!

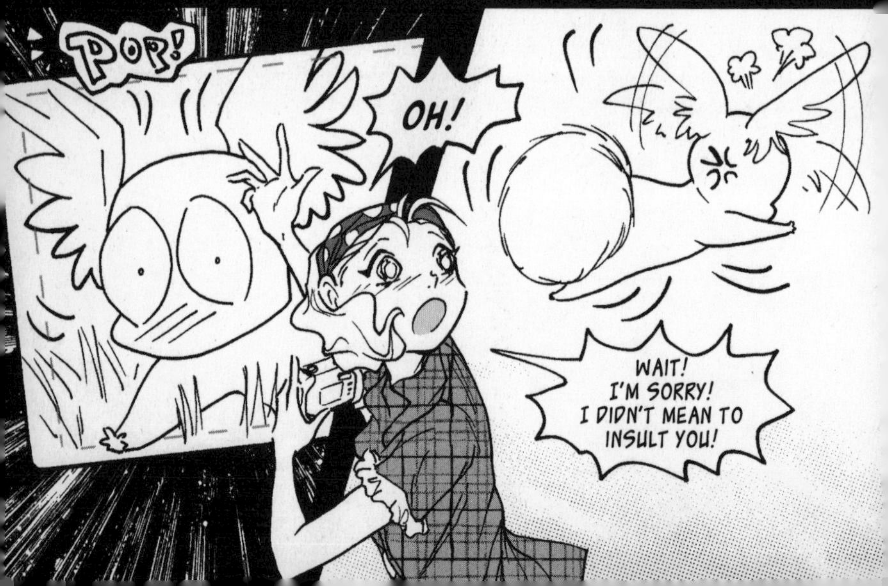
POP!
OH!
WAIT! I'M SORRY! I DIDN'T MEAN TO INSULT YOU!

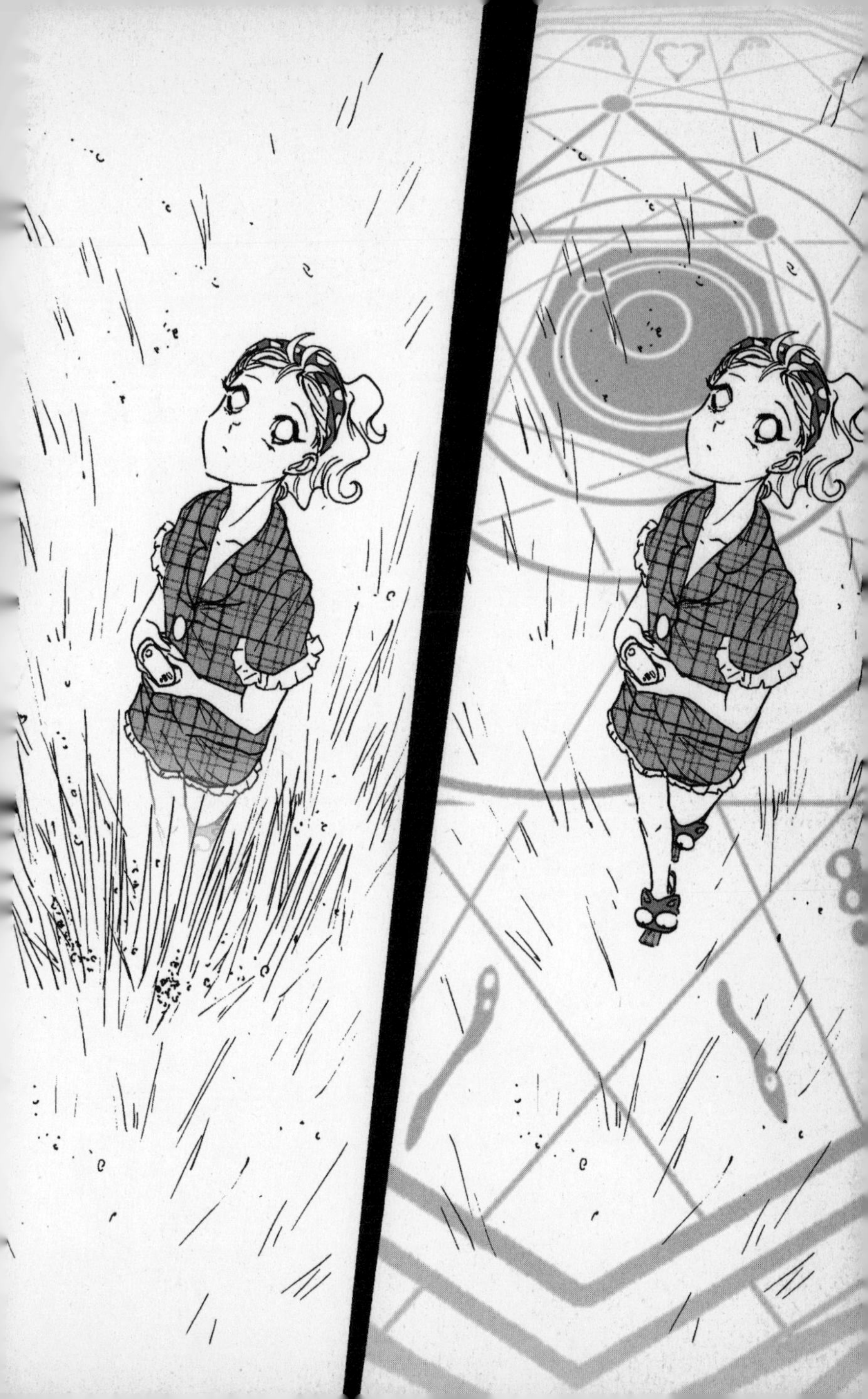

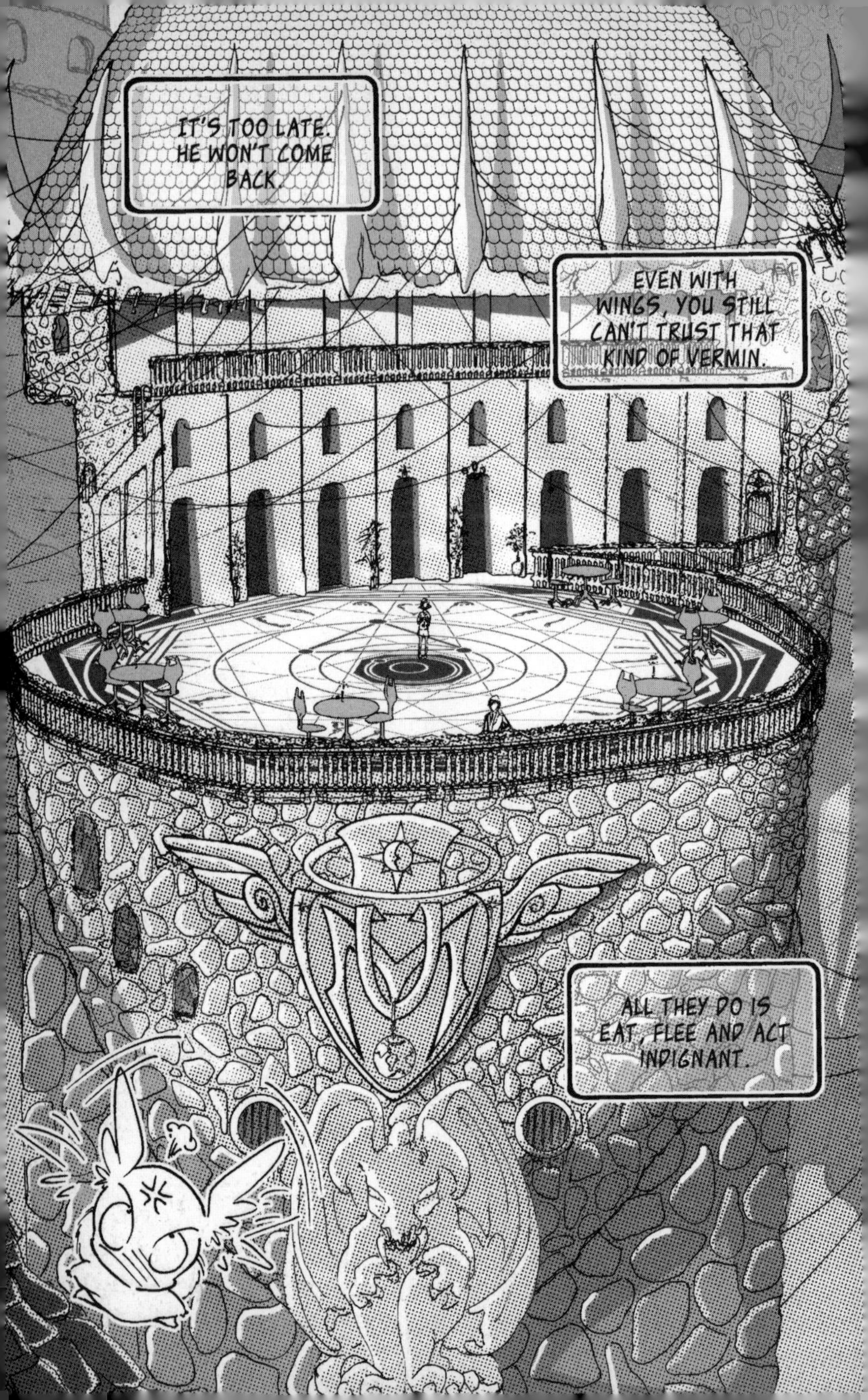
IT'S TOO LATE. HE WON'T COME BACK.
EVEN WITH WINGS, YOU STILL CAN'T TRUST THAT KIND OF VERMIN.
ALL THEY DO IS EAT, FLEE AND ACT INDIGNANT.

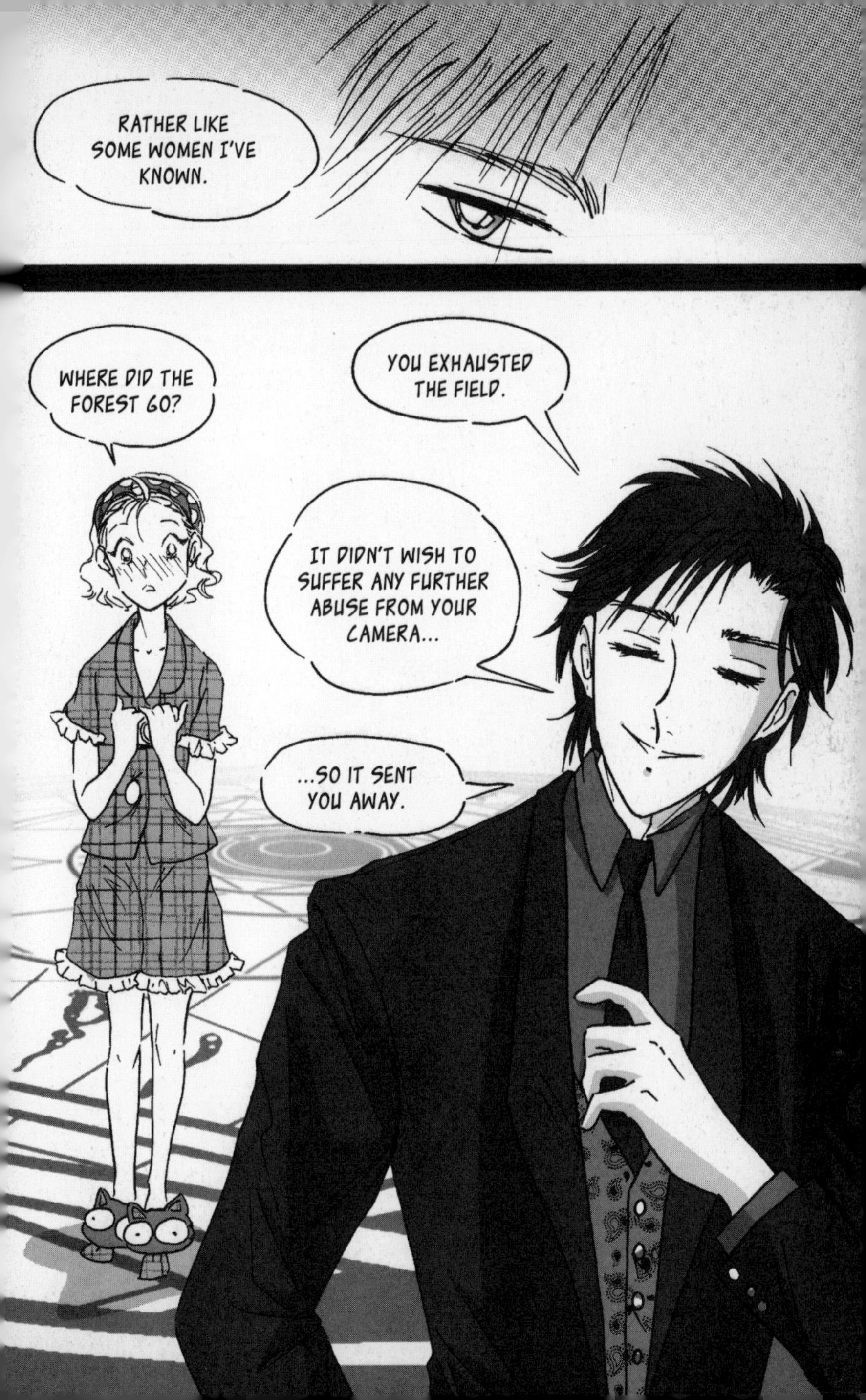
RATHER LIKE SOME WOMEN I'VE KNOWN.
WHERE DID THE FOREST GO?
YOU EXHAUSTED THE FIELD.
IT DIDN'T WISH TO SUFFER ANY FURTHER ABUSE FROM YOUR CAMERA...
...SO IT SENT YOU AWAY.

CHAPTER FOUR:
IT IS RHETORICAL

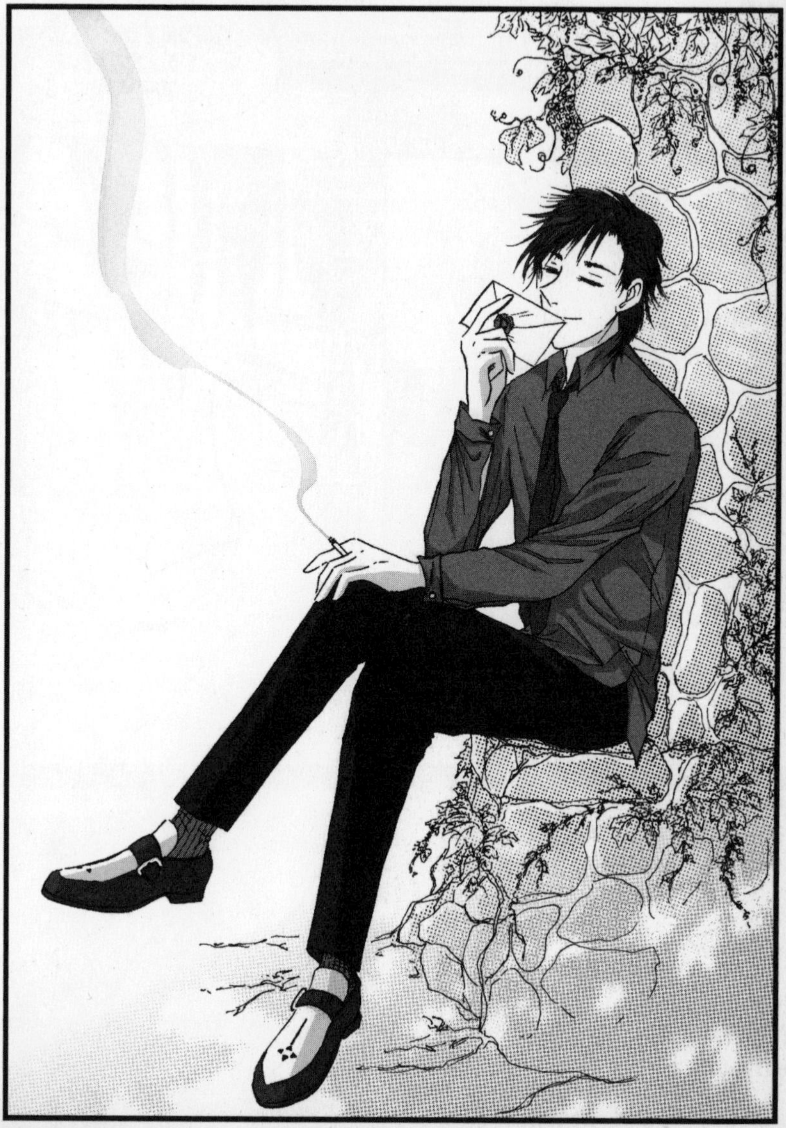

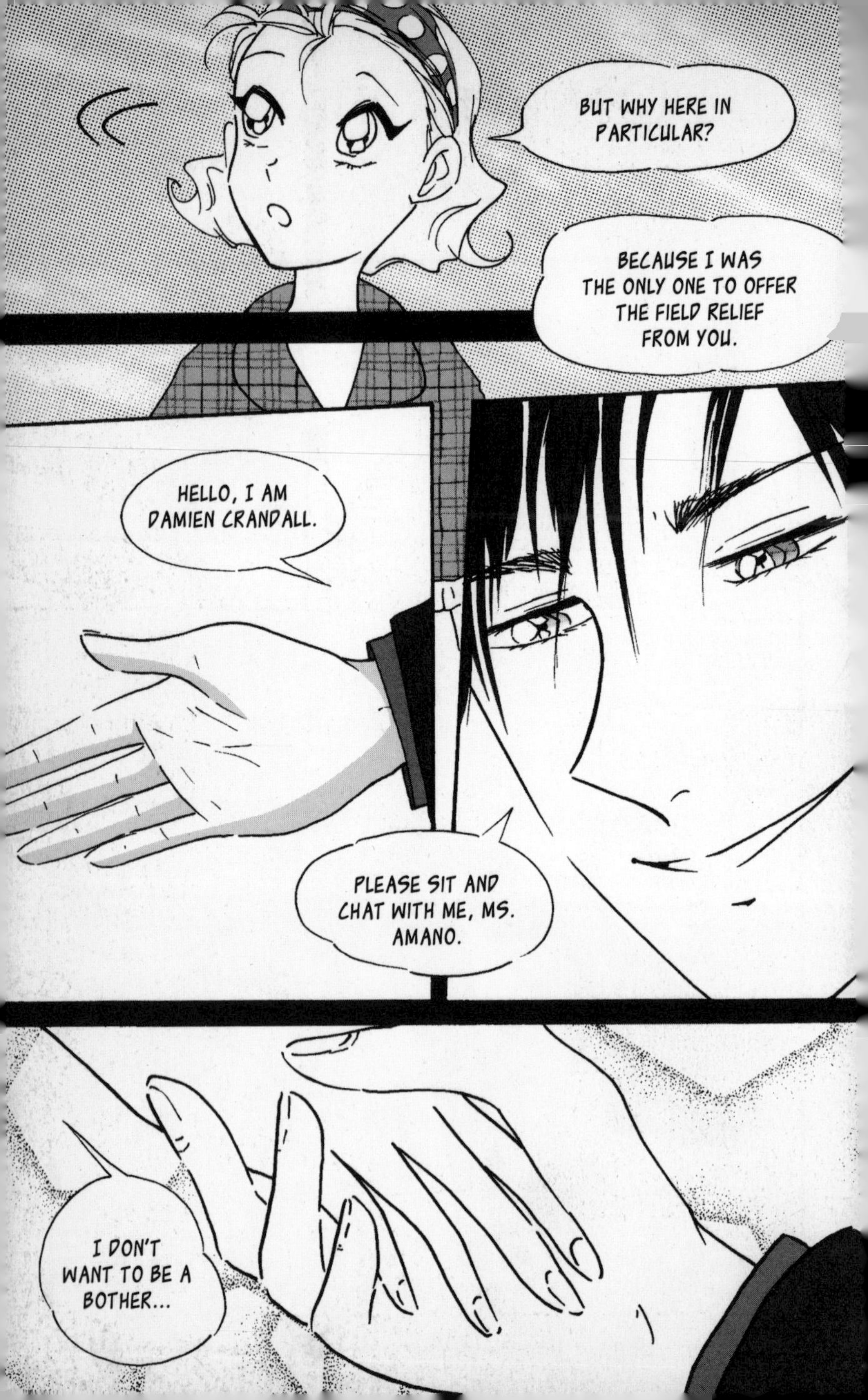
BUT WHY HERE IN PARTICULAR?
BECAUSE I WAS THE ONLY ONE TO OFFER THE FIELD RELIEF FROM YOU.
HELLO, I AM DAMIEN CRANDALL.
PLEASE SIT AND CHAT WITH ME, MS. AMANO.
I DON'T WANT TO BE A BOTHER...

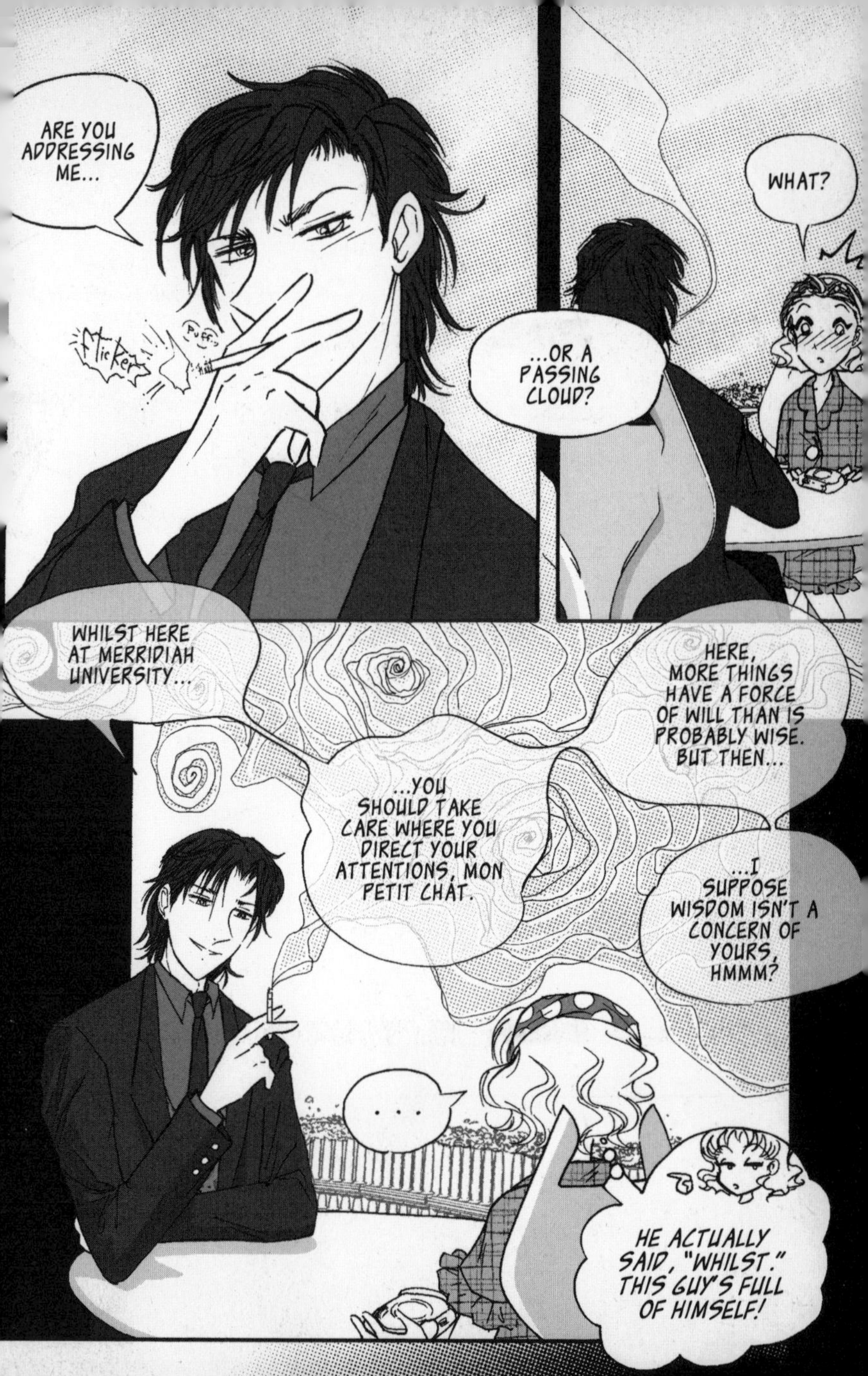
ARE YOU ADDRESSING ME...
Flicker
Puff
WHAT?
...OR A PASSING CLOUD?
WHILST HERE AT MERRIDIAH UNIVERSITY...
...YOU SHOULD TAKE CARE WHERE YOU DIRECT YOUR ATTENTIONS, MON PETIT CHAT.
HERE, MORE THINGS HAVE A FORCE OF WILL THAN IS PROBABLY WISE. BUT THEN...
...I SUPPOSE WISDOM ISN'T A CONCERN OF YOURS, HMMM?
. . .
HE ACTUALLY SAID, "WHILST." THIS GUY'S FULL OF HIMSELF!

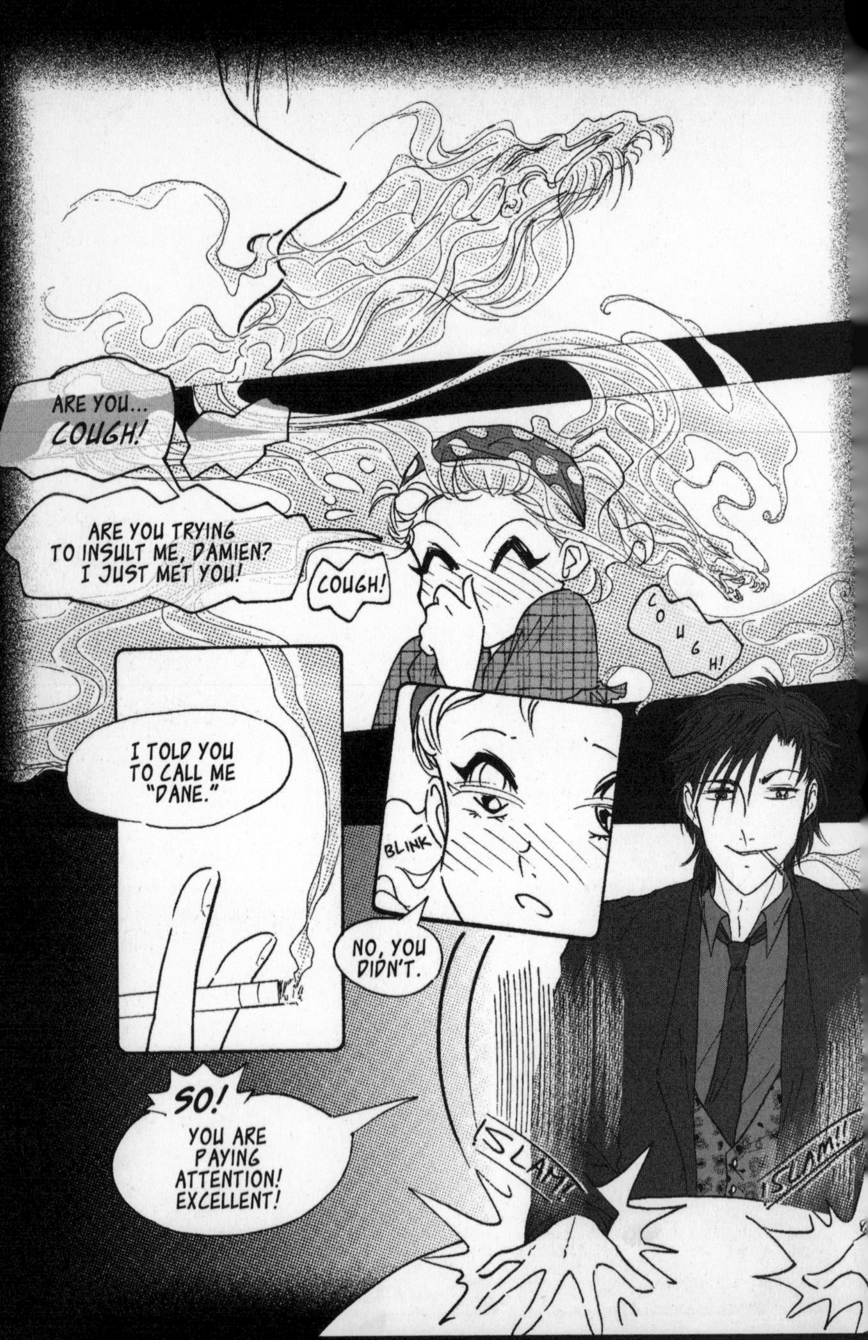
ARE YOU... COUGH!
ARE YOU TRYING TO INSULT ME, DAMIEN? I JUST MET YOU!
COUGH!
COUGH!
I TOLD YOU TO CALL ME "DANE."
BLINK
NO, YOU DIDN'T.
SO! YOU ARE PAYING ATTENTION! EXCELLENT!
SLAM!
SLAM!!

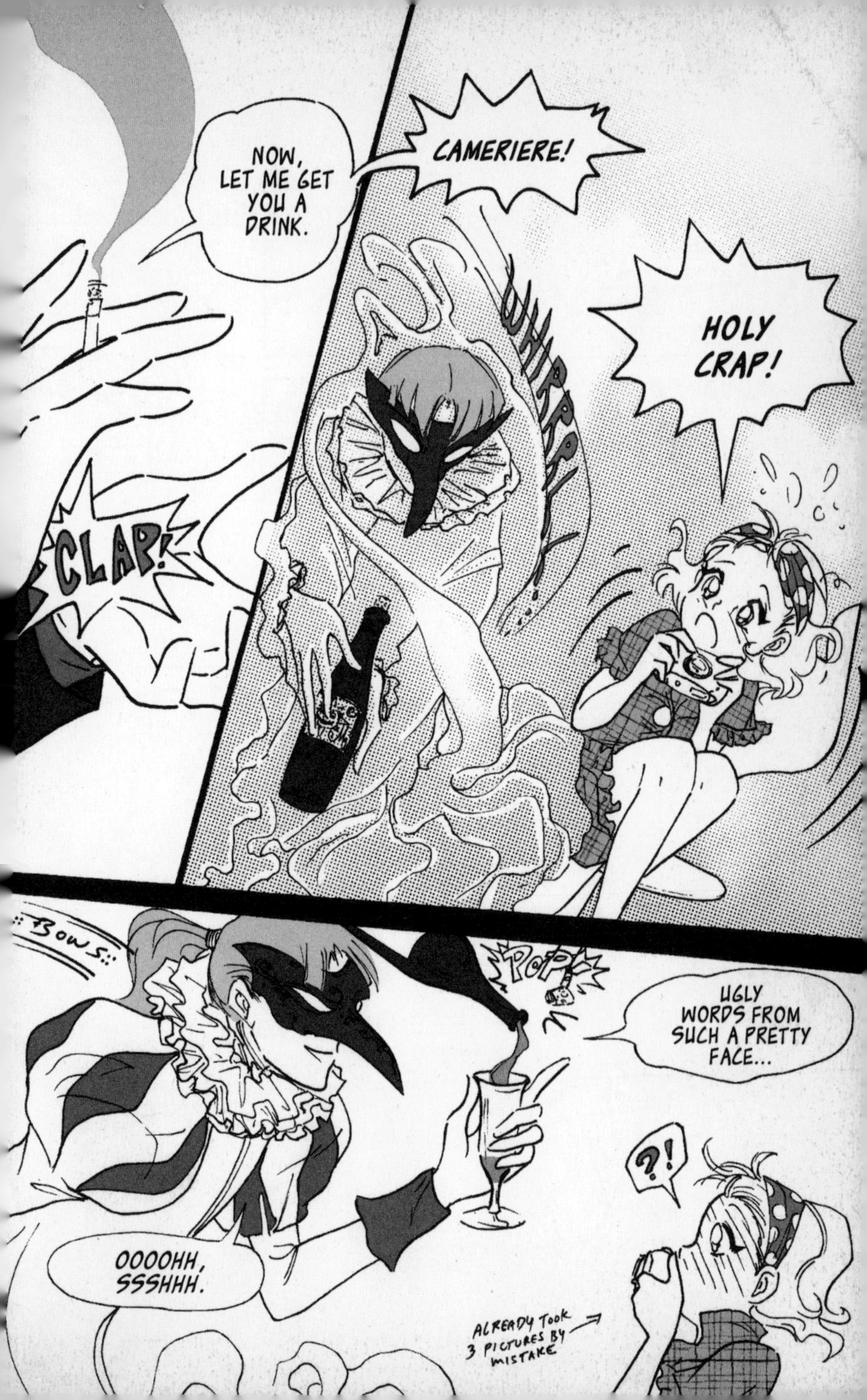
NOW, LET ME GET YOU A DRINK.
CLAP!
CAMERIERE!
WHIRRR!
HOLY CRAP!
BOWS
POP!
UGLY WORDS FROM SUCH A PRETTY FACE...
?!
OOOOHH, SSSHHH.
ALREADY TOOK 3 PICTURES BY MISTAKE

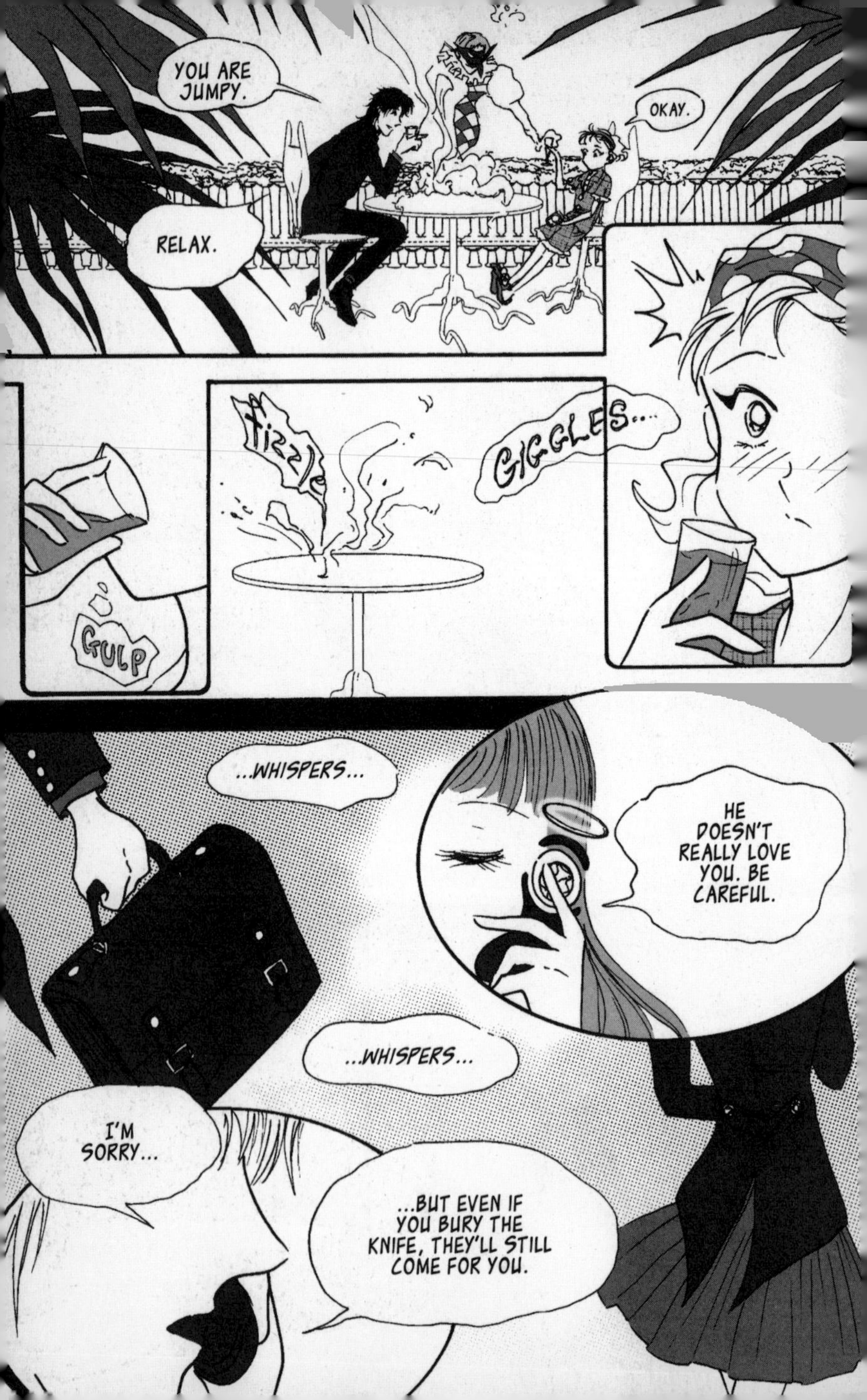
YOU ARE JUMPY.
RELAX.
OKAY.
GULP
fizzle
GIGGLES....
...WHISPERS...
HE DOESN'T REALLY LOVE YOU. BE CAREFUL.
...WHISPERS...
I'M SORRY...
...BUT EVEN IF YOU BURY THE KNIFE, THEY'LL STILL COME FOR YOU.

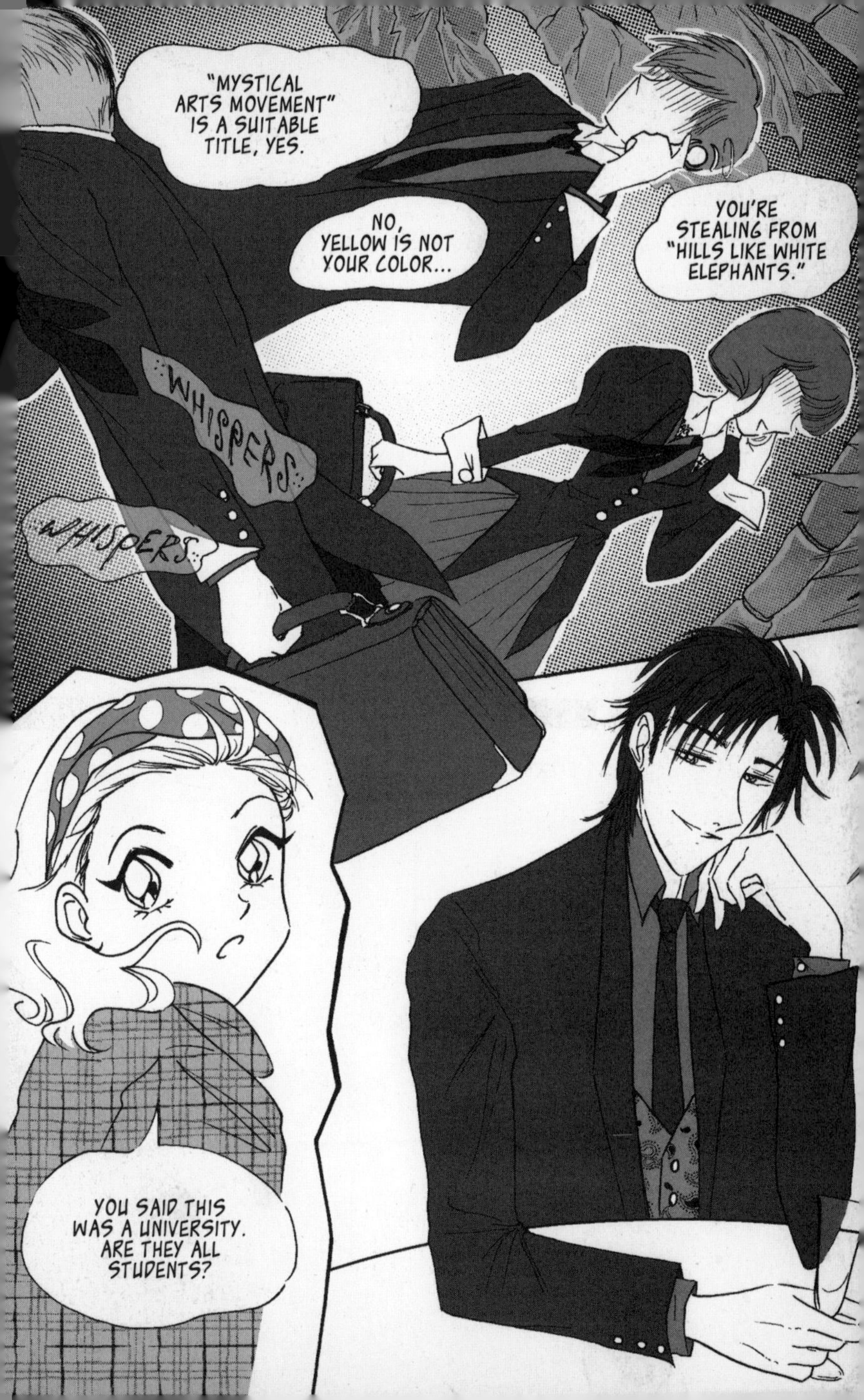
"MYSTICAL ARTS MOVEMENT" IS A SUITABLE TITLE, YES.
NO, YELLOW IS NOT YOUR COLOR...
YOU'RE STEALING FROM "HILLS LIKE WHITE ELEPHANTS."
WHISPERS
WHISPERS
YOU SAID THIS WAS A UNIVERSITY. ARE THEY ALL STUDENTS?

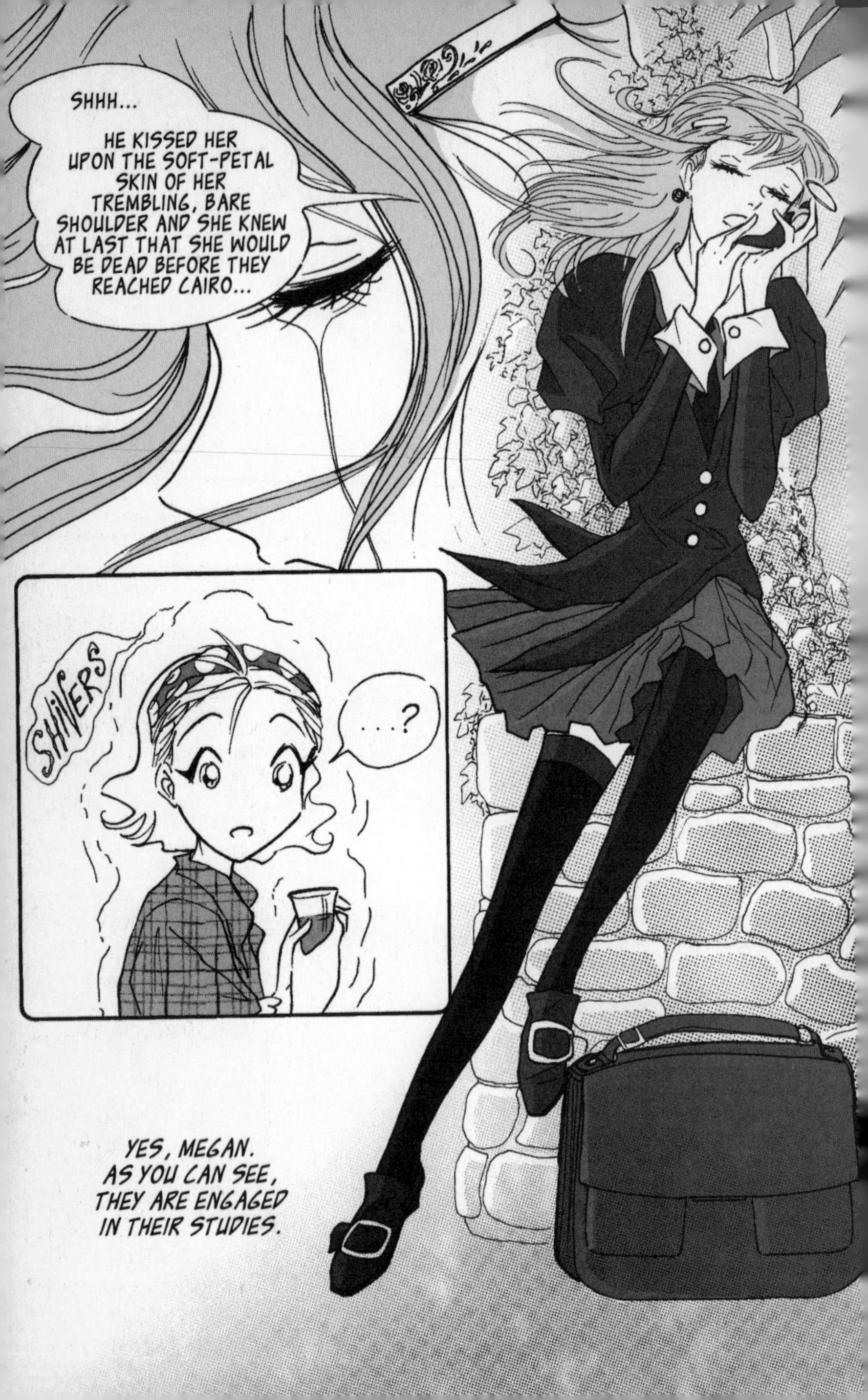
SHHH...
HE KISSED HER UPON THE SOFT-PETAL SKIN OF HER TREMBLING, BARE SHOULDER AND SHE KNEW AT LAST THAT SHE WOULD BE DEAD BEFORE THEY REACHED CAIRO...
SHIVERS
...?
YES, MEGAN. AS YOU CAN SEE, THEY ARE ENGAGED IN THEIR STUDIES.

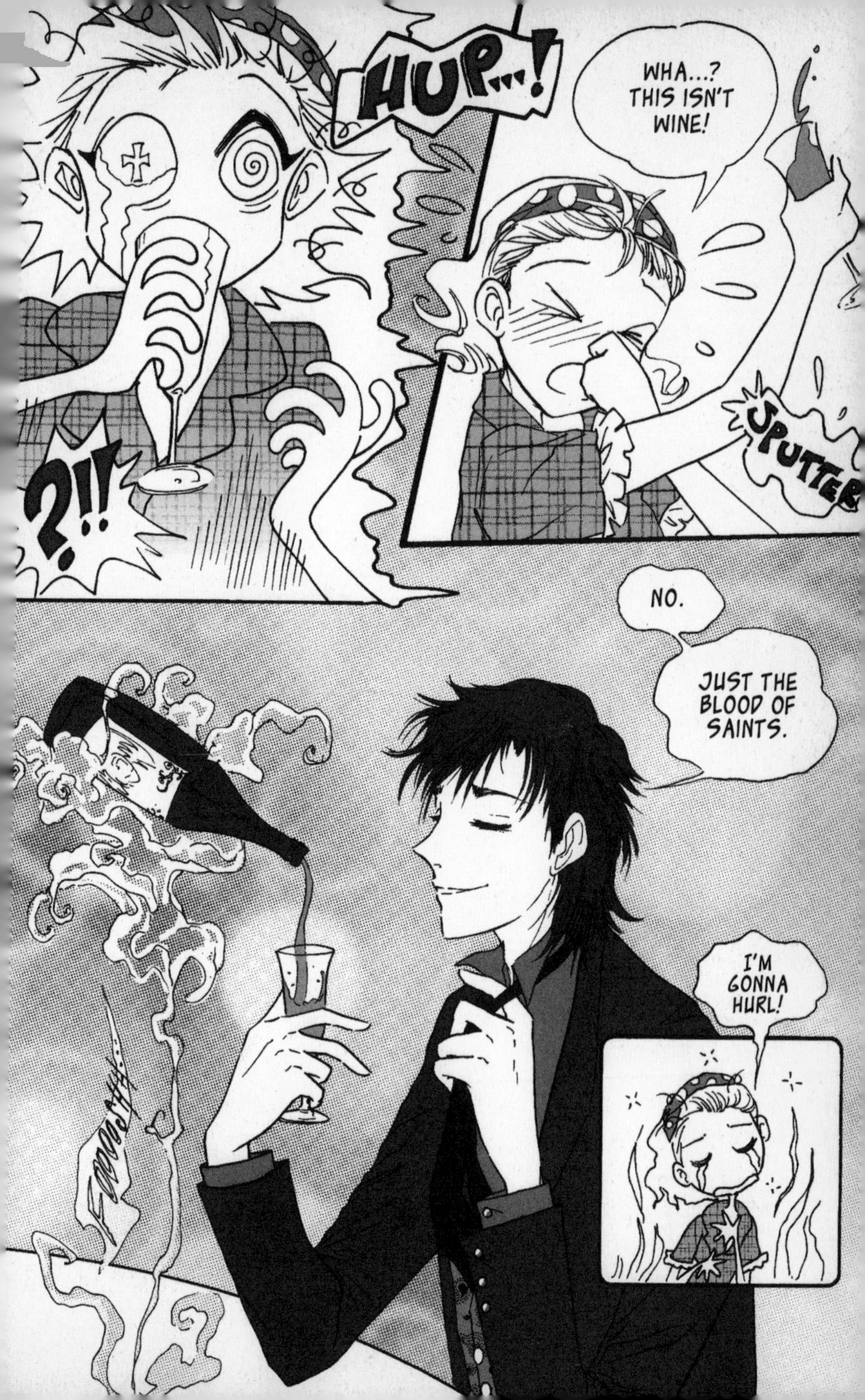
HUP...!
?!!
WHA...? THIS ISN'T WINE!
SPUTTER
NO.
JUST THE BLOOD OF SAINTS.
I'M GONNA HURL!

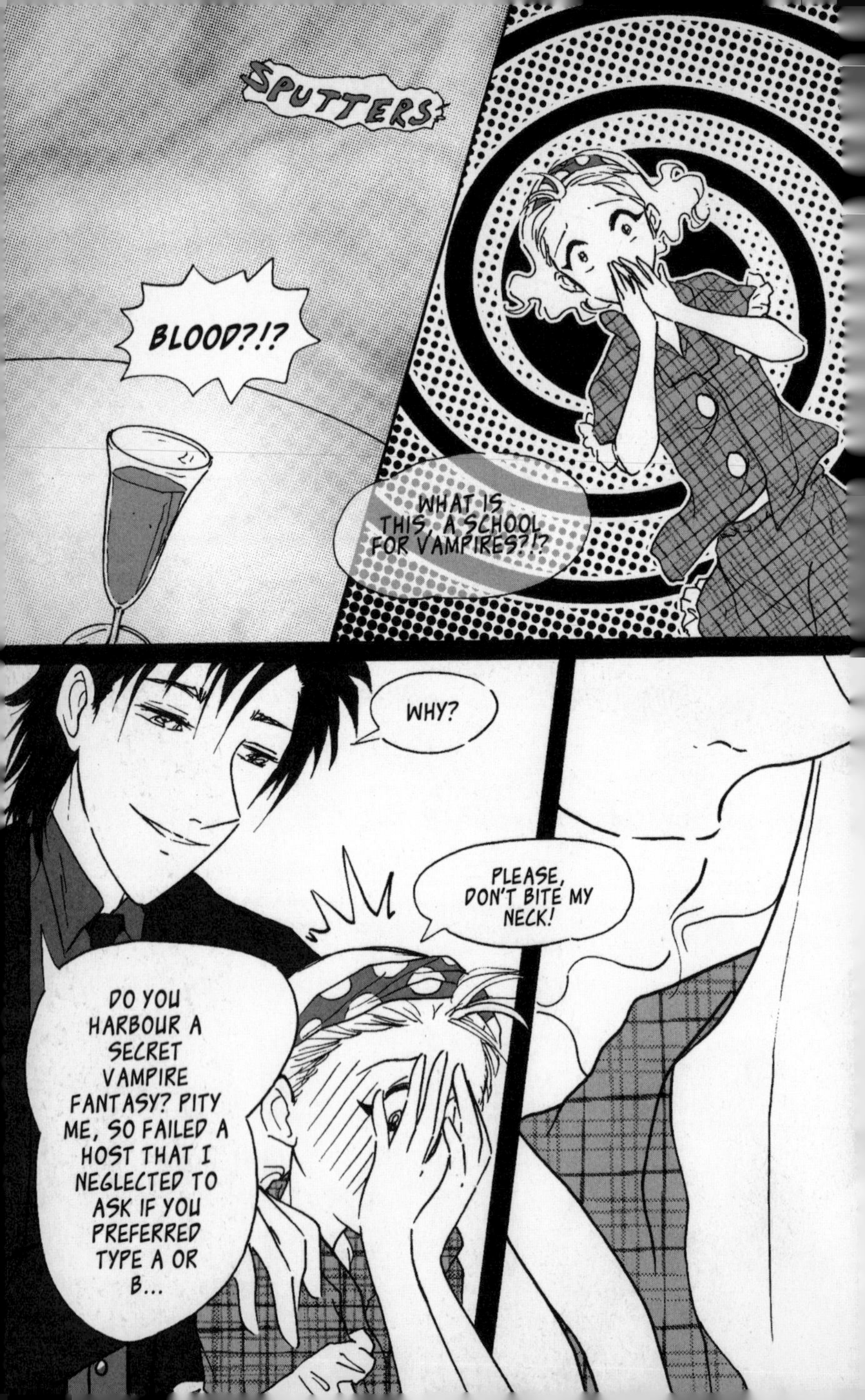
SPUTTERS
BLOOD?!?
WHAT IS THIS, A SCHOOL FOR VAMPIRES?!?
WHY?
DO YOU HARBOUR A SECRET VAMPIRE FANTASY? PITY ME, SO FAILED A HOST THAT I NEGLECTED TO ASK IF YOU PREFERRED TYPE A OR B...
PLEASE, DON'T BITE MY NECK!

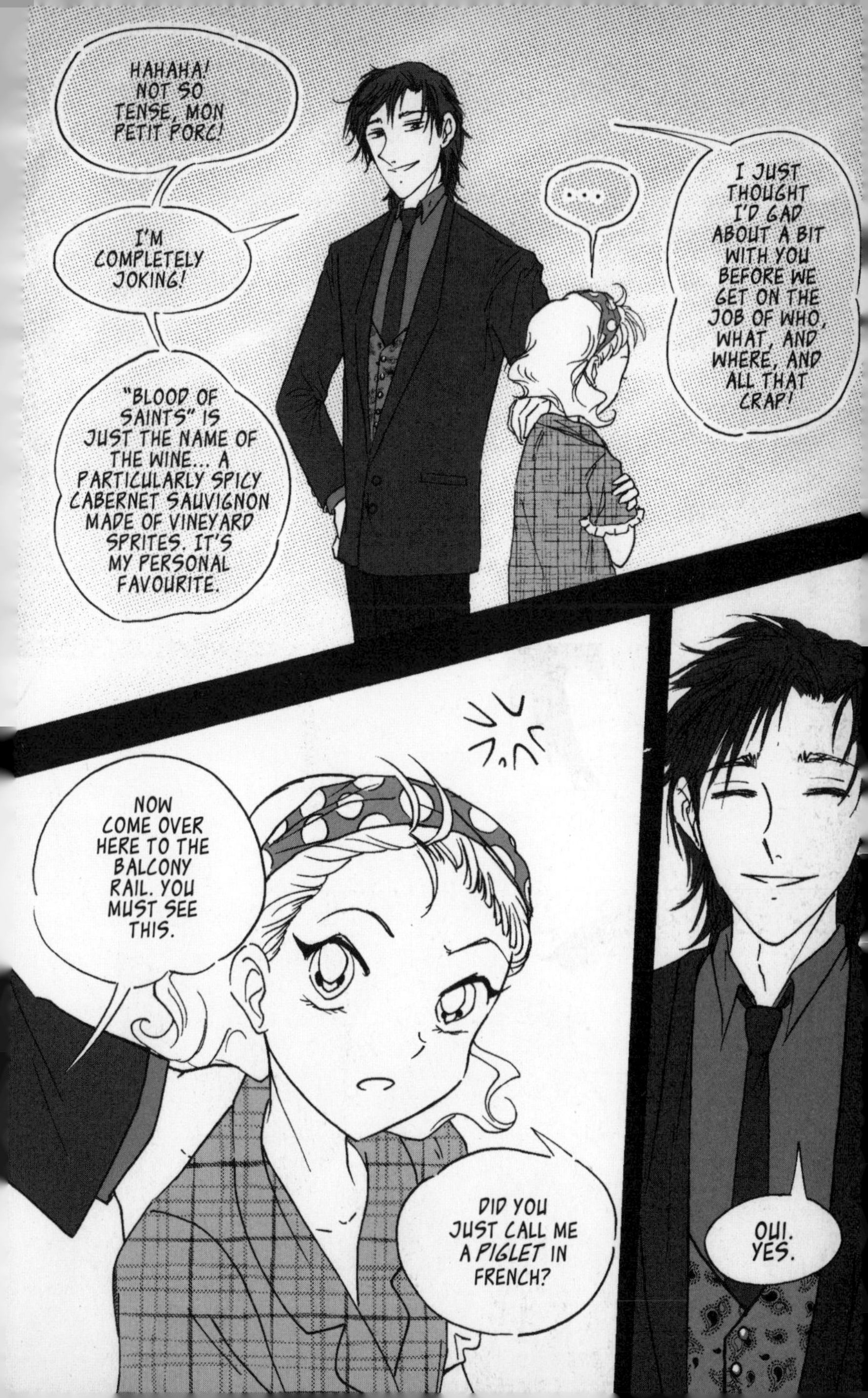
HAHAHA! NOT SO TENSE, MON PETIT PORC!
I'M COMPLETELY JOKING!
"BLOOD OF SAINTS" IS JUST THE NAME OF THE WINE... A PARTICULARLY SPICY CABERNET SAUVIGNON MADE OF VINEYARD SPRITES. IT'S MY PERSONAL FAVOURITE.
...
I JUST THOUGHT I'D GAD ABOUT A BIT WITH YOU BEFORE WE GET ON THE JOB OF WHO, WHAT, AND WHERE, AND ALL THAT CRAP!
NOW COME OVER HERE TO THE BALCONY RAIL. YOU MUST SEE THIS.
DID YOU JUST CALL ME A *PIGLET* IN FRENCH?
OUI. YES.

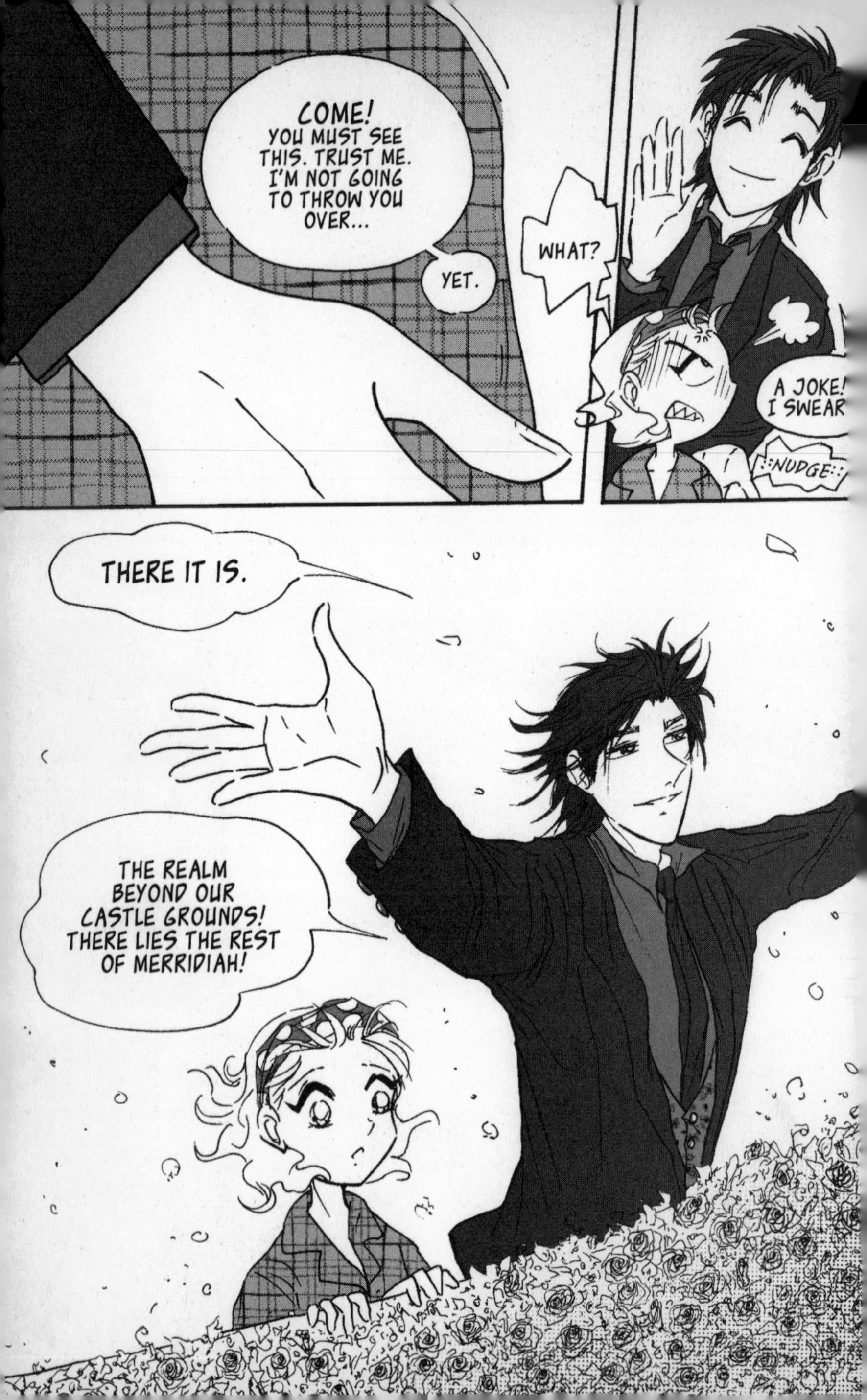
COME! YOU MUST SEE THIS. TRUST ME. I'M NOT GOING TO THROW YOU OVER...
YET.
WHAT?
A JOKE! I SWEAR
NUDGE
THERE IT IS.
THE REALM BEYOND OUR CASTLE GROUNDS! THERE LIES THE REST OF MERRIDIAH!

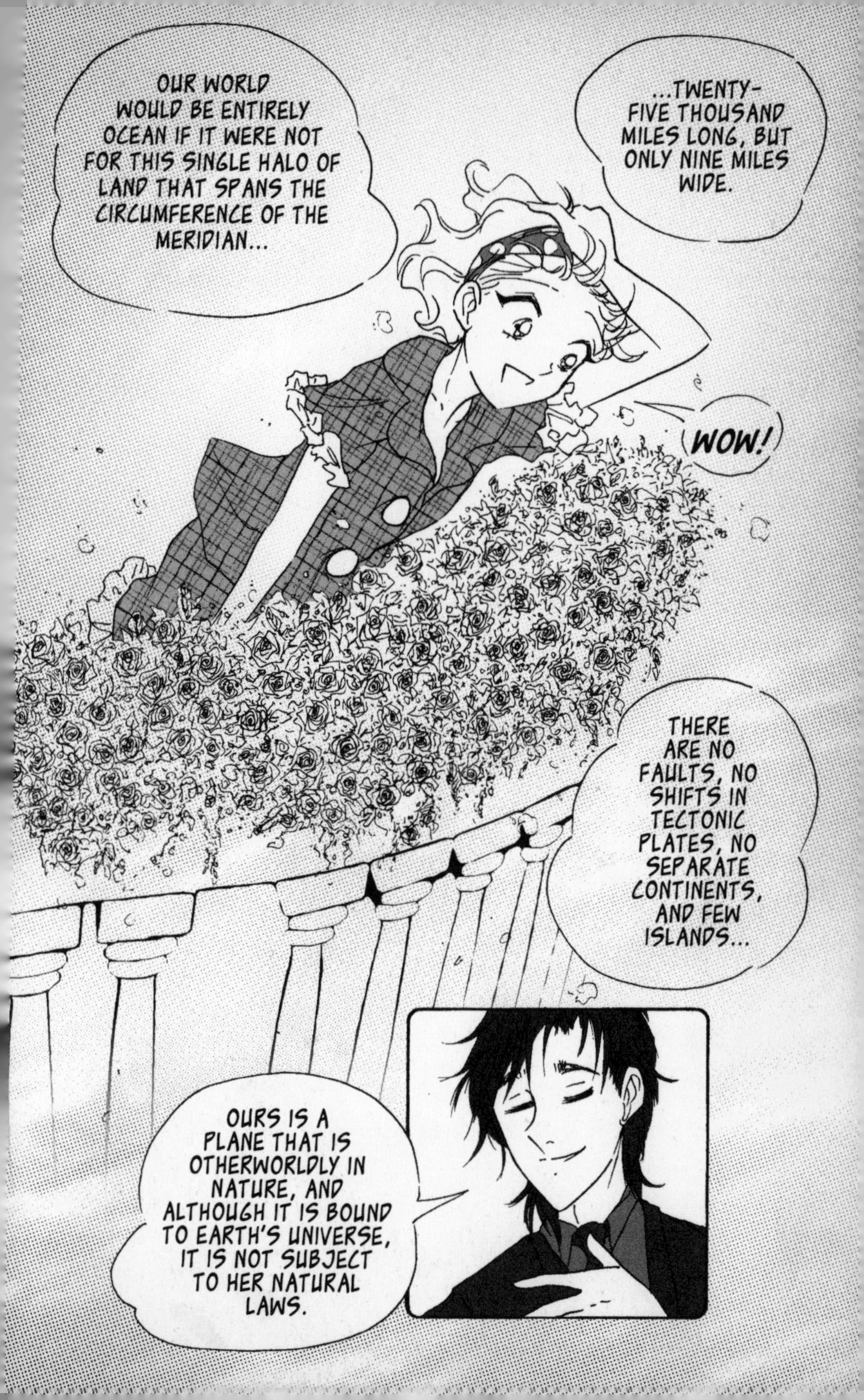
OUR WORLD WOULD BE ENTIRELY OCEAN IF IT WERE NOT FOR THIS SINGLE HALO OF LAND THAT SPANS THE CIRCUMFERENCE OF THE MERIDIAN...
...TWENTY-FIVE THOUSAND MILES LONG, BUT ONLY NINE MILES WIDE.
WOW!
THERE ARE NO FAULTS, NO SHIFTS IN TECTONIC PLATES, NO SEPARATE CONTINENTS, AND FEW ISLANDS...
OURS IS A PLANE THAT IS OTHERWORLDLY IN NATURE, AND ALTHOUGH IT IS BOUND TO EARTH'S UNIVERSE, IT IS NOT SUBJECT TO HER NATURAL LAWS.

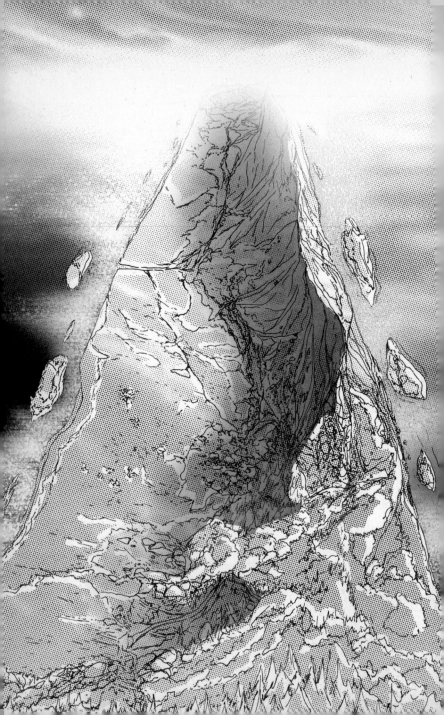

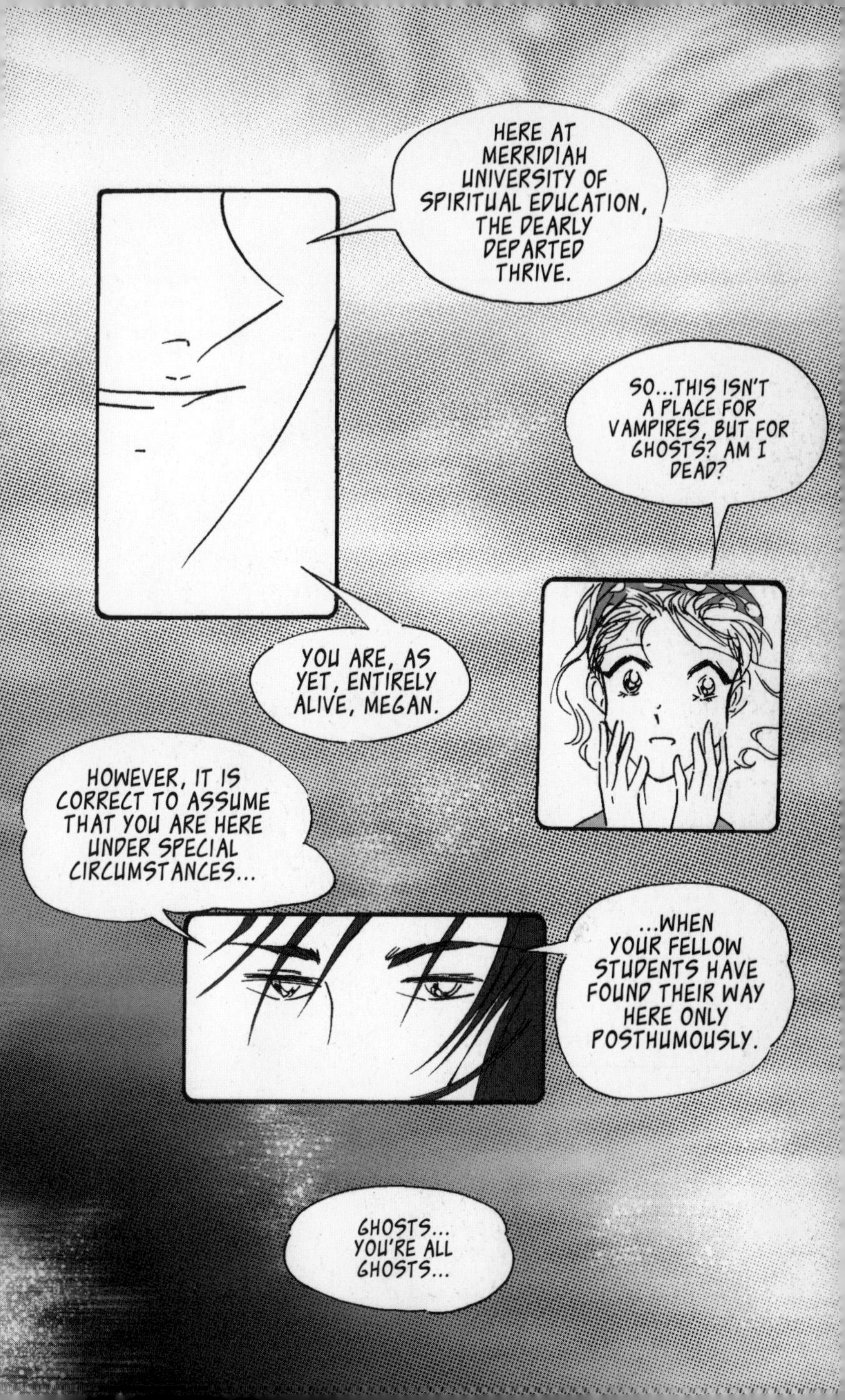
HERE AT MERRIDIAH UNIVERSITY OF SPIRITUAL EDUCATION, THE DEARLY DEPARTED THRIVE.
SO...THIS ISN'T A PLACE FOR VAMPIRES, BUT FOR GHOSTS? AM I DEAD?
YOU ARE, AS YET, ENTIRELY ALIVE, MEGAN.
HOWEVER, IT IS CORRECT TO ASSUME THAT YOU ARE HERE UNDER SPECIAL CIRCUMSTANCES...
...WHEN YOUR FELLOW STUDENTS HAVE FOUND THEIR WAY HERE ONLY POSTHUMOUSLY.
GHOSTS... YOU'RE ALL GHOSTS...

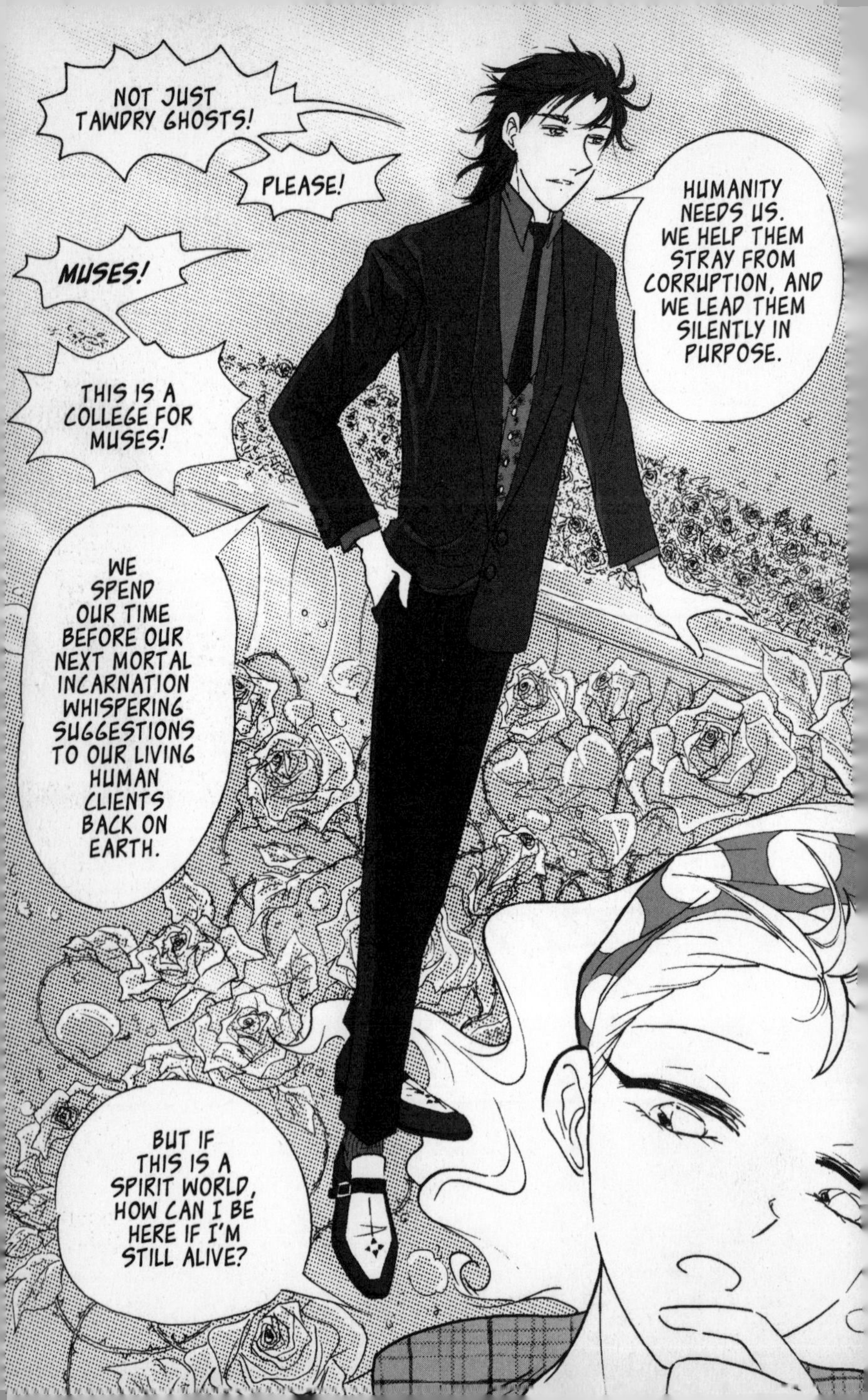
NOT JUST TAWDRY GHOSTS!
PLEASE!
MUSES!
THIS IS A COLLEGE FOR MUSES!
WE SPEND OUR TIME BEFORE OUR NEXT MORTAL INCARNATION WHISPERING SUGGESTIONS TO OUR LIVING HUMAN CLIENTS BACK ON EARTH.
HUMANITY NEEDS US. WE HELP THEM STRAY FROM CORRUPTION, AND WE LEAD THEM SILENTLY IN PURPOSE.
BUT IF THIS IS A SPIRIT WORLD, HOW CAN I BE HERE IF I'M STILL ALIVE?

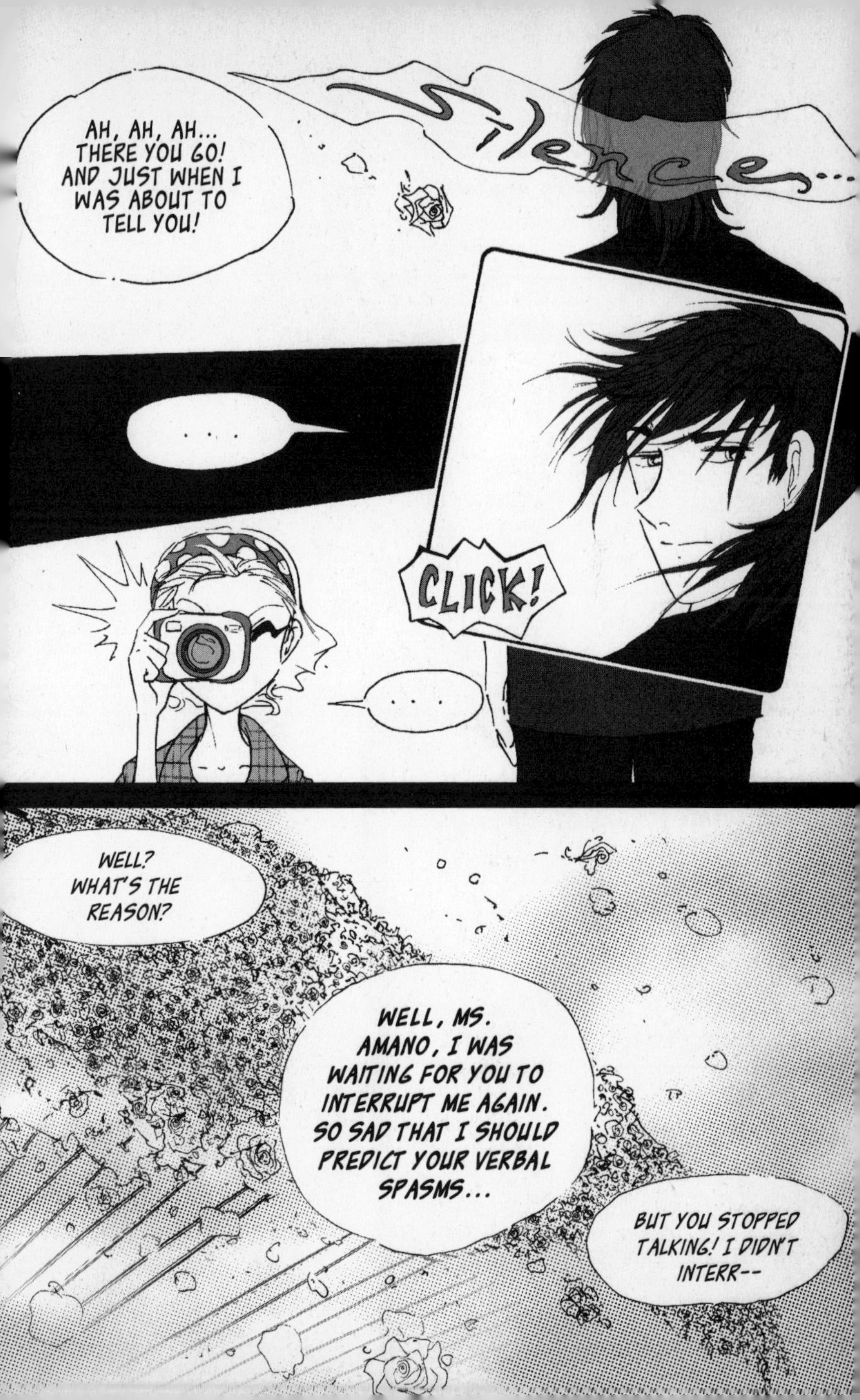
AH, AH, AH... THERE YOU GO! AND JUST WHEN I WAS ABOUT TO TELL YOU!
Silence...
. . .
CLICK!
. . .
WELL? WHAT'S THE REASON?
WELL, MS. AMANO, I WAS WAITING FOR YOU TO INTERRUPT ME AGAIN. SO SAD THAT I SHOULD PREDICT YOUR VERBAL SPASMS...
BUT YOU STOPPED TALKING! I DIDN'T INTERR--

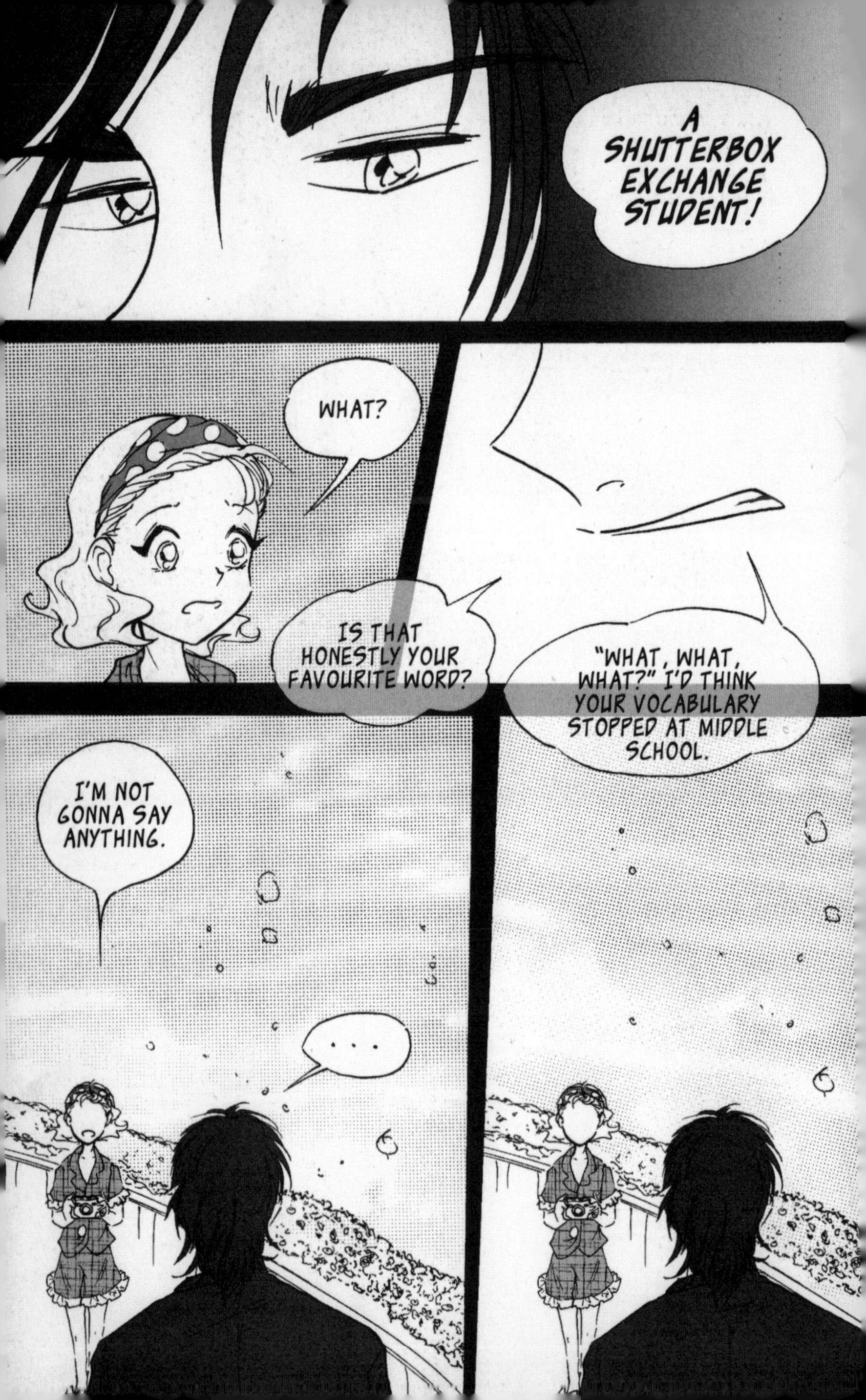
A SHUTTERBOX EXCHANGE STUDENT!
WHAT?
IS THAT HONESTLY YOUR FAVOURITE WORD?
"WHAT, WHAT, WHAT?" I'D THINK YOUR VOCABULARY STOPPED AT MIDDLE SCHOOL.
I'M NOT GONNA SAY ANYTHING.
...

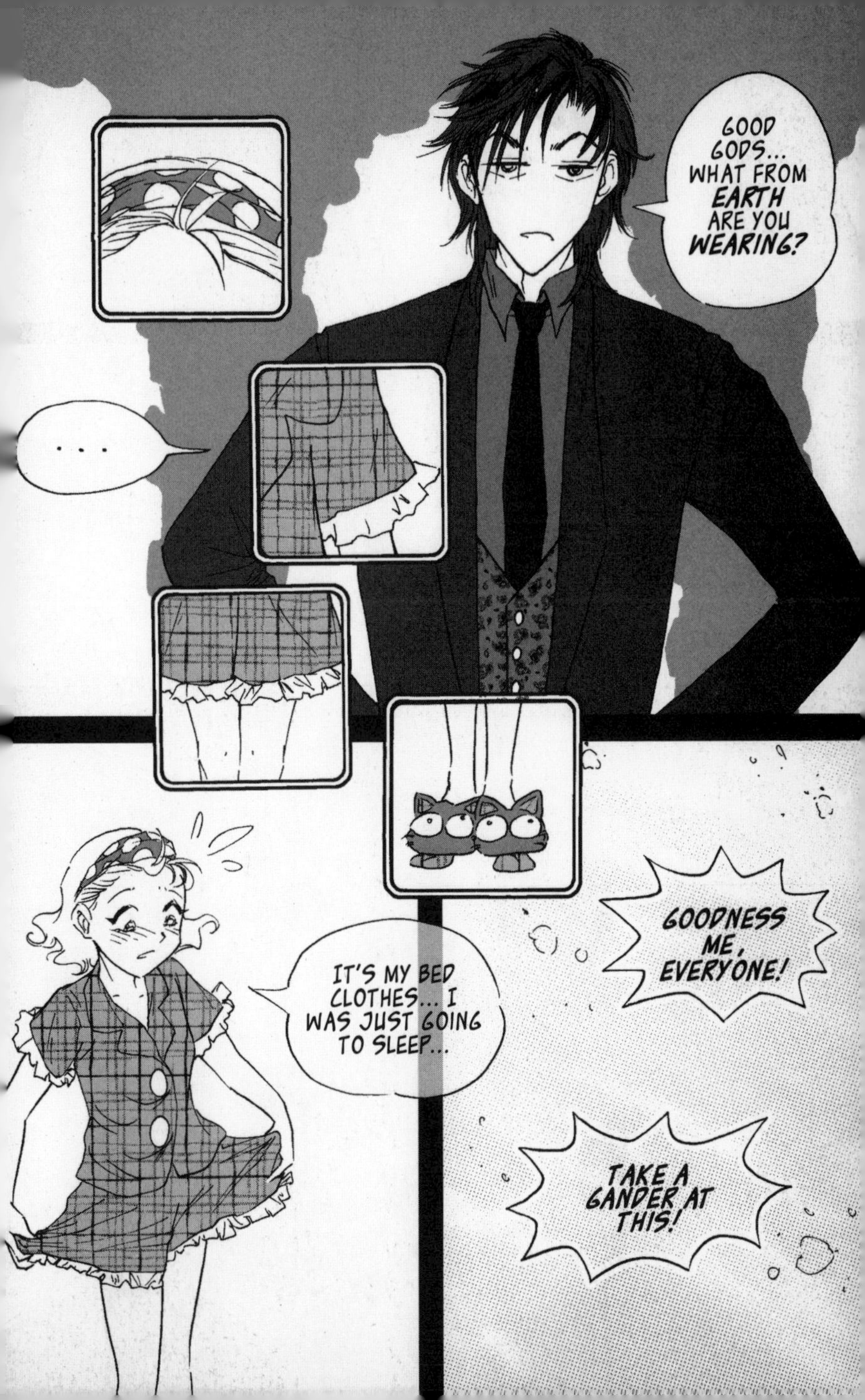
GOOD GODS... WHAT FROM EARTH ARE YOU WEARING?
...
IT'S MY BED CLOTHES... I WAS JUST GOING TO SLEEP...
GOODNESS ME, EVERYONE!
TAKE A GANDER AT THIS!

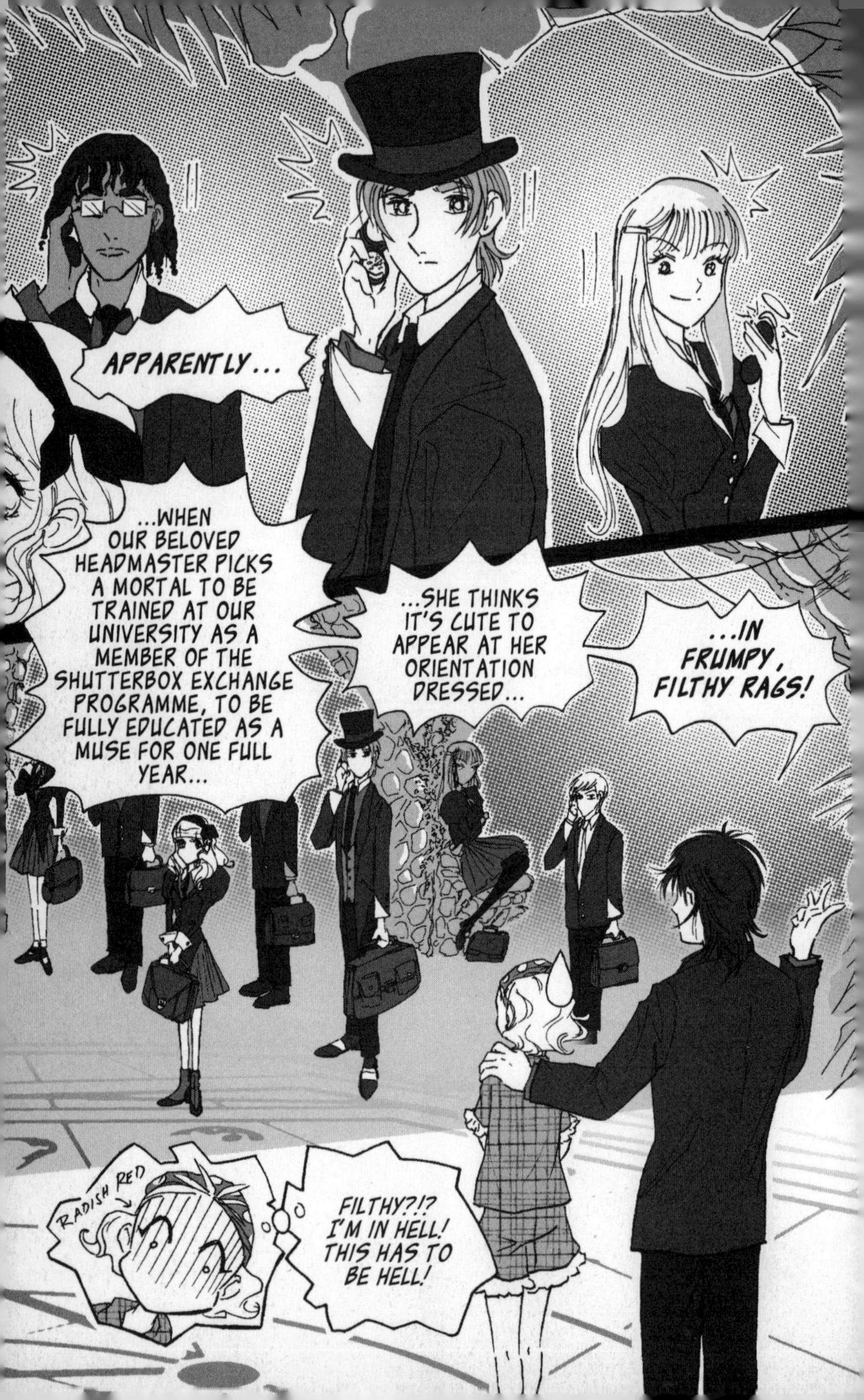
APPARENTLY...
...WHEN OUR BELOVED HEADMASTER PICKS A MORTAL TO BE TRAINED AT OUR UNIVERSITY AS A MEMBER OF THE SHUTTERBOX EXCHANGE PROGRAMME, TO BE FULLY EDUCATED AS A MUSE FOR ONE FULL YEAR...
...SHE THINKS IT'S CUTE TO APPEAR AT HER ORIENTATION DRESSED...
...IN FRUMPY, FILTHY RAGS!
RADISH RED
FILTHY?!? I'M IN HELL! THIS HAS TO BE HELL!

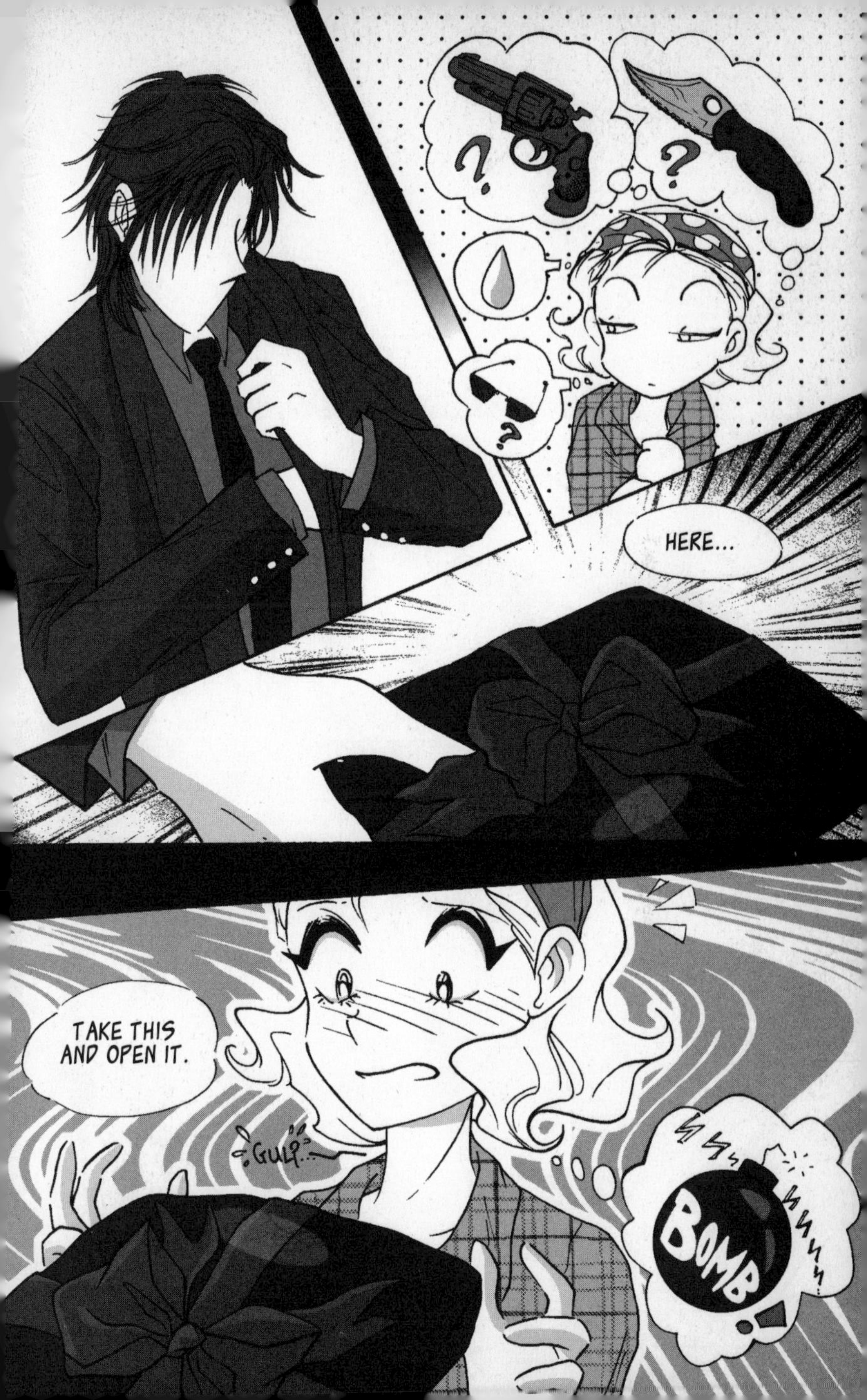
HERE...
TAKE THIS AND OPEN IT.
GULP
BOMB

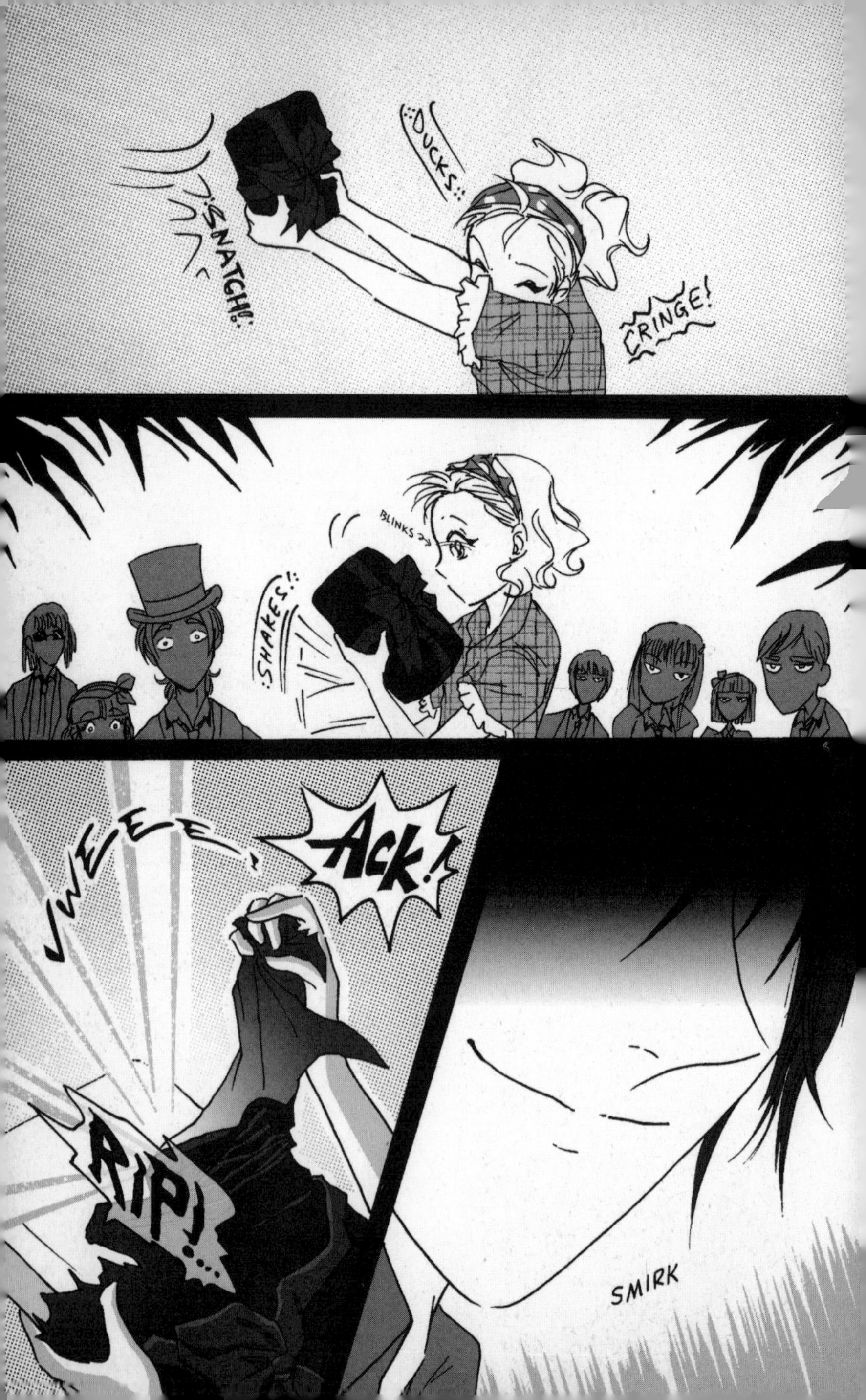
::SNATCH!::
::DUCKS::
CRINGE!
BLINKS
::SHAKES::
WEEE
Ack!
RIP!...
SMIRK

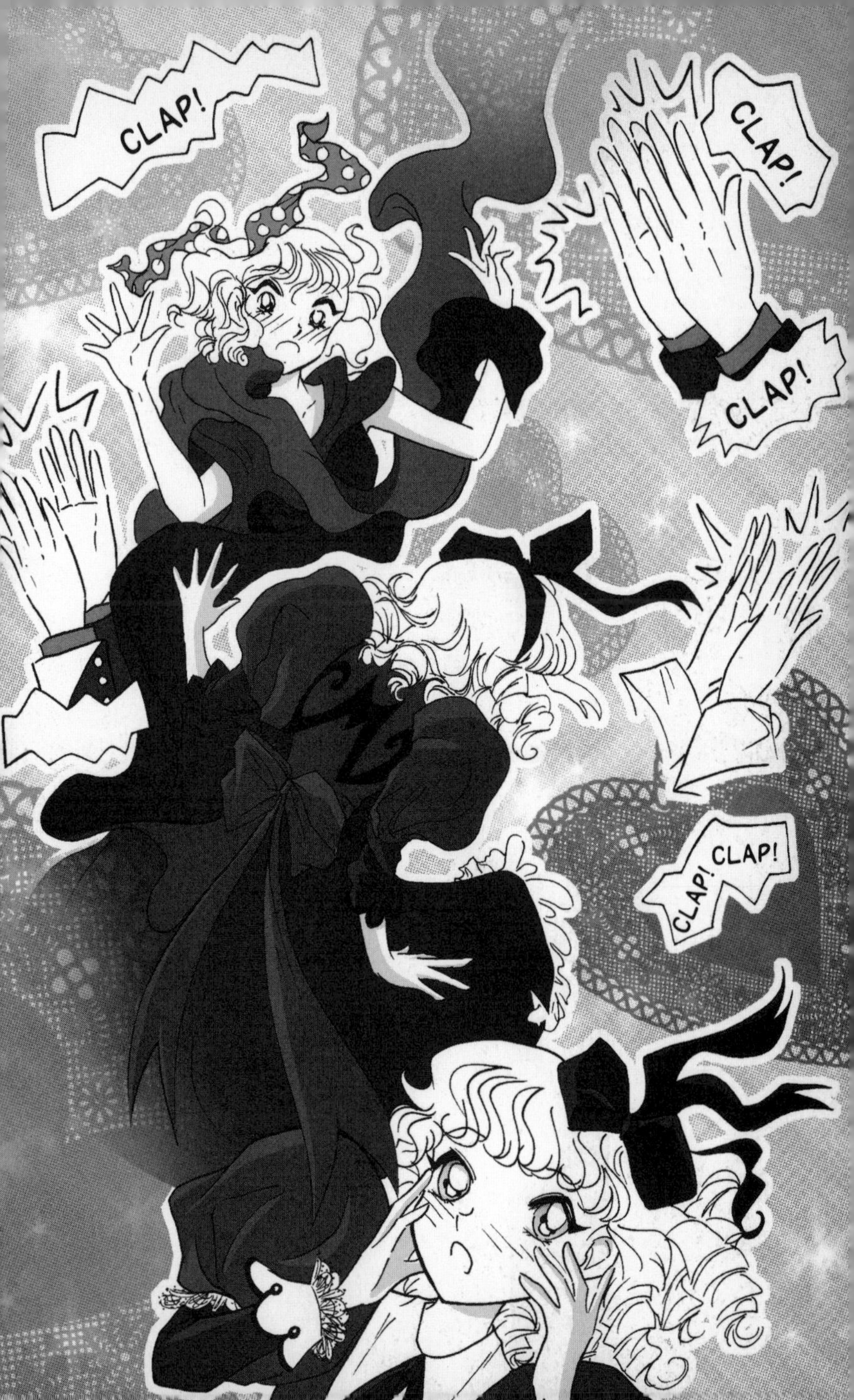
CLAP!
CLAP!
CLAP!
CLAP!
CLAP!

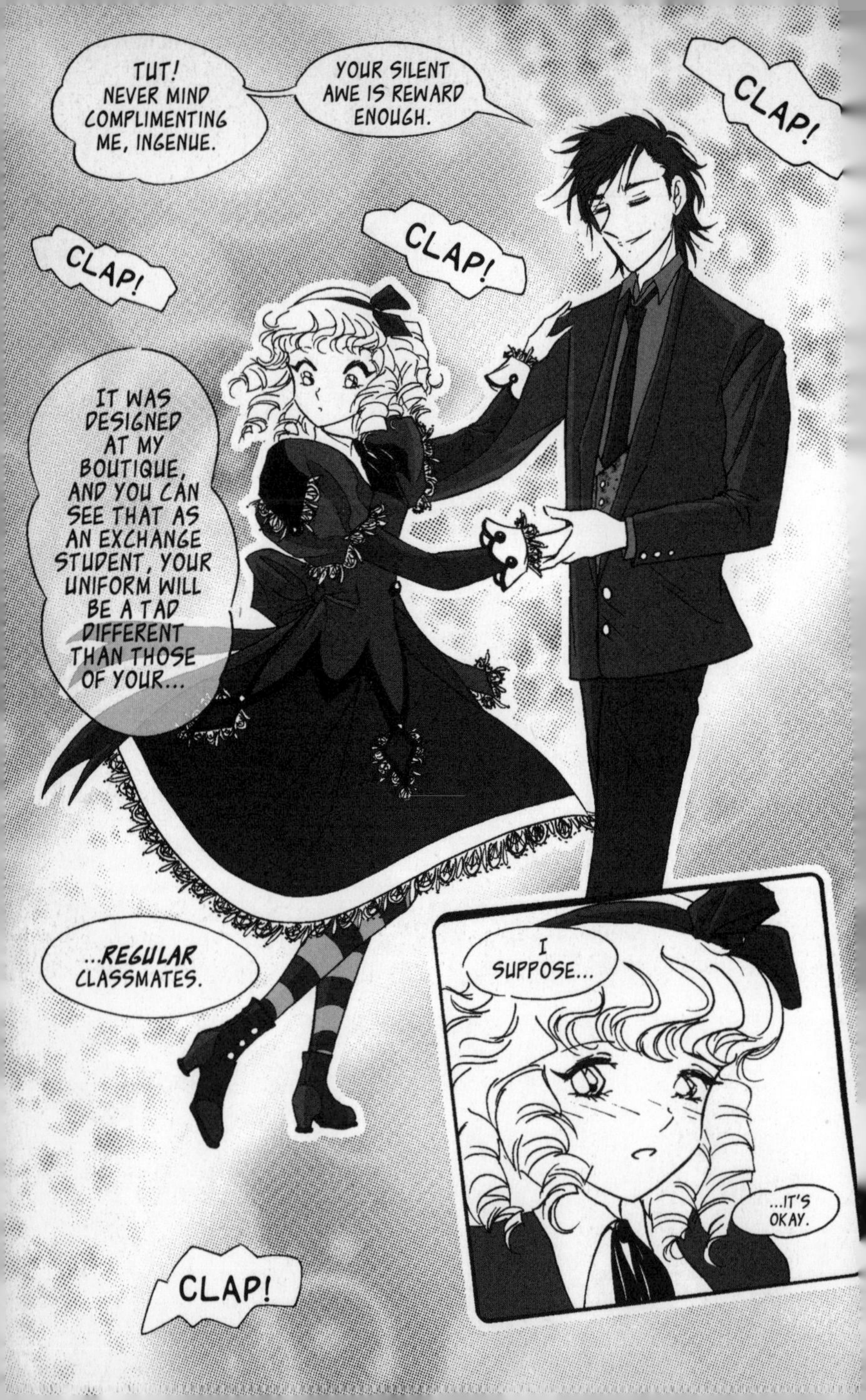
TUT! NEVER MIND COMPLIMENTING ME, INGENUE.
YOUR SILENT AWE IS REWARD ENOUGH.
CLAP!
CLAP!
CLAP!
IT WAS DESIGNED AT MY BOUTIQUE, AND YOU CAN SEE THAT AS AN EXCHANGE STUDENT, YOUR UNIFORM WILL BE A TAD DIFFERENT THAN THOSE OF YOUR...
...REGULAR CLASSMATES.
CLAP!
I SUPPOSE...
...IT'S OKAY.

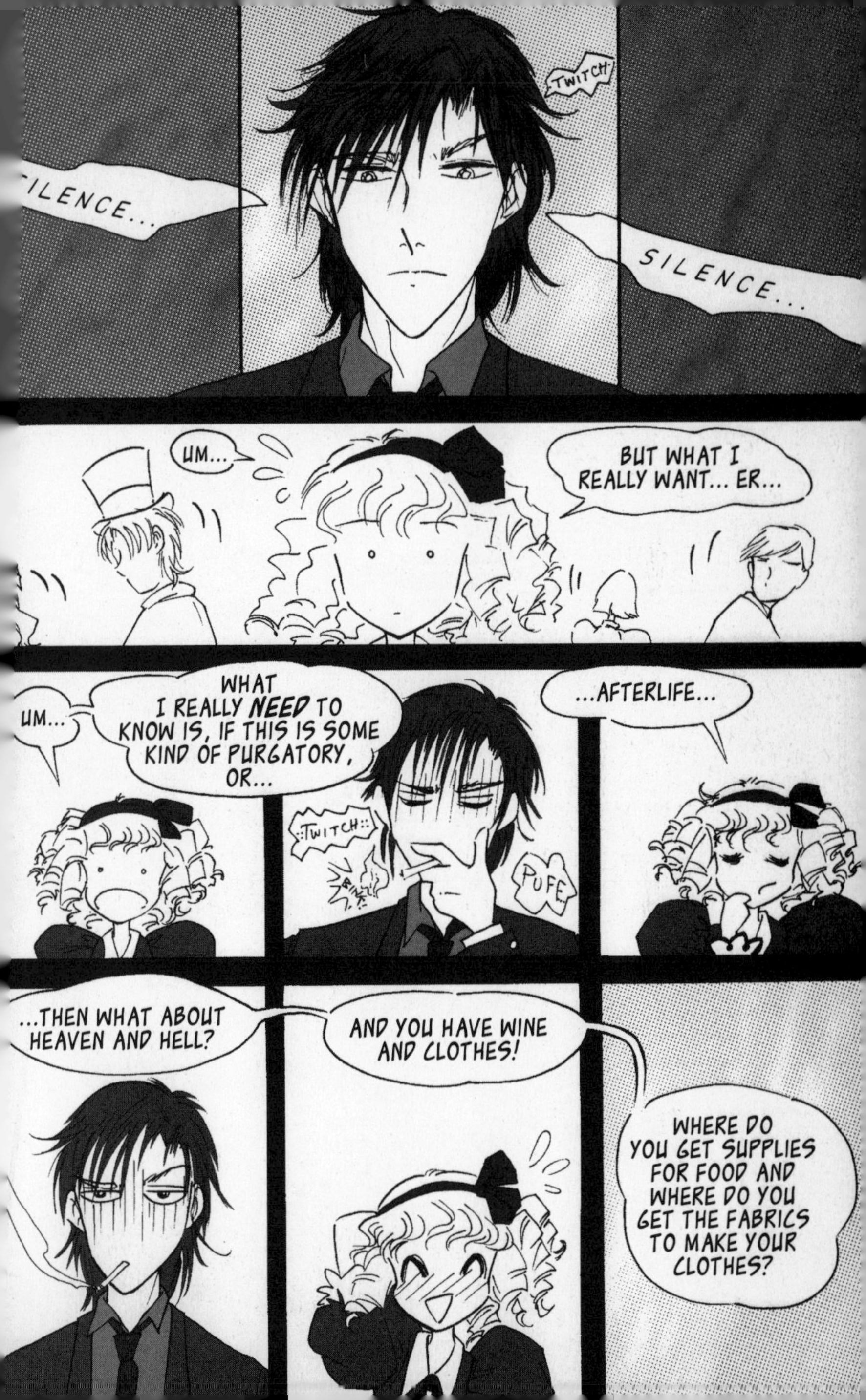
ILENCE...
TWITCH
SILENCE...
UM...
BUT WHAT I REALLY WANT... ER...
UM...
WHAT I REALLY *NEED* TO KNOW IS, IF THIS IS SOME KIND OF PURGATORY, OR...
TWITCH
PUFF
...AFTERLIFE...
...THEN WHAT ABOUT HEAVEN AND HELL?
AND YOU HAVE WINE AND CLOTHES!
WHERE DO YOU GET SUPPLIES FOR FOOD AND WHERE DO YOU GET THE FABRICS TO MAKE YOUR CLOTHES?

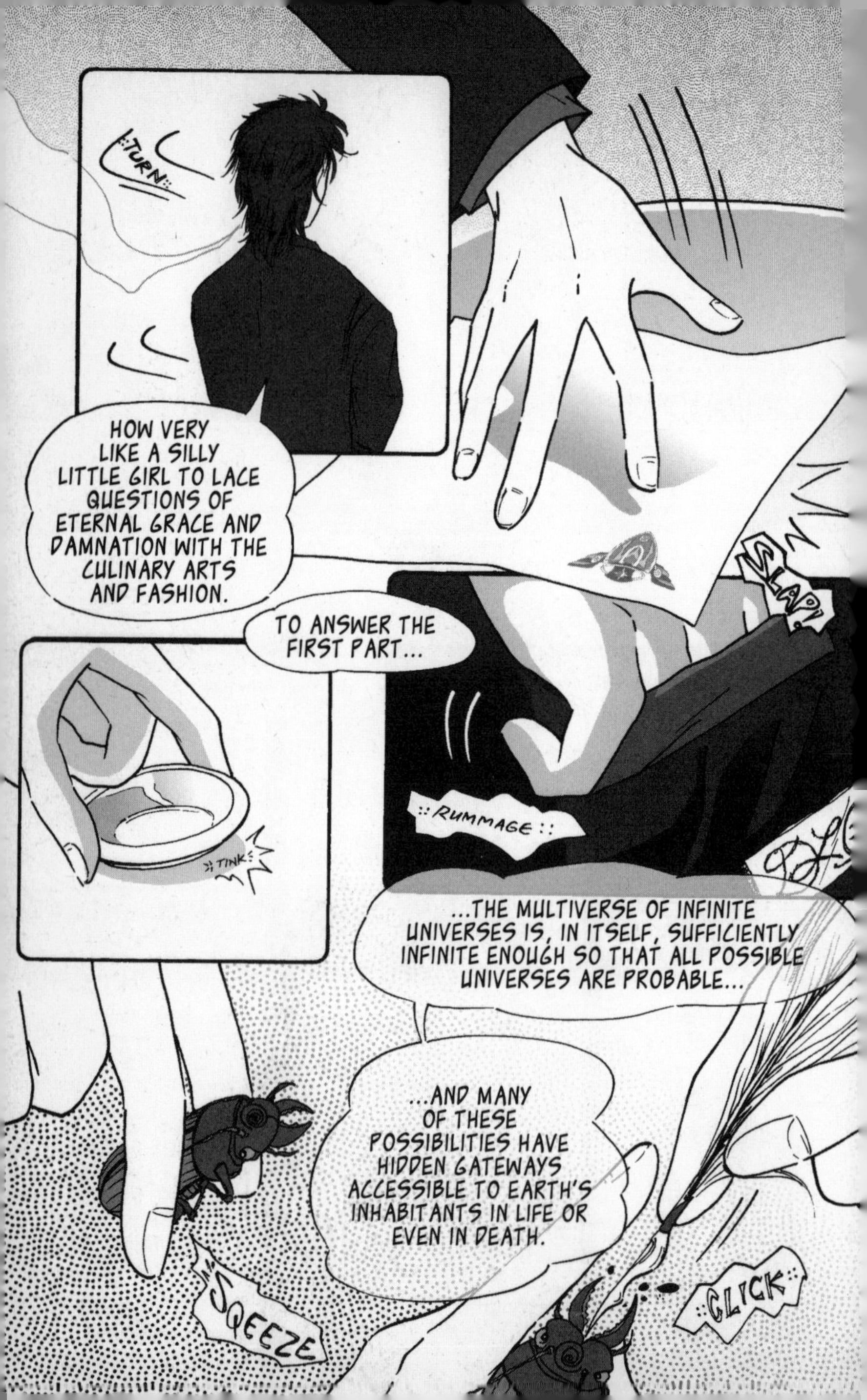

TURN
HOW VERY LIKE A SILLY LITTLE GIRL TO LACE QUESTIONS OF ETERNAL GRACE AND DAMNATION WITH THE CULINARY ARTS AND FASHION.
TO ANSWER THE FIRST PART...
SLAP!
TINK
RUMMAGE
...THE MULTIVERSE OF INFINITE UNIVERSES IS, IN ITSELF, SUFFICIENTLY INFINITE ENOUGH SO THAT ALL POSSIBLE UNIVERSES ARE PROBABLE...
...AND MANY OF THESE POSSIBILITIES HAVE HIDDEN GATEWAYS ACCESSIBLE TO EARTH'S INHABITANTS IN LIFE OR EVEN IN DEATH.
SQEEZE
CLICK

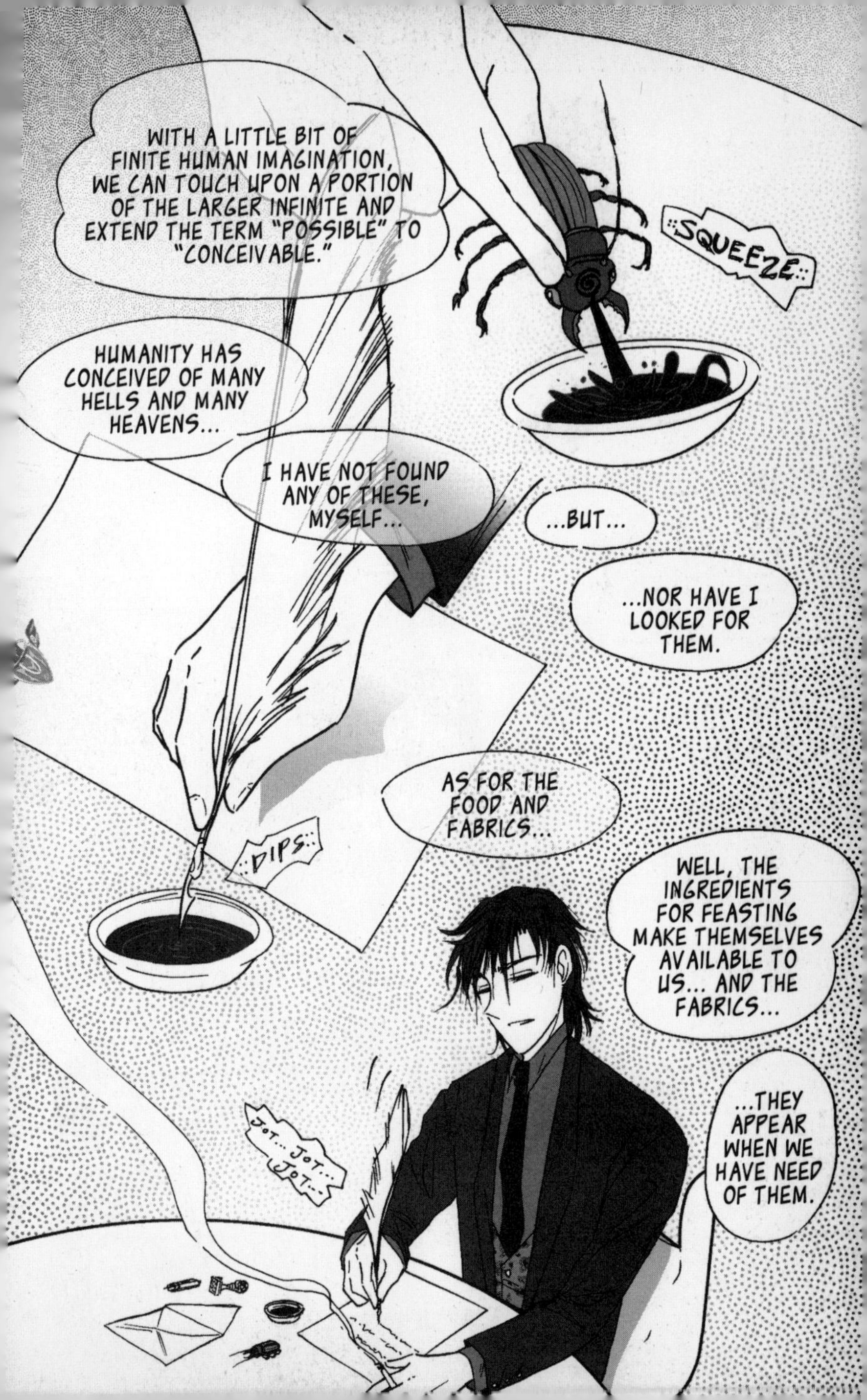
WITH A LITTLE BIT OF FINITE HUMAN IMAGINATION, WE CAN TOUCH UPON A PORTION OF THE LARGER INFINITE AND EXTEND THE TERM "POSSIBLE" TO "CONCEIVABLE."
SQUEEZE
HUMANITY HAS CONCEIVED OF MANY HELLS AND MANY HEAVENS...
I HAVE NOT FOUND ANY OF THESE, MYSELF...
...BUT...
...NOR HAVE I LOOKED FOR THEM.
AS FOR THE FOOD AND FABRICS...
DIPS
WELL, THE INGREDIENTS FOR FEASTING MAKE THEMSELVES AVAILABLE TO US... AND THE FABRICS...
JOT... JOT... JOT...
...THEY APPEAR WHEN WE HAVE NEED OF THEM.

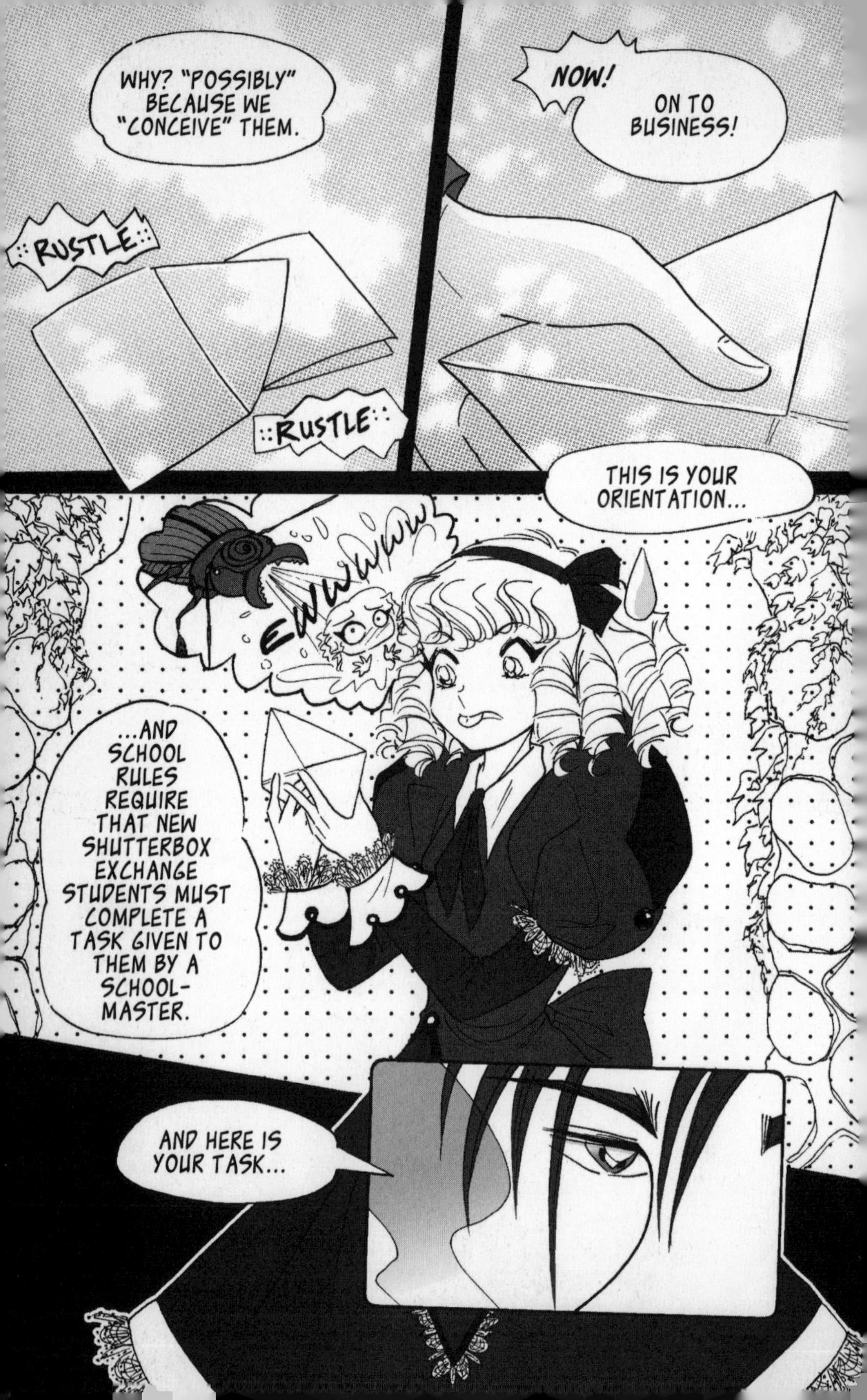
WHY? "POSSIBLY" BECAUSE WE "CONCEIVE" THEM.
RUSTLE
RUSTLE
NOW!
ON TO BUSINESS!
THIS IS YOUR ORIENTATION...
EWWWWWW
...AND SCHOOL RULES REQUIRE THAT NEW SHUTTERBOX EXCHANGE STUDENTS MUST COMPLETE A TASK GIVEN TO THEM BY A SCHOOL-MASTER.
AND HERE IS YOUR TASK...

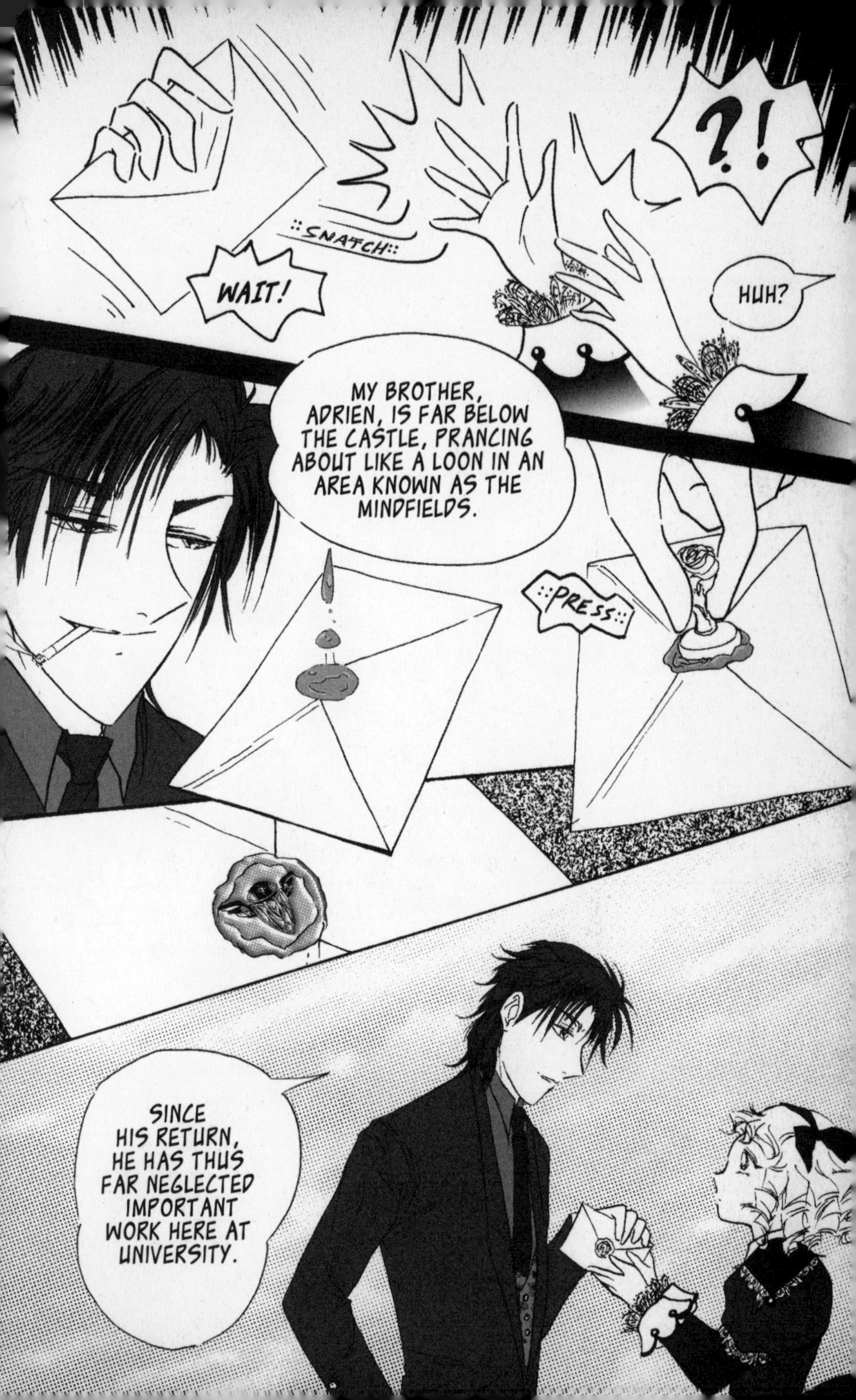

::SNATCH::
?!
WAIT!
HUH?
MY BROTHER, ADRIEN, IS FAR BELOW THE CASTLE, PRANCING ABOUT LIKE A LOON IN AN AREA KNOWN AS THE MINDFIELDS.
::PRESS::
SINCE HIS RETURN, HE HAS THUS FAR NEGLECTED IMPORTANT WORK HERE AT UNIVERSITY.

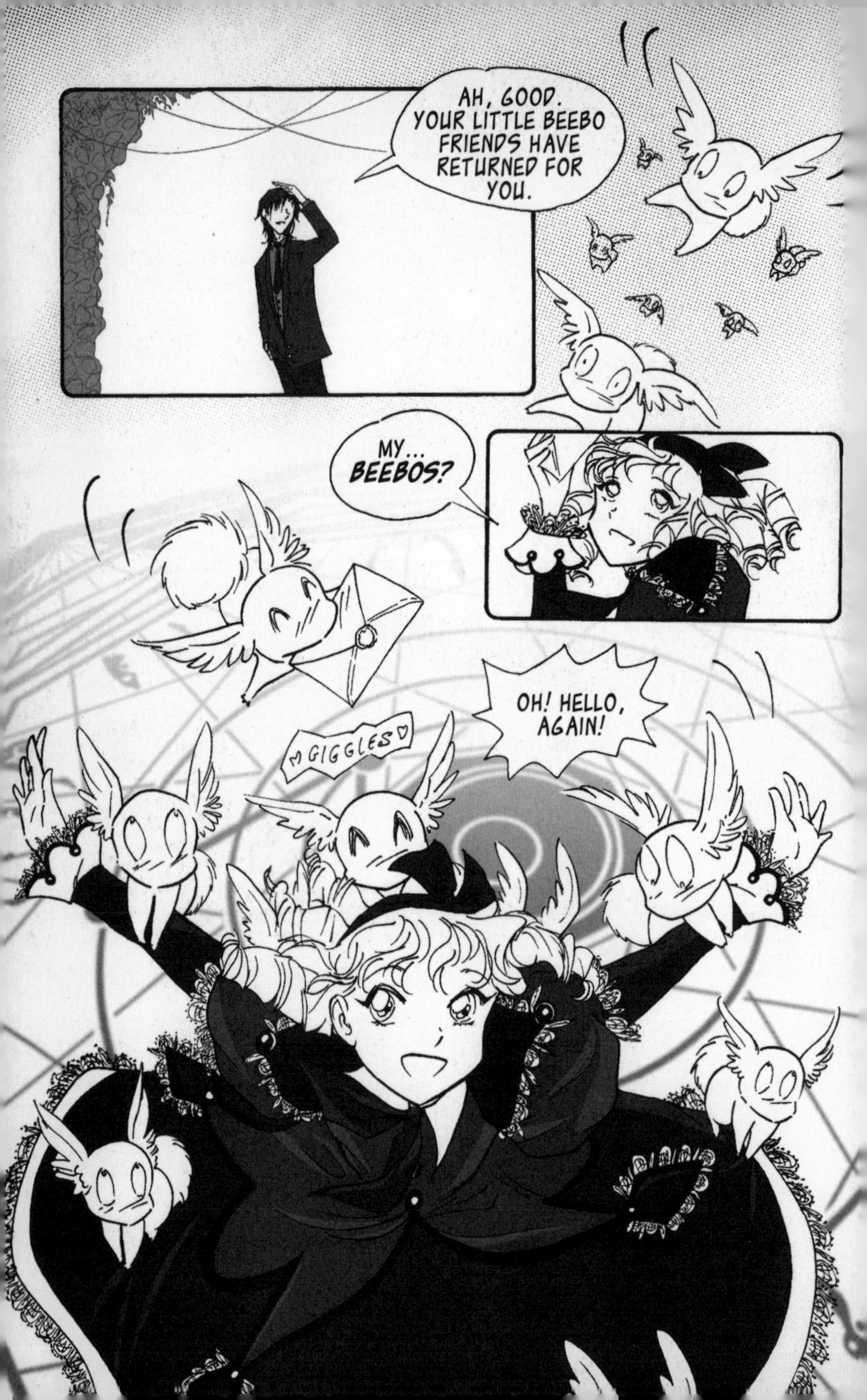
AH, GOOD. YOUR LITTLE BEEBO FRIENDS HAVE RETURNED FOR YOU.
MY... BEEBOS?
GIGGLES
OH! HELLO, AGAIN!

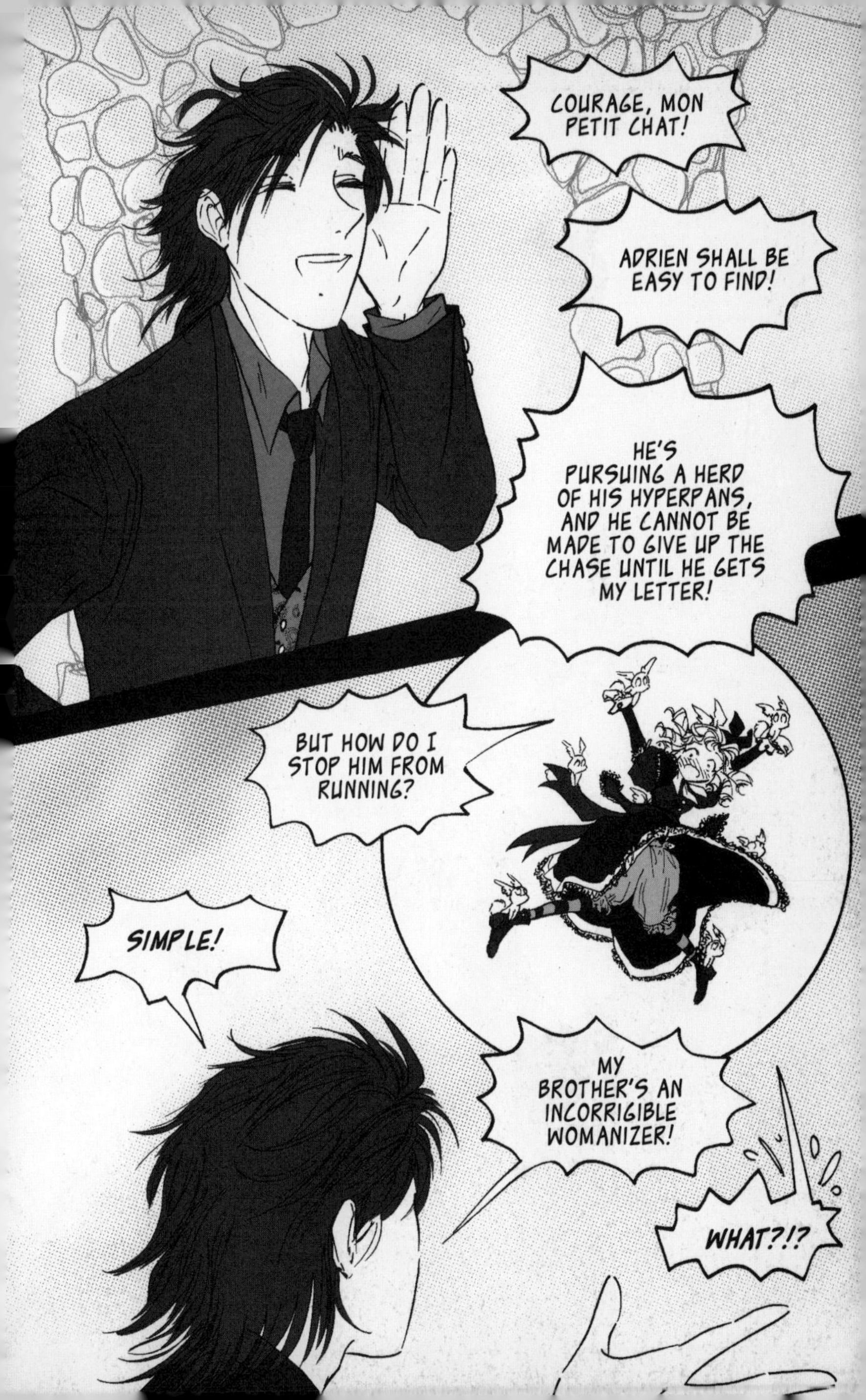
COURAGE, MON PETIT CHAT!
ADRIEN SHALL BE EASY TO FIND!
HE'S PURSUING A HERD OF HIS HYPERPANS, AND HE CANNOT BE MADE TO GIVE UP THE CHASE UNTIL HE GETS MY LETTER!
BUT HOW DO I STOP HIM FROM RUNNING?
SIMPLE!
MY BROTHER'S AN INCORRIGIBLE WOMANIZER!
WHAT?!?

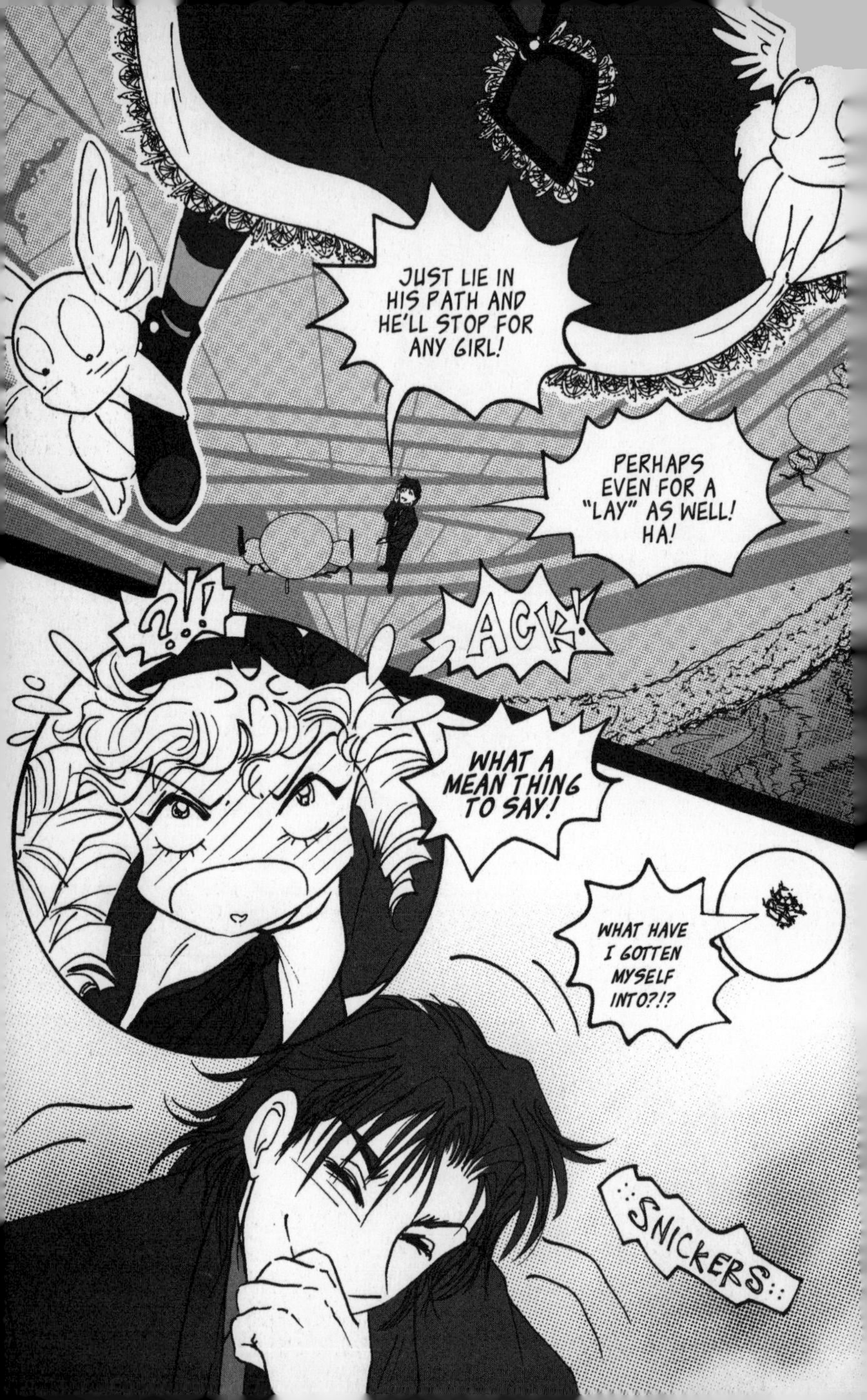
JUST LIE IN HIS PATH AND HE'LL STOP FOR ANY GIRL!
PERHAPS EVEN FOR A "LAY" AS WELL! HA!
?!!
ACK!
WHAT A MEAN THING TO SAY!
WHAT HAVE I GOTTEN MYSELF INTO?!?
::SNICKERS::

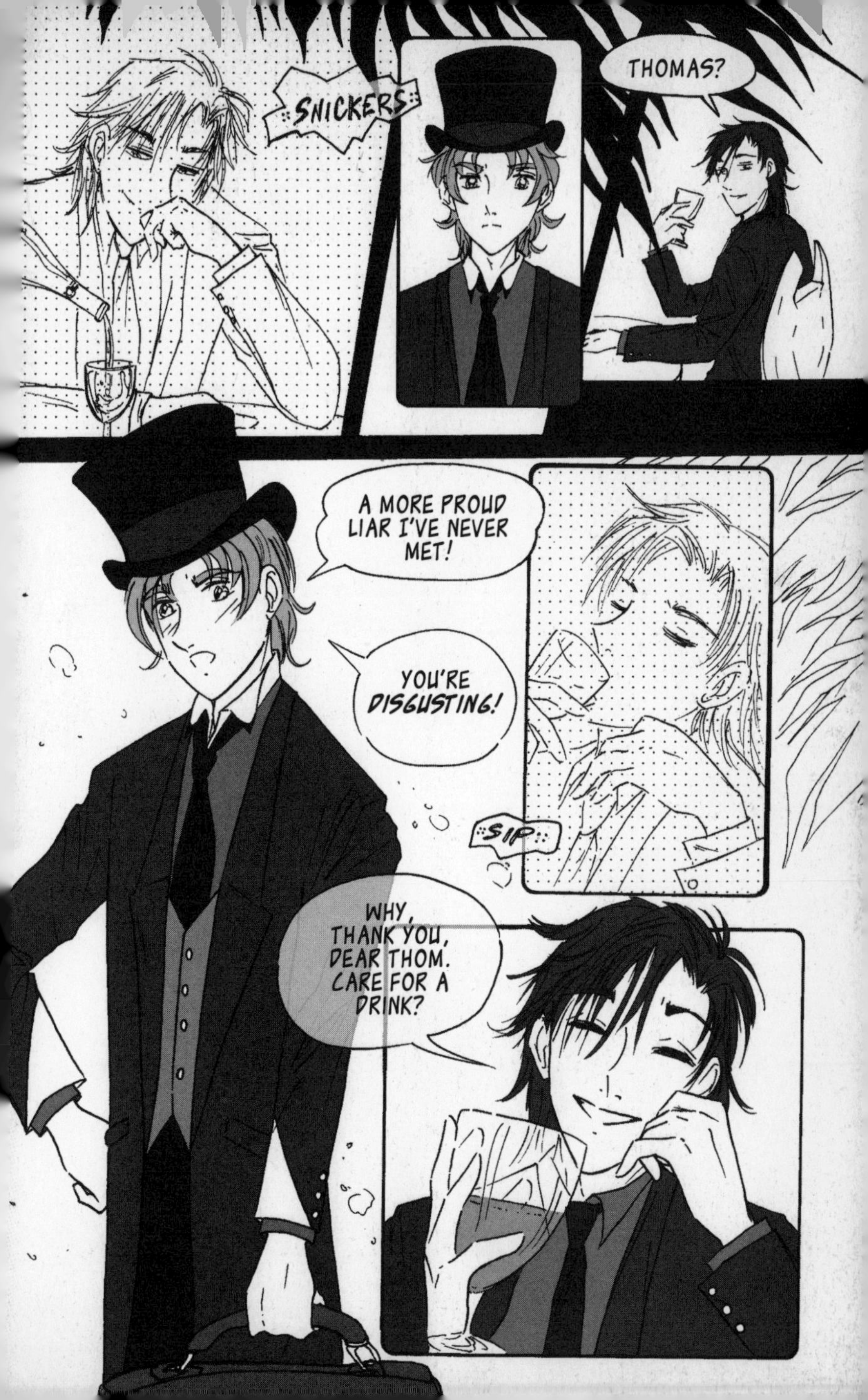
SNICKERS
THOMAS?
A MORE PROUD LIAR I'VE NEVER MET!
YOU'RE DISGUSTING!
SIP
WHY, THANK YOU, DEAR THOM. CARE FOR A DRINK?

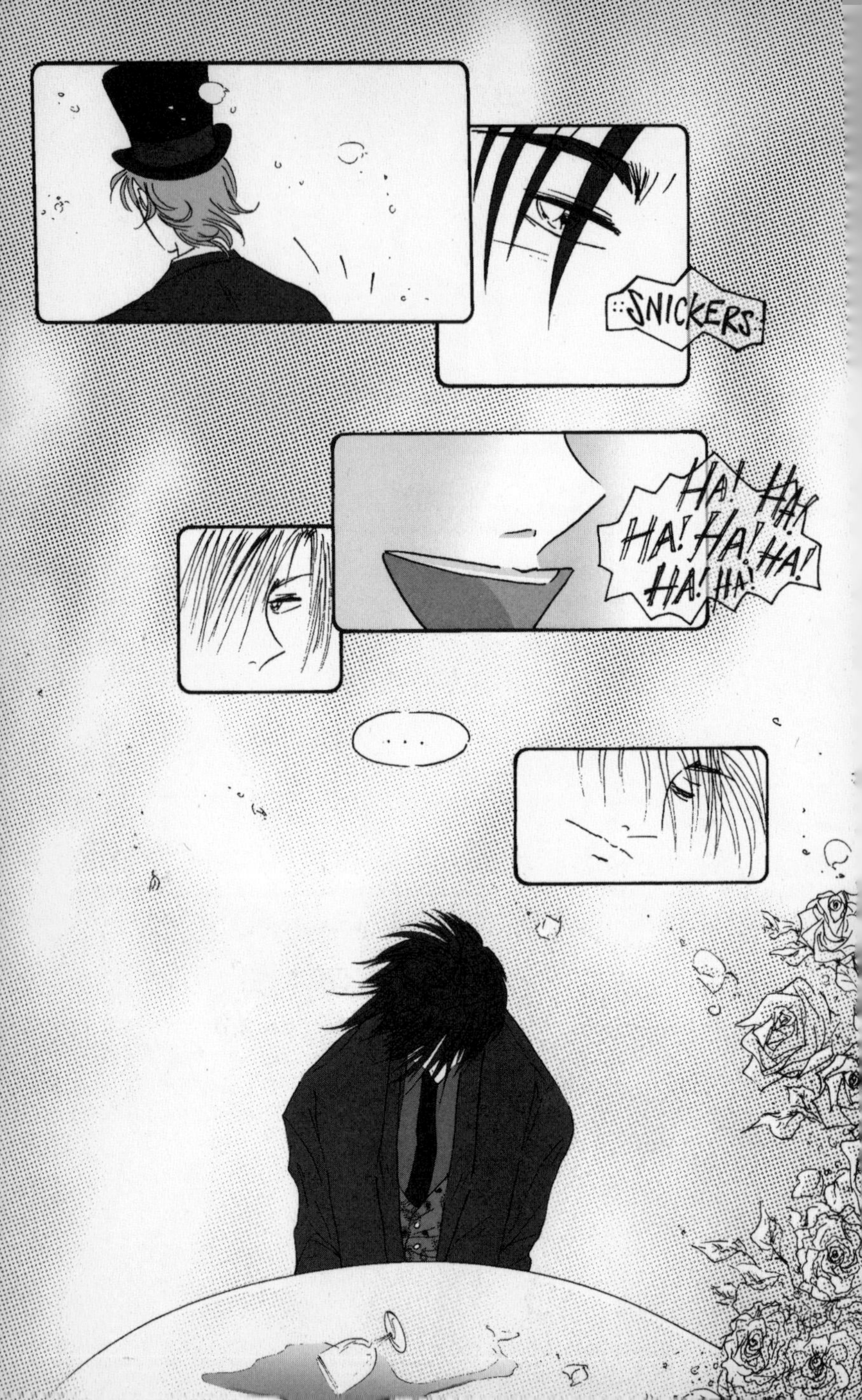
SNICKERS
HA! HA! HA! HA! HA! HA! HA! HA!
. . .

Chapter Five:

It is Higgledy-Piggledy

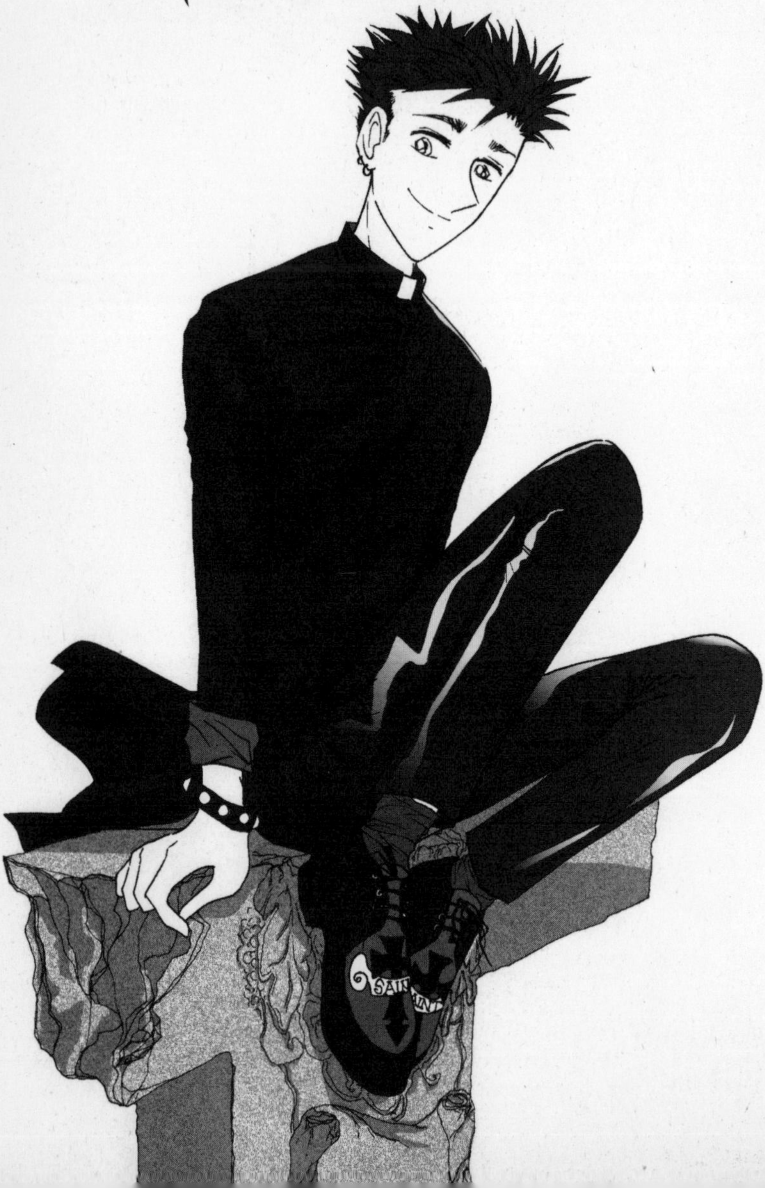

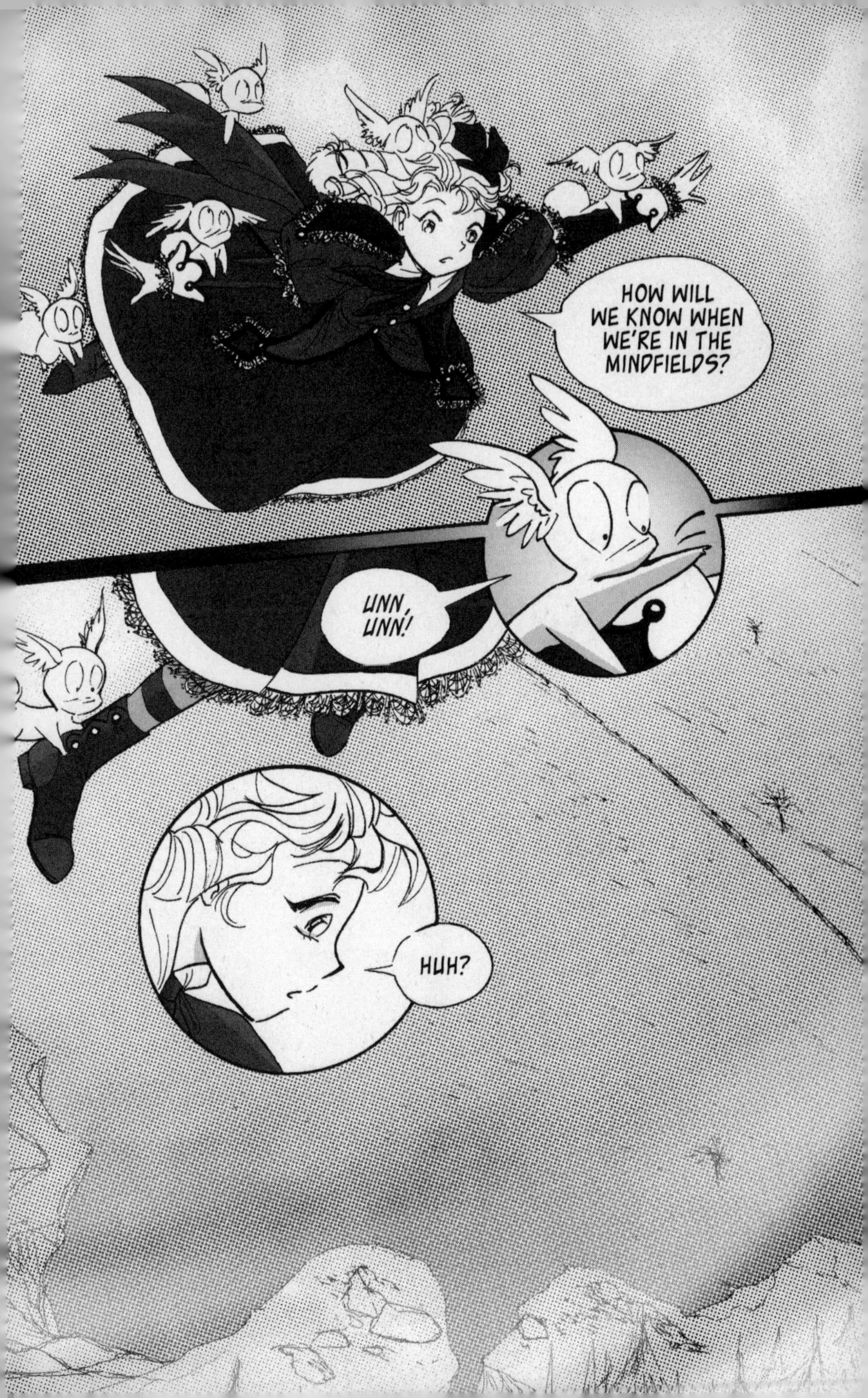
HOW WILL WE KNOW WHEN WE'RE IN THE MINDFIELDS?
UNN, UNN!
HUH?

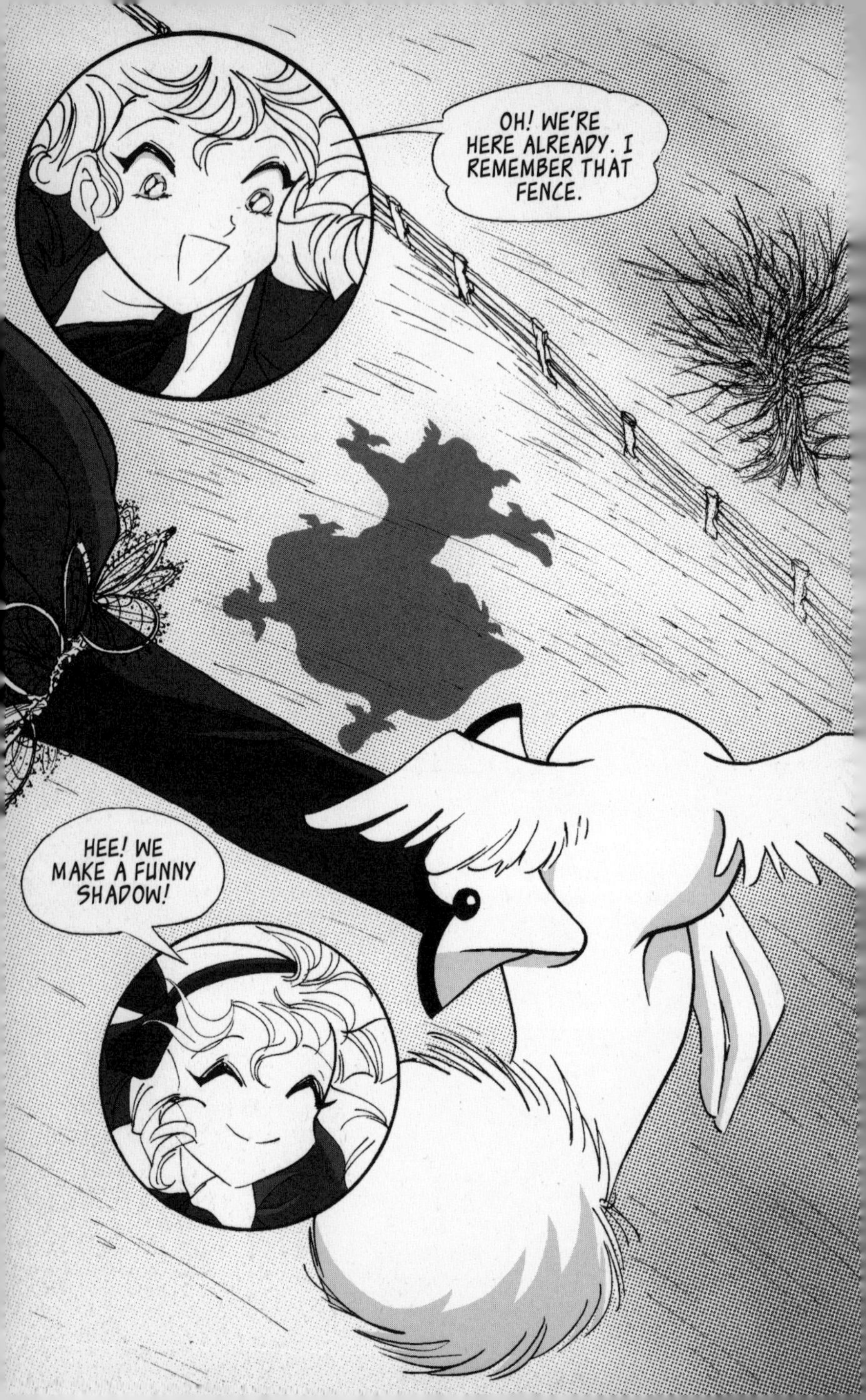
OH! WE'RE HERE ALREADY. I REMEMBER THAT FENCE.
HEE! WE MAKE A FUNNY SHADOW!

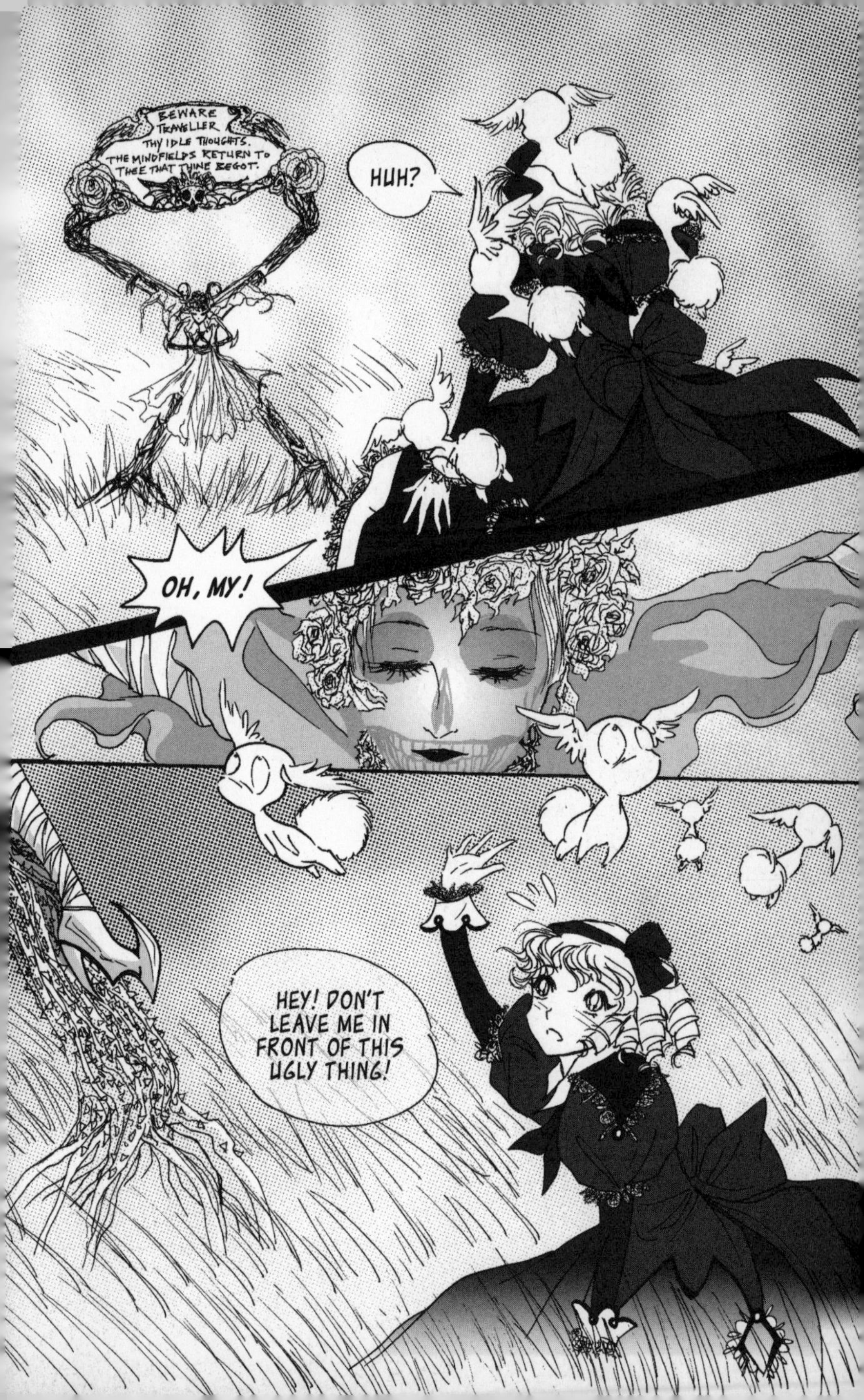
BEWARE TRAVELLER THY IDLE THOUGHTS. THE MINDFIELDS RETURN TO THEE THAT THINE BEGOT.
HUH?
OH, MY!
HEY! DON'T LEAVE ME IN FRONT OF THIS UGLY THING!

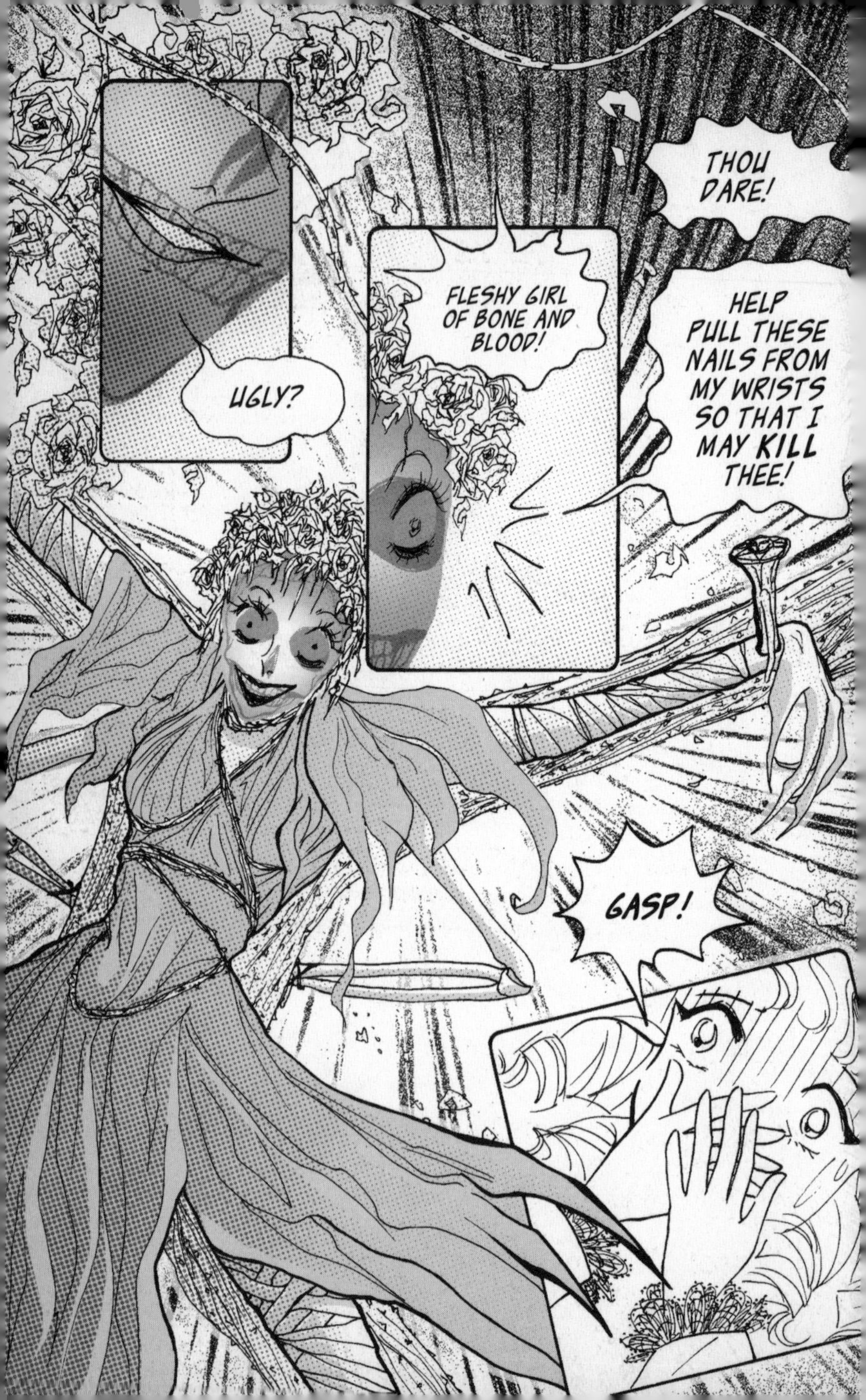
UGLY?
FLESHY GIRL OF BONE AND BLOOD!
THOU DARE!
HELP PULL THESE NAILS FROM MY WRISTS SO THAT I MAY **KILL** THEE!
GASP!

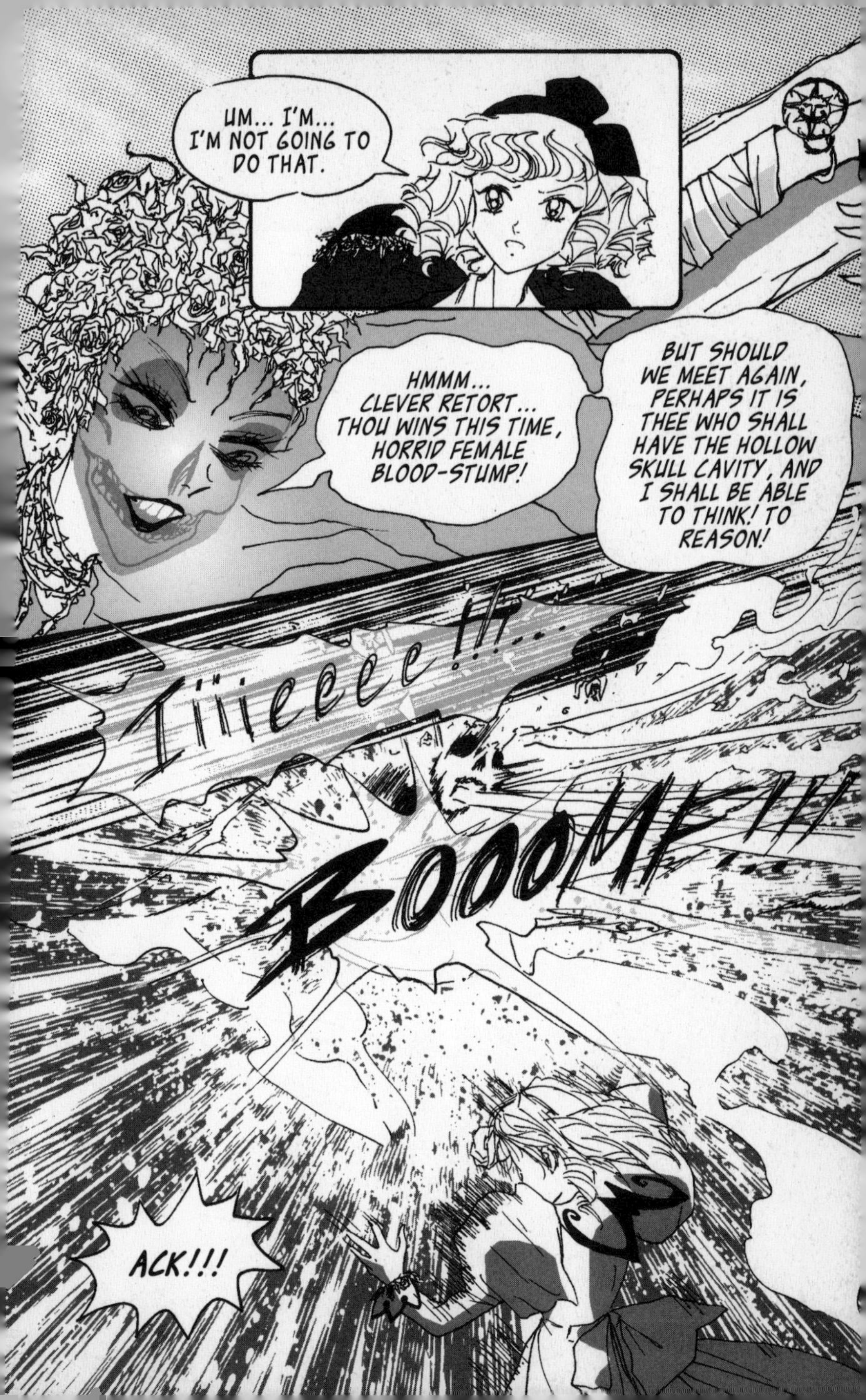
UM... I'M... I'M NOT GOING TO DO THAT.
HMMM... CLEVER RETORT... THOU WINS THIS TIME, HORRID FEMALE BLOOD-STUMP!
BUT SHOULD WE MEET AGAIN, PERHAPS IT IS THEE WHO SHALL HAVE THE HOLLOW SKULL CAVITY, AND I SHALL BE ABLE TO THINK! TO REASON!
Iiiieeee!!!...
BOOOMF!!!
ACK!!!

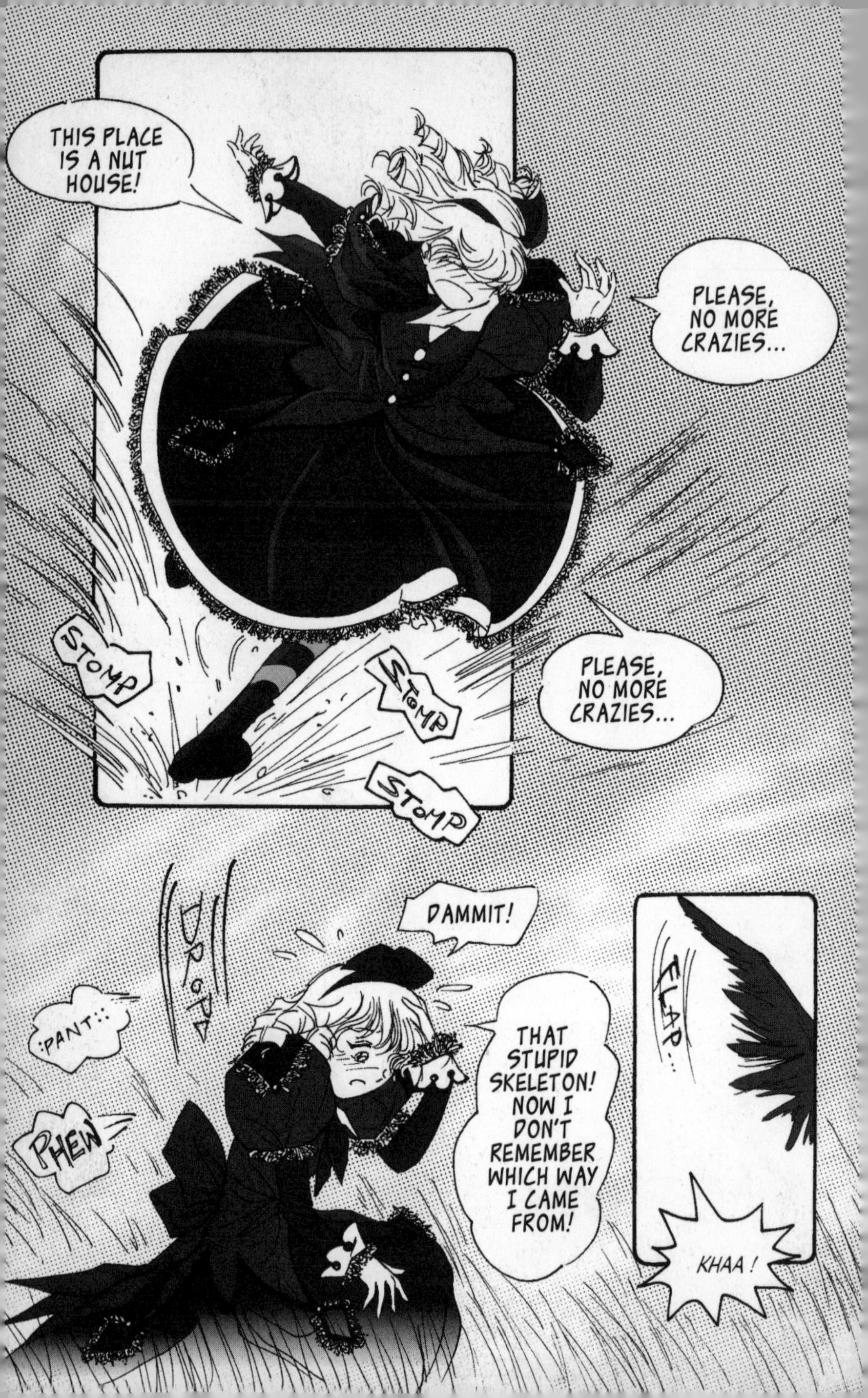
THIS PLACE IS A NUT HOUSE!
PLEASE, NO MORE CRAZIES...
STOMP
STOMP
PLEASE, NO MORE CRAZIES...
STOMP
DROP
DAMMIT!
PANT
PHEW
THAT STUPID SKELETON! NOW I DON'T REMEMBER WHICH WAY I CAME FROM!
FLAP...
KHAA!

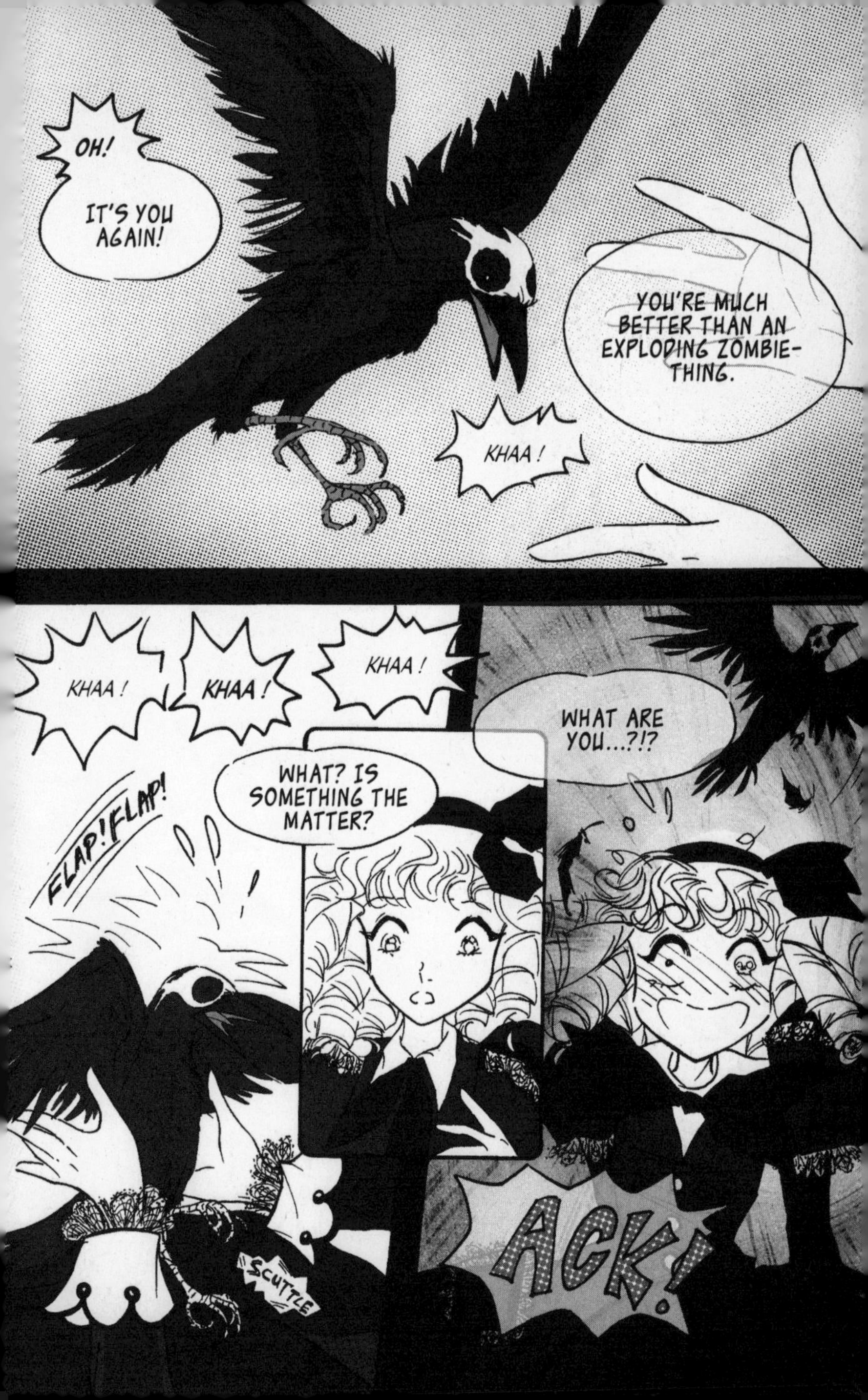
OH!
IT'S YOU AGAIN!
YOU'RE MUCH BETTER THAN AN EXPLODING ZOMBIE-THING.
KHAA!
KHAA!
KHAA!
KHAA!
FLAP! FLAP!
SCUTTLE
WHAT? IS SOMETHING THE MATTER?
WHAT ARE YOU...?!?
ACK!

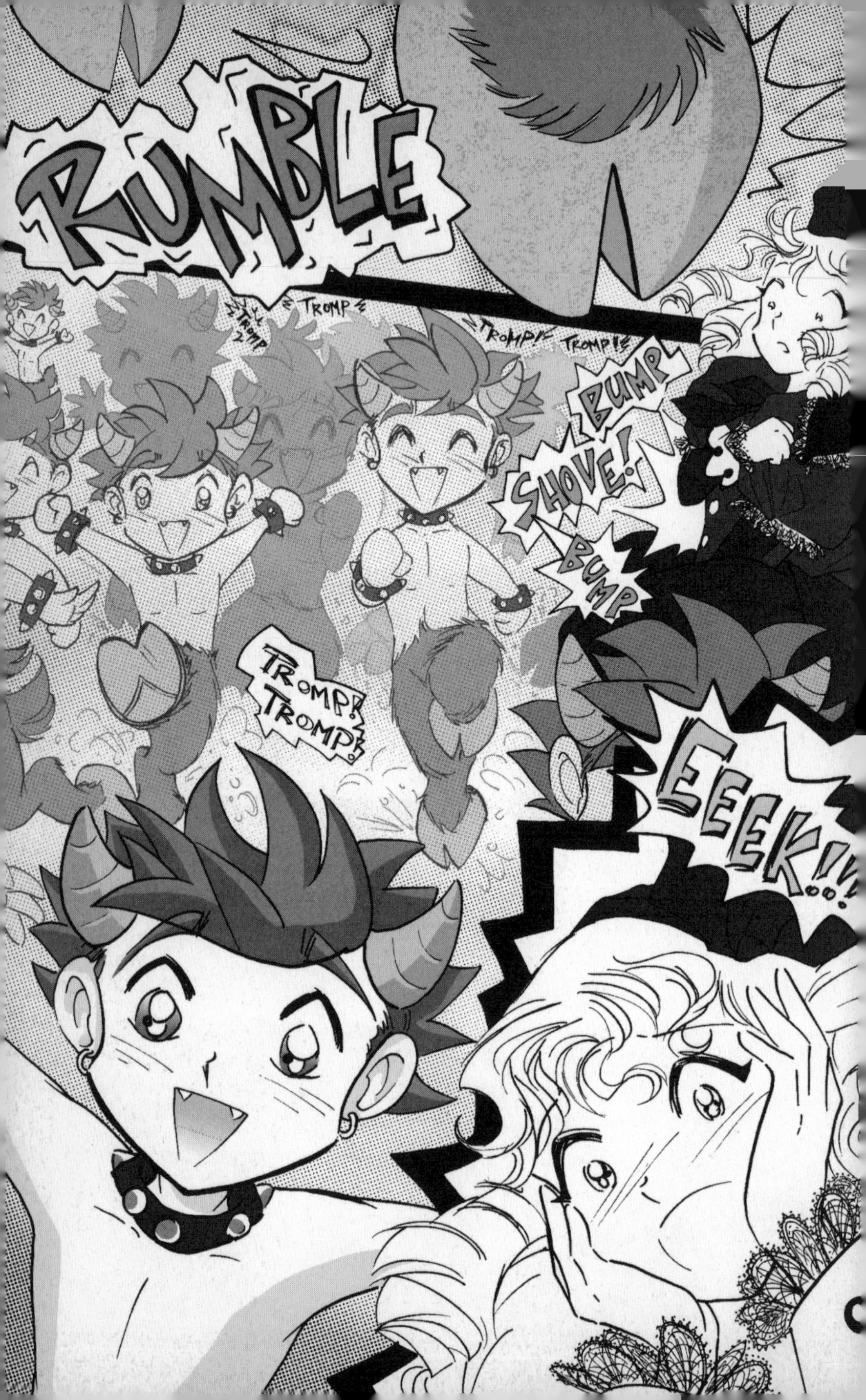
RUMBLE
TROMP
TROMP
TROMP!
TROMP!
BUMP
SHOVE!
BUMP
TROMP! TROMP!
EEEEK!!!

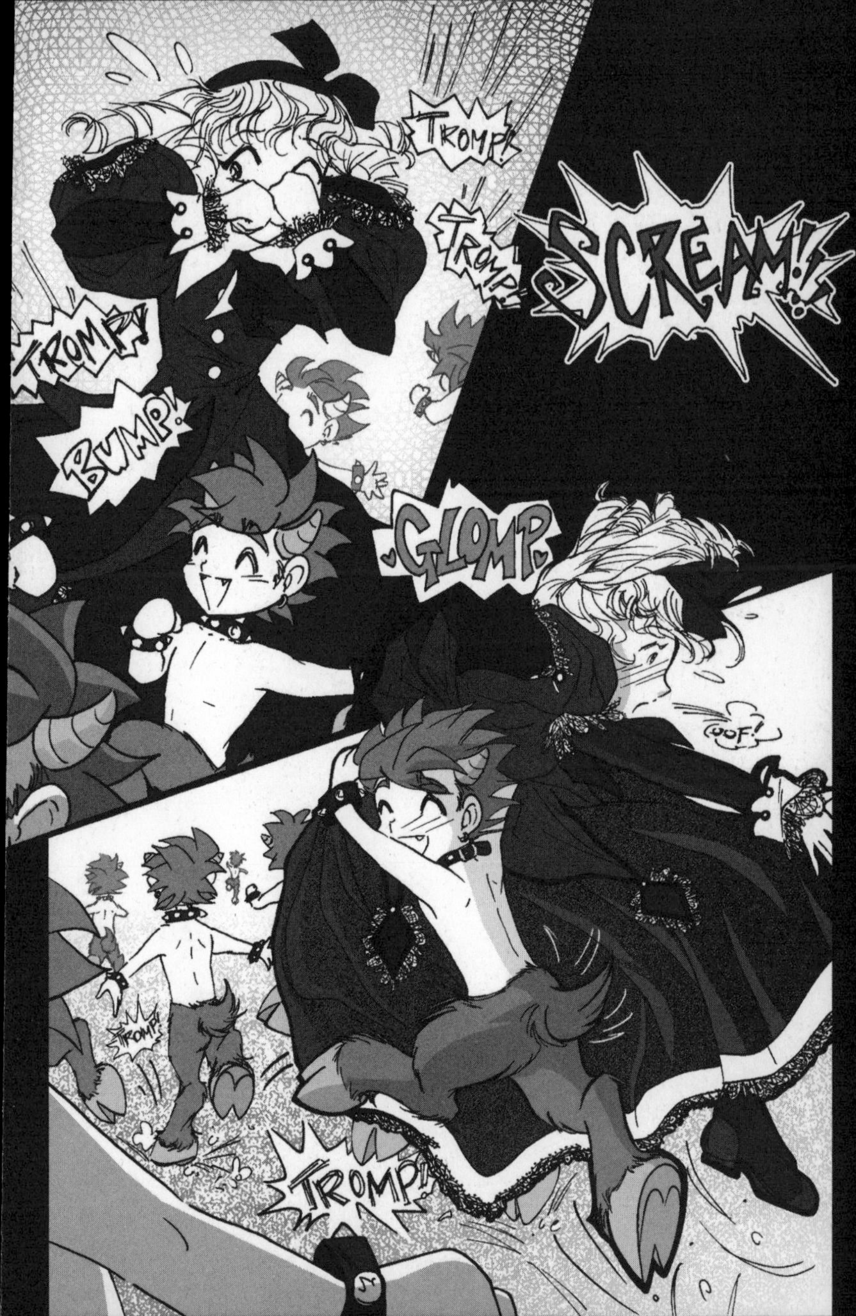
TROMP!
TROMP!
TROMP!
BUMP!
SCREAM!!
GLOMP
UOF!
TROMP!
TROMP!!

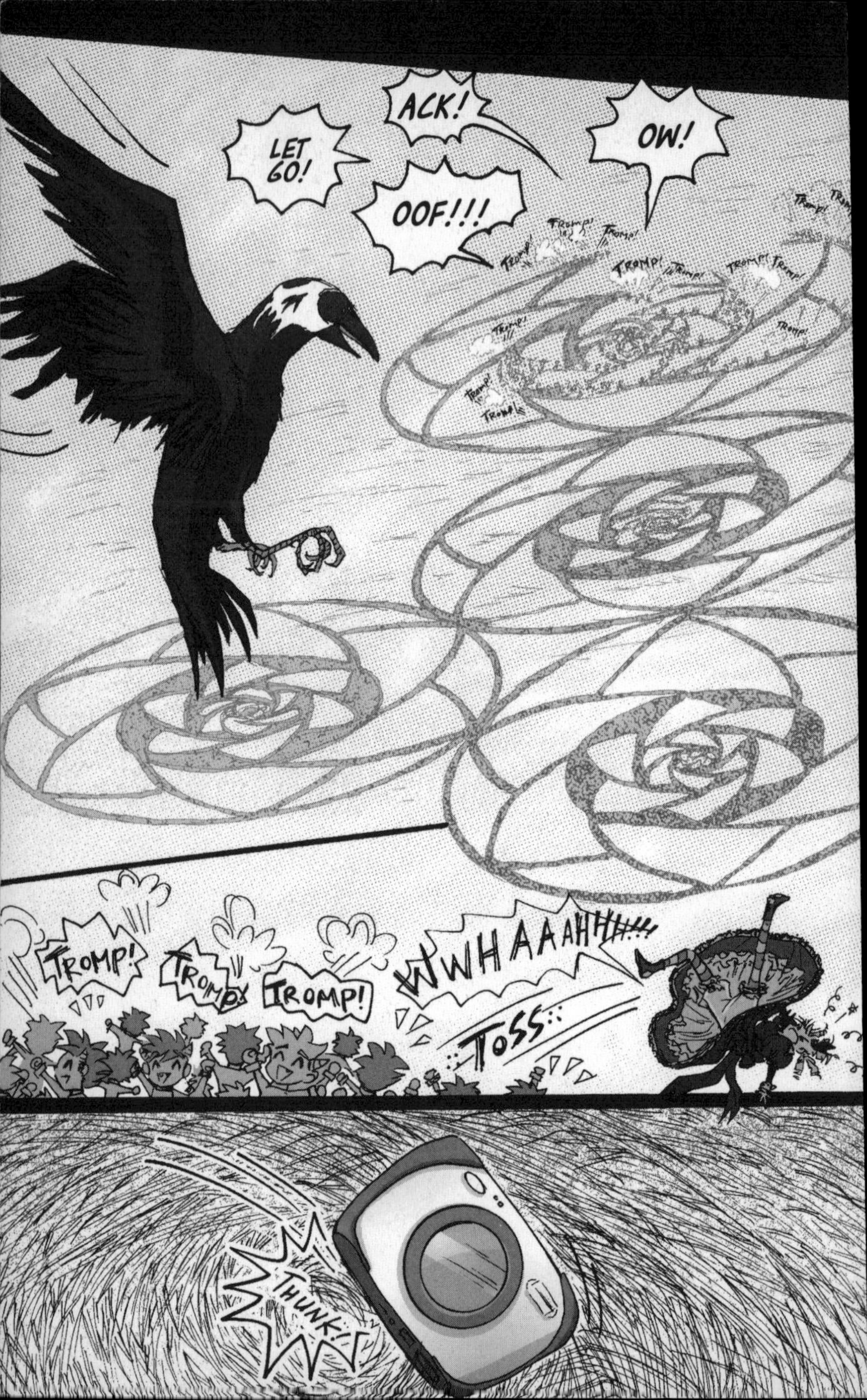
LET GO!
ACK!
OOF!!!
OW!
TROMP!
TROMP!
TROMP!
WWHAAAAHH!!!!
TOSS
THUNK

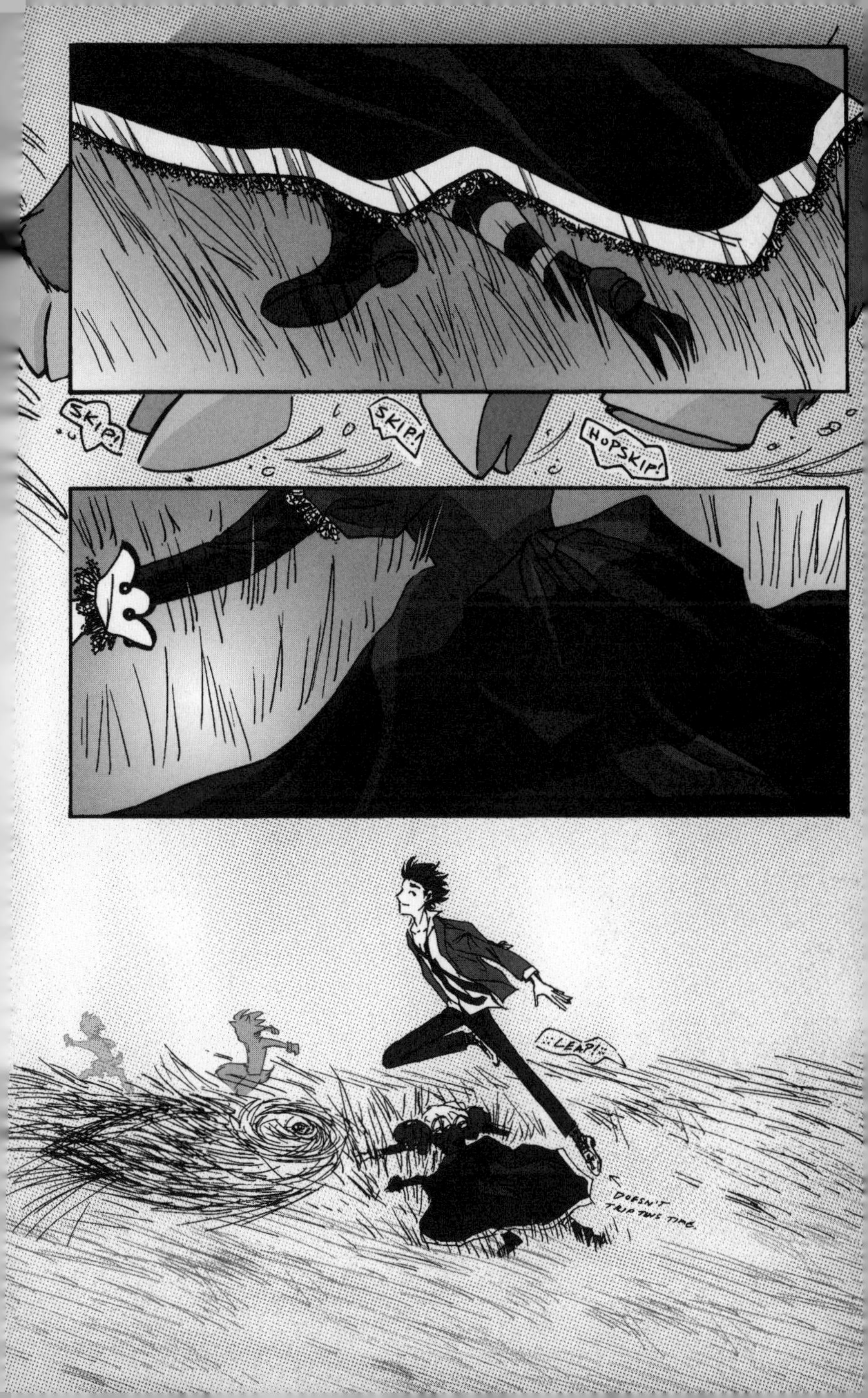
SKIP!
SKIP!
HOPSKIP!
::LEAP!::
DOESN'T TRIP THIS TIME.

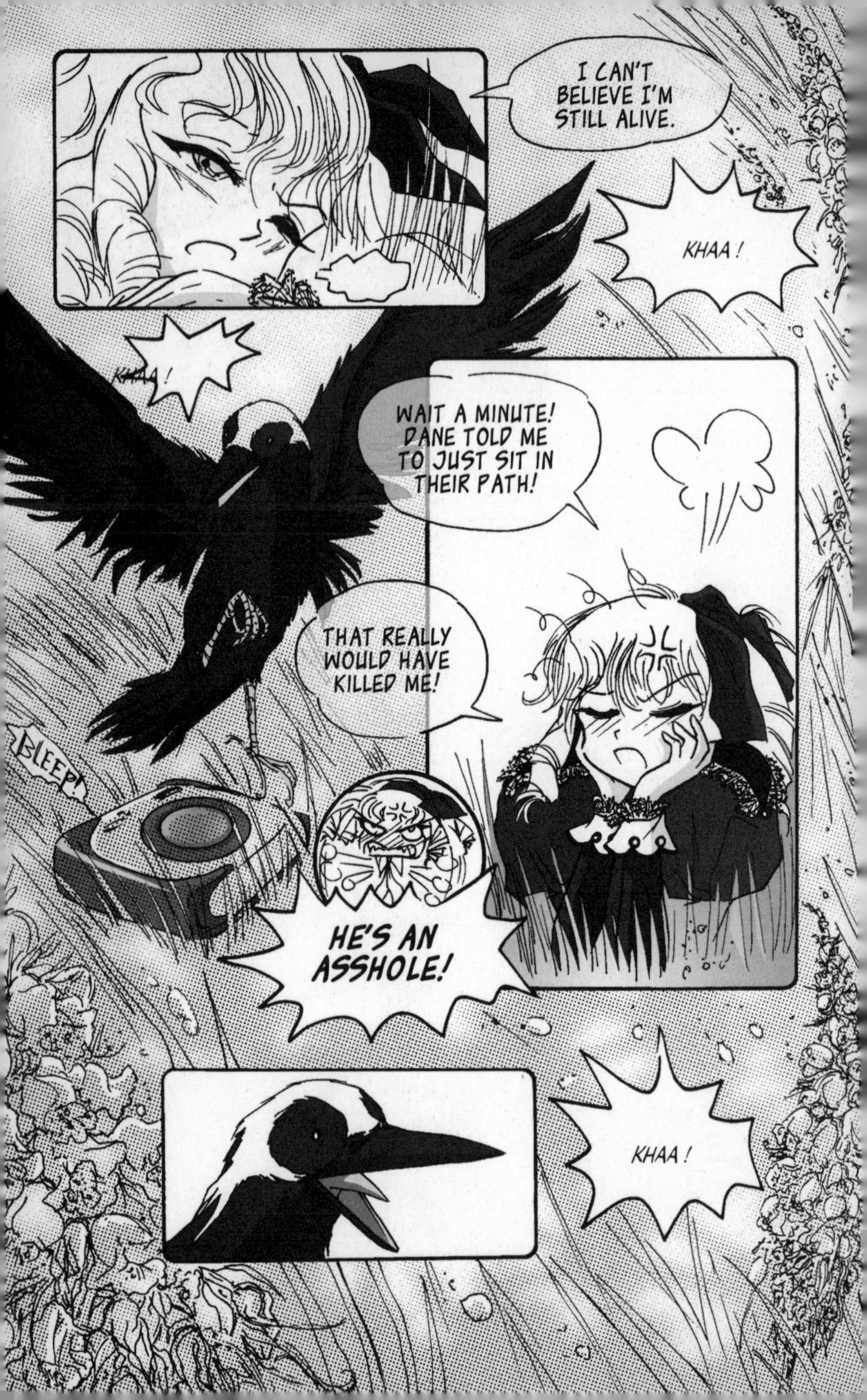
I CAN'T BELIEVE I'M STILL ALIVE.
KHAA!
KHAA!
WAIT A MINUTE! DANE TOLD ME TO JUST SIT IN THEIR PATH!
THAT REALLY WOULD HAVE KILLED ME!
BLEEP!
HE'S AN ASSHOLE!
KHAA!

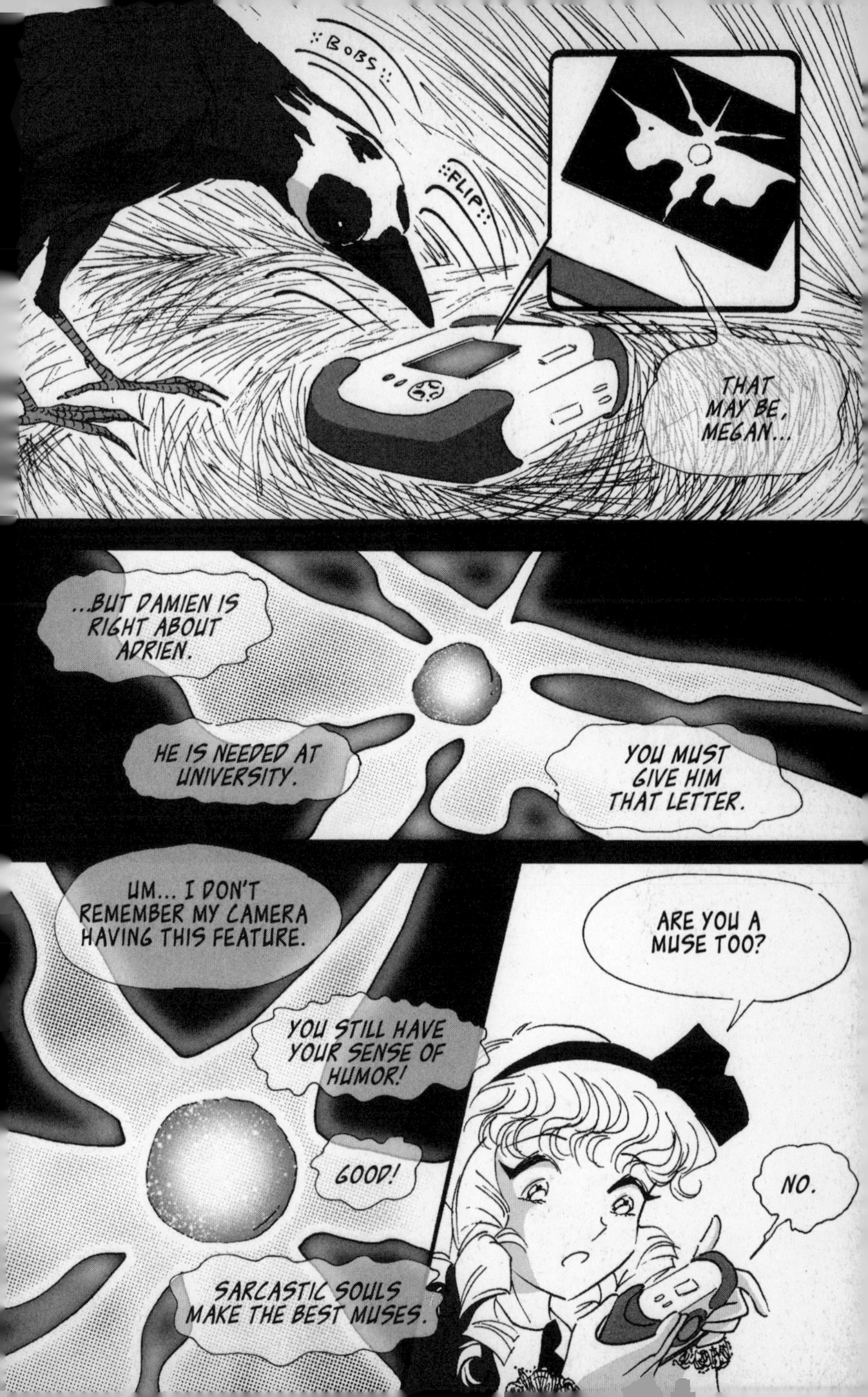
::BOBS::
::FLIP::
THAT MAY BE, MEGAN...
...BUT DAMIEN IS RIGHT ABOUT ADRIEN.
HE IS NEEDED AT UNIVERSITY.
YOU MUST GIVE HIM THAT LETTER.
UM... I DON'T REMEMBER MY CAMERA HAVING THIS FEATURE.
YOU STILL HAVE YOUR SENSE OF HUMOR!
GOOD!
SARCASTIC SOULS MAKE THE BEST MUSES.
ARE YOU A MUSE TOO?
NO.

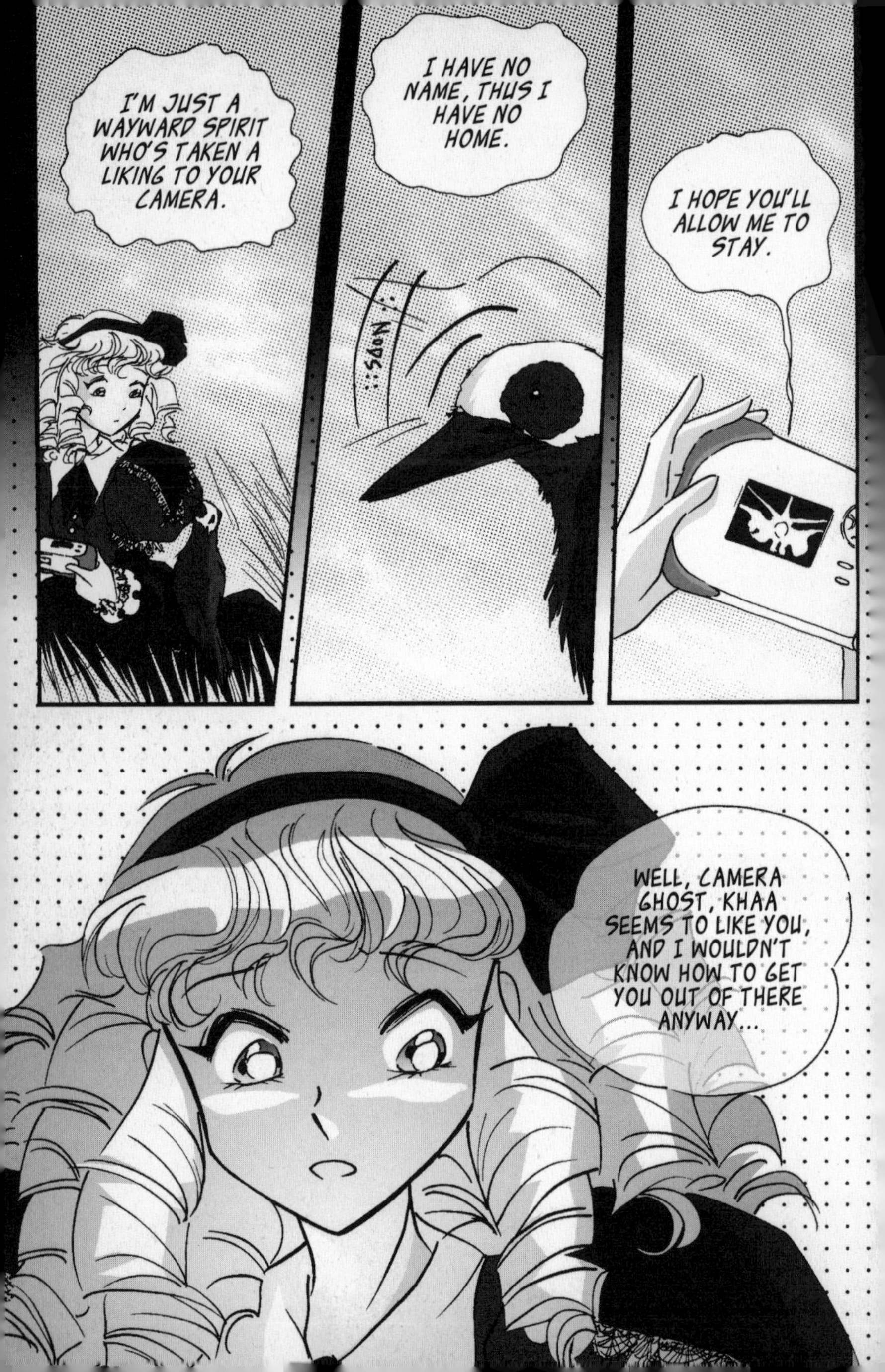
I'M JUST A WAYWARD SPIRIT WHO'S TAKEN A LIKING TO YOUR CAMERA.
I HAVE NO NAME, THUS I HAVE NO HOME.
I HOPE YOU'LL ALLOW ME TO STAY.
WELL, CAMERA GHOST, KHAA SEEMS TO LIKE YOU, AND I WOULDN'T KNOW HOW TO GET YOU OUT OF THERE ANYWAY...

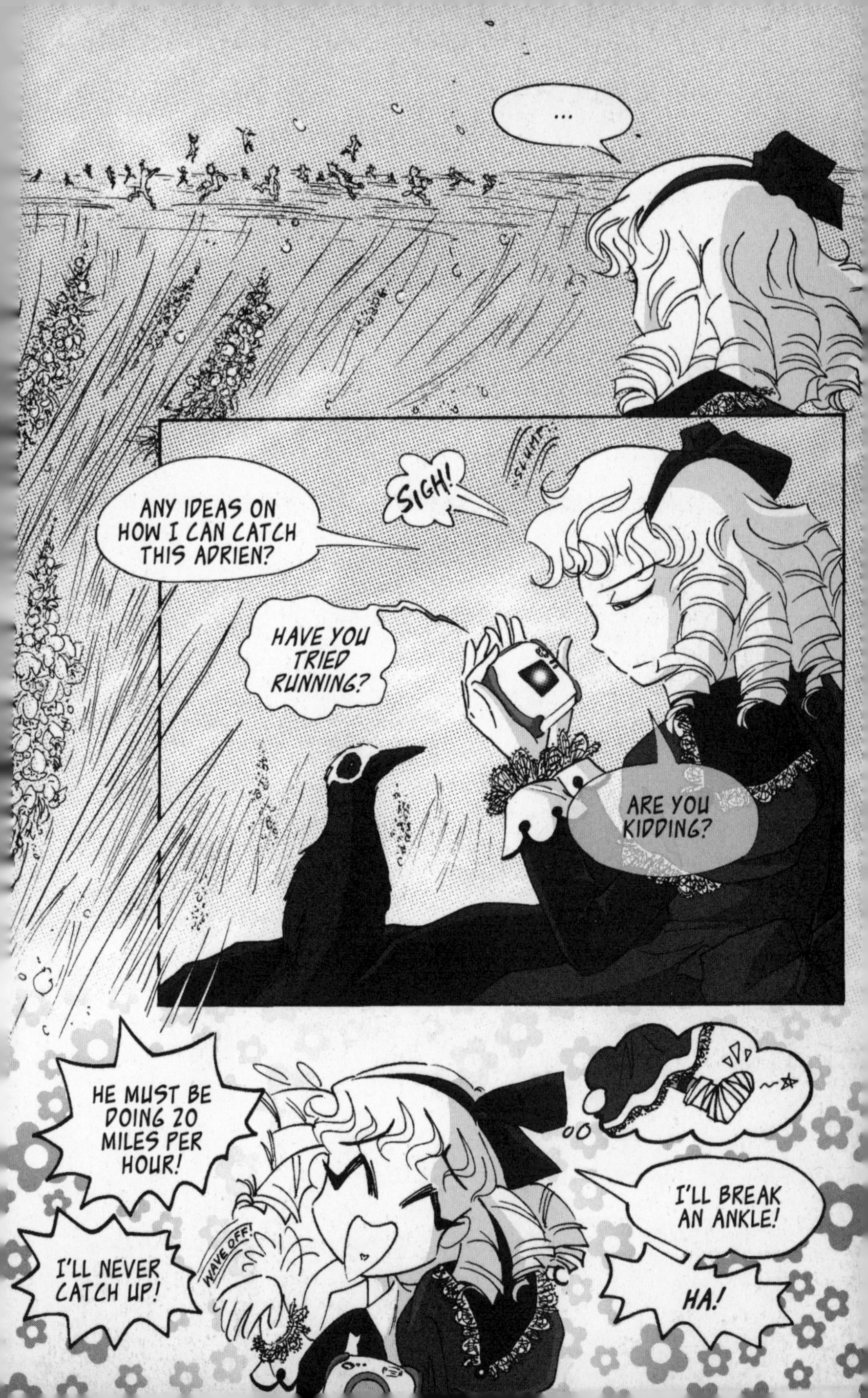
...
ANY IDEAS ON HOW I CAN CATCH THIS ADRIEN?
SIGH!
SLUMP...
HAVE YOU TRIED RUNNING?
ARE YOU KIDDING?
HE MUST BE DOING 20 MILES PER HOUR!
I'LL BREAK AN ANKLE!
I'LL NEVER CATCH UP!
WAVE OFF!
HA!

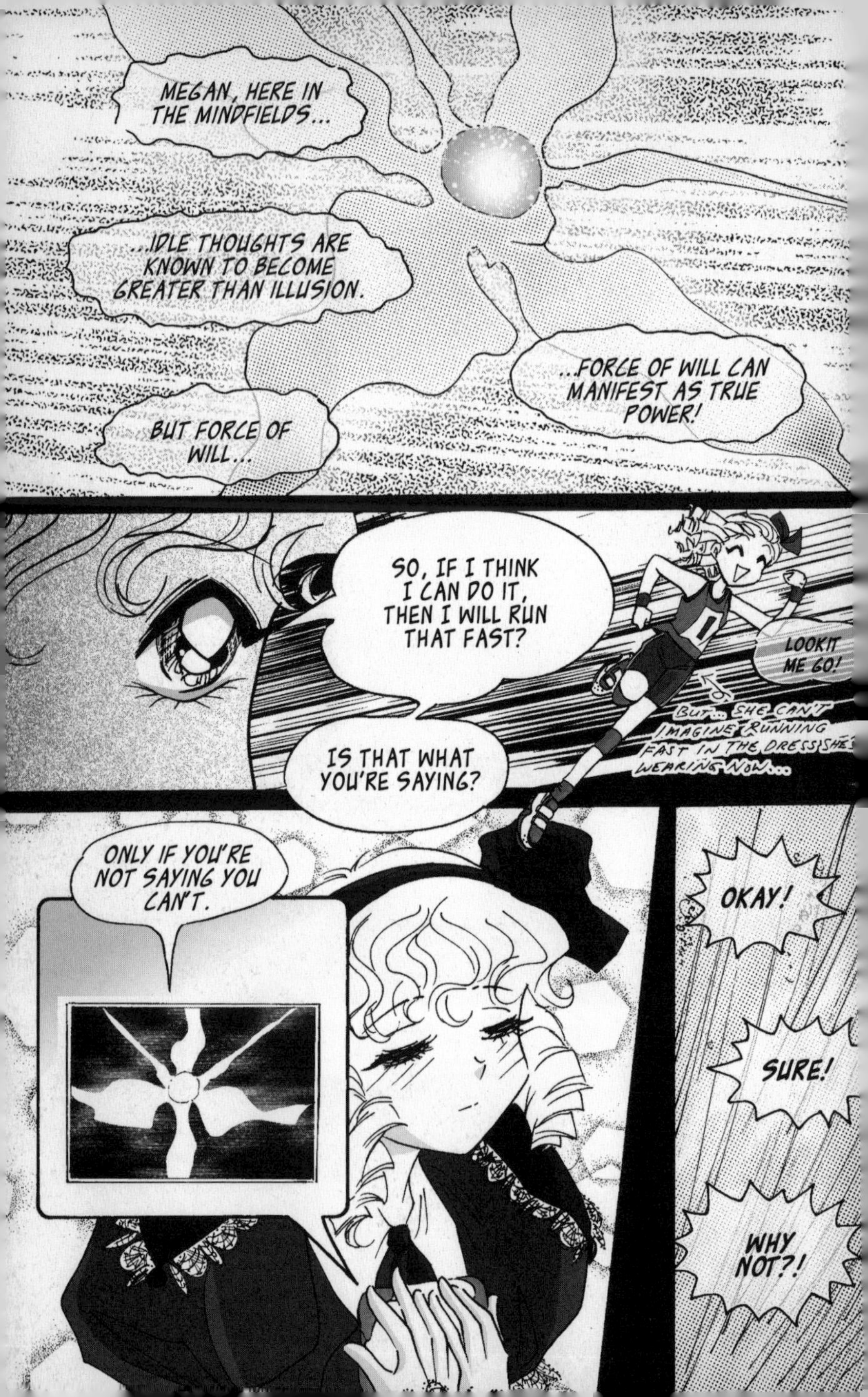
MEGAN, HERE IN THE MINDFIELDS...
...IDLE THOUGHTS ARE KNOWN TO BECOME GREATER THAN ILLUSION.
BUT FORCE OF WILL...
...FORCE OF WILL CAN MANIFEST AS TRUE POWER!
SO, IF I THINK I CAN DO IT, THEN I WILL RUN THAT FAST?
IS THAT WHAT YOU'RE SAYING?
LOOKIT ME GO!
BUT... SHE CAN'T IMAGINE RUNNING FAST IN THE DRESS SHE'S WEARING NOW...
ONLY IF YOU'RE NOT SAYING YOU CAN'T.
OKAY!
SURE!
WHY NOT?!

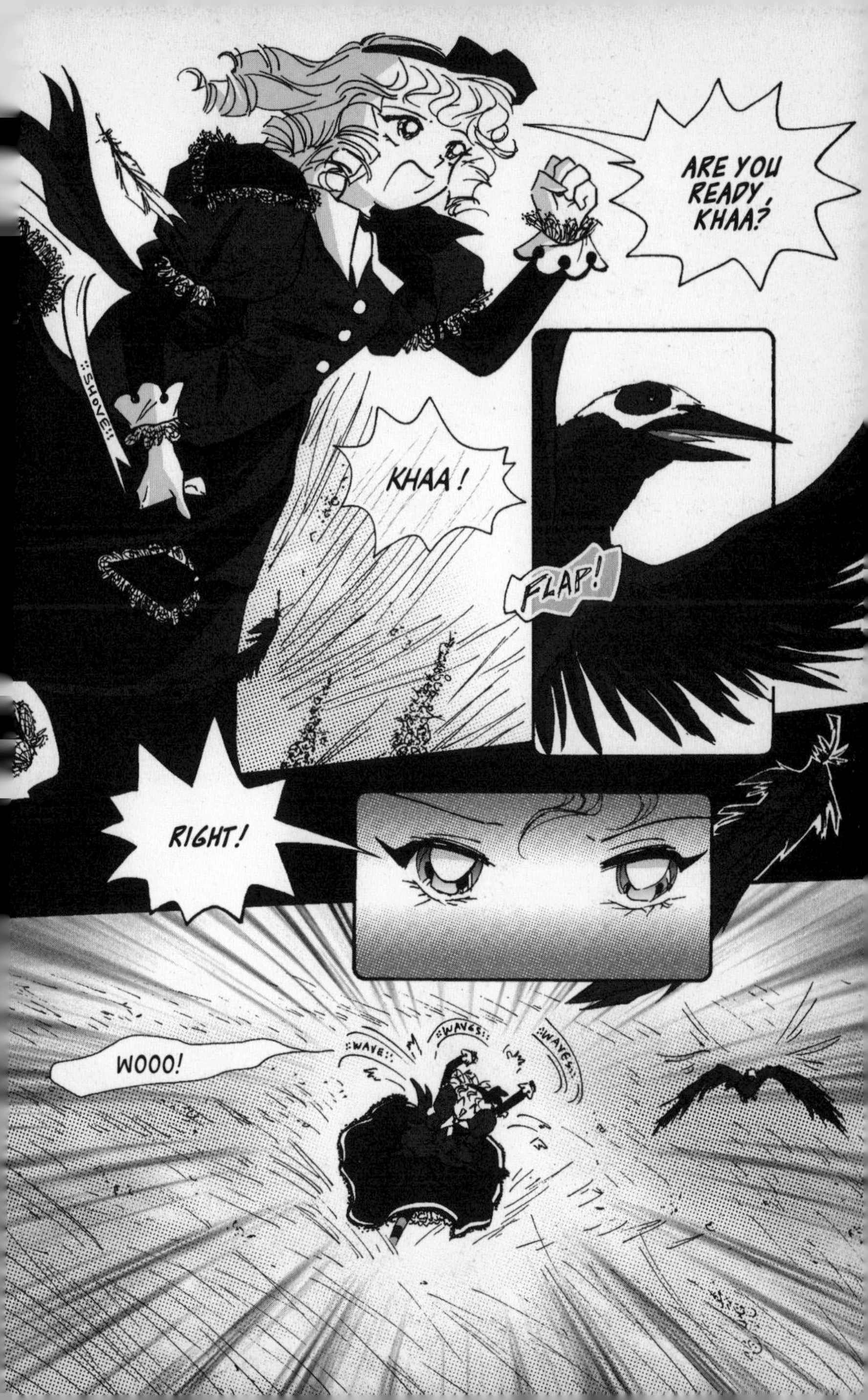
ARE YOU READY, KHAA?
::SHOVE::
KHAA!
FLAP!
RIGHT!
WOOO!
::WAVE::
::WAVES::
::WAVES::

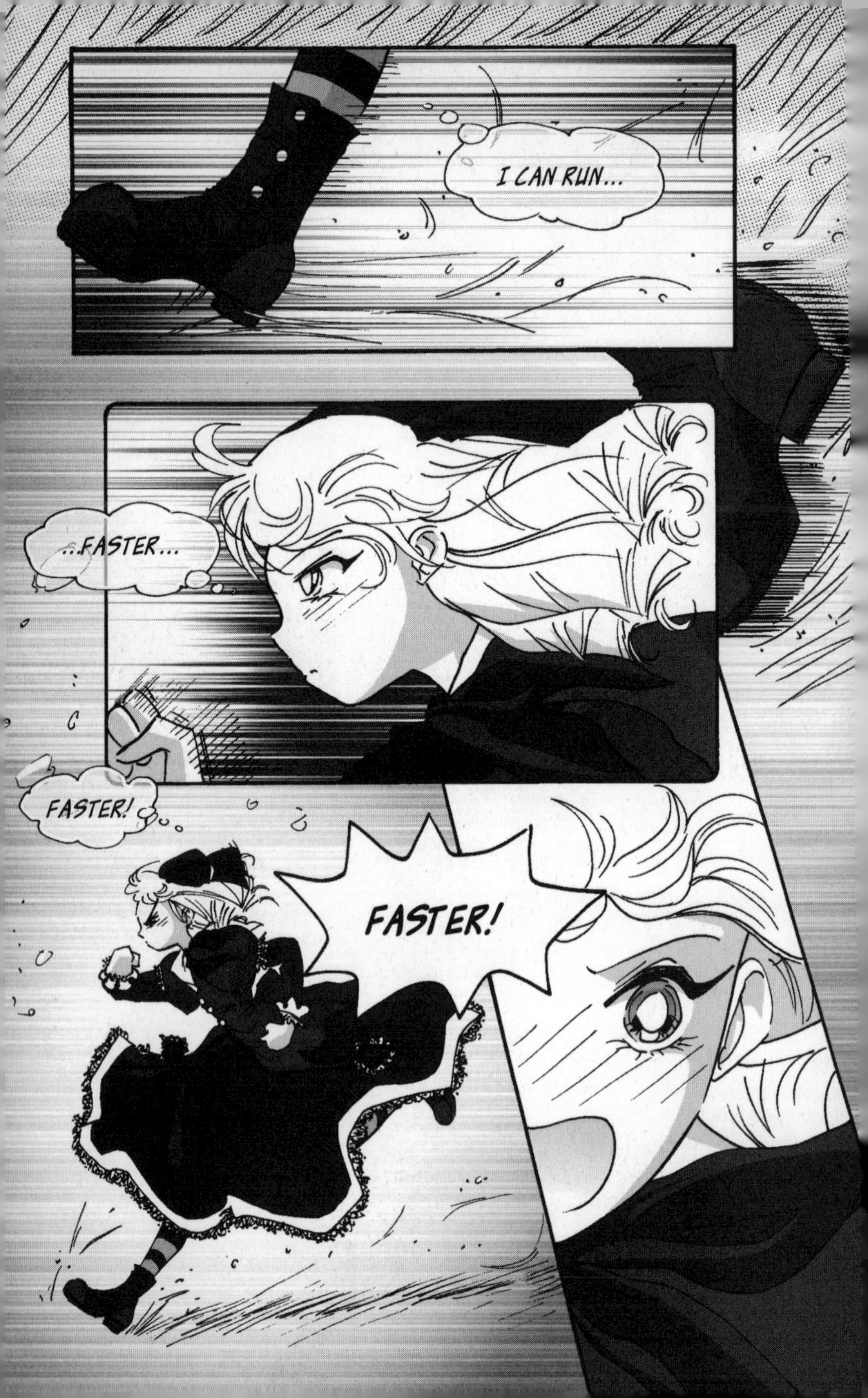
I CAN RUN...
...FASTER...
FASTER!
FASTER!

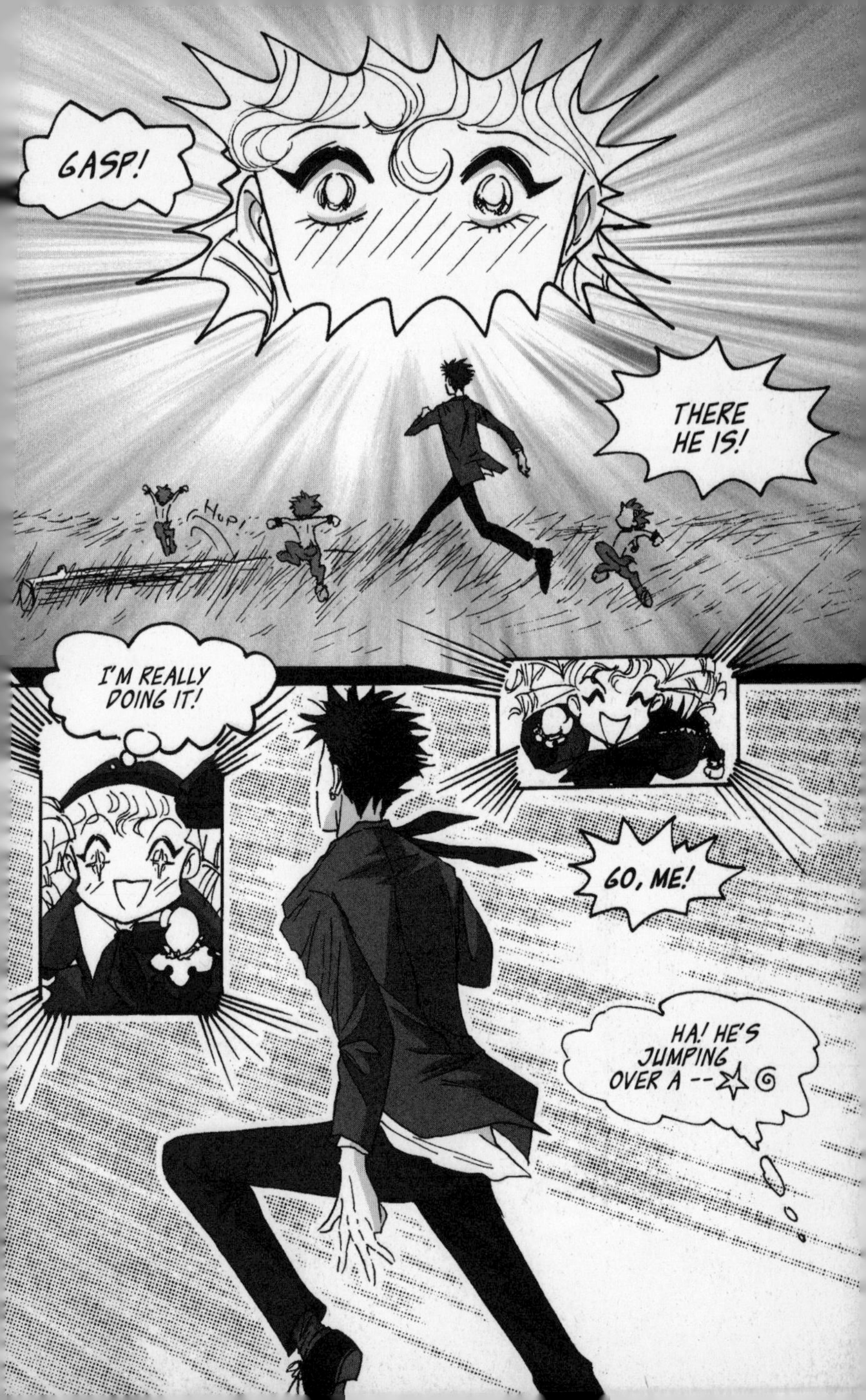
GASP!
THERE HE IS!
HUP!
I'M REALLY DOING IT!
GO, ME!
HA! HE'S JUMPING OVER A --

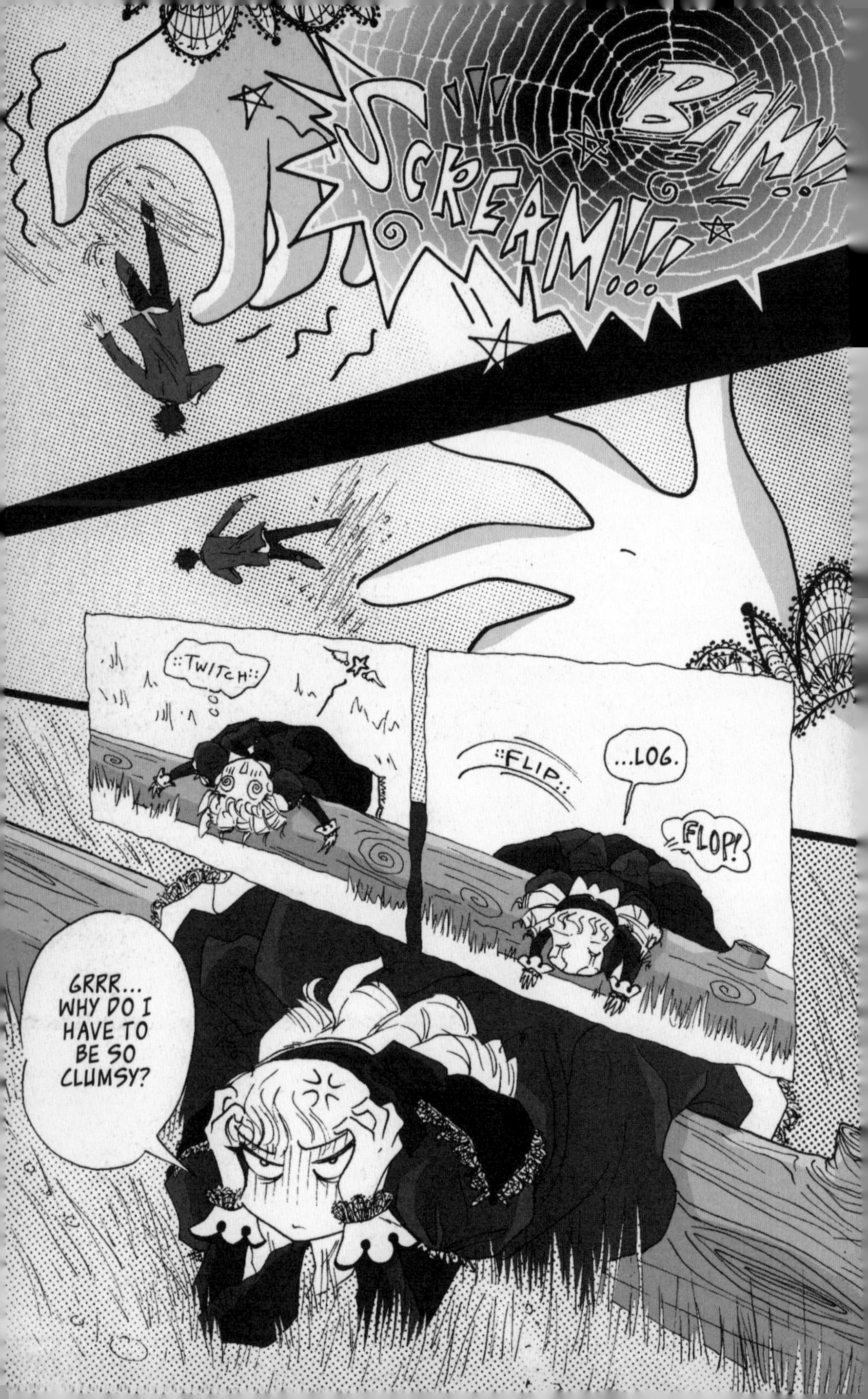
SCREAM!!!...
BAM!!
::TWITCH::
::FLIP::
...LOG.
FLOP!
GRRR... WHY DO I HAVE TO BE SO CLUMSY?

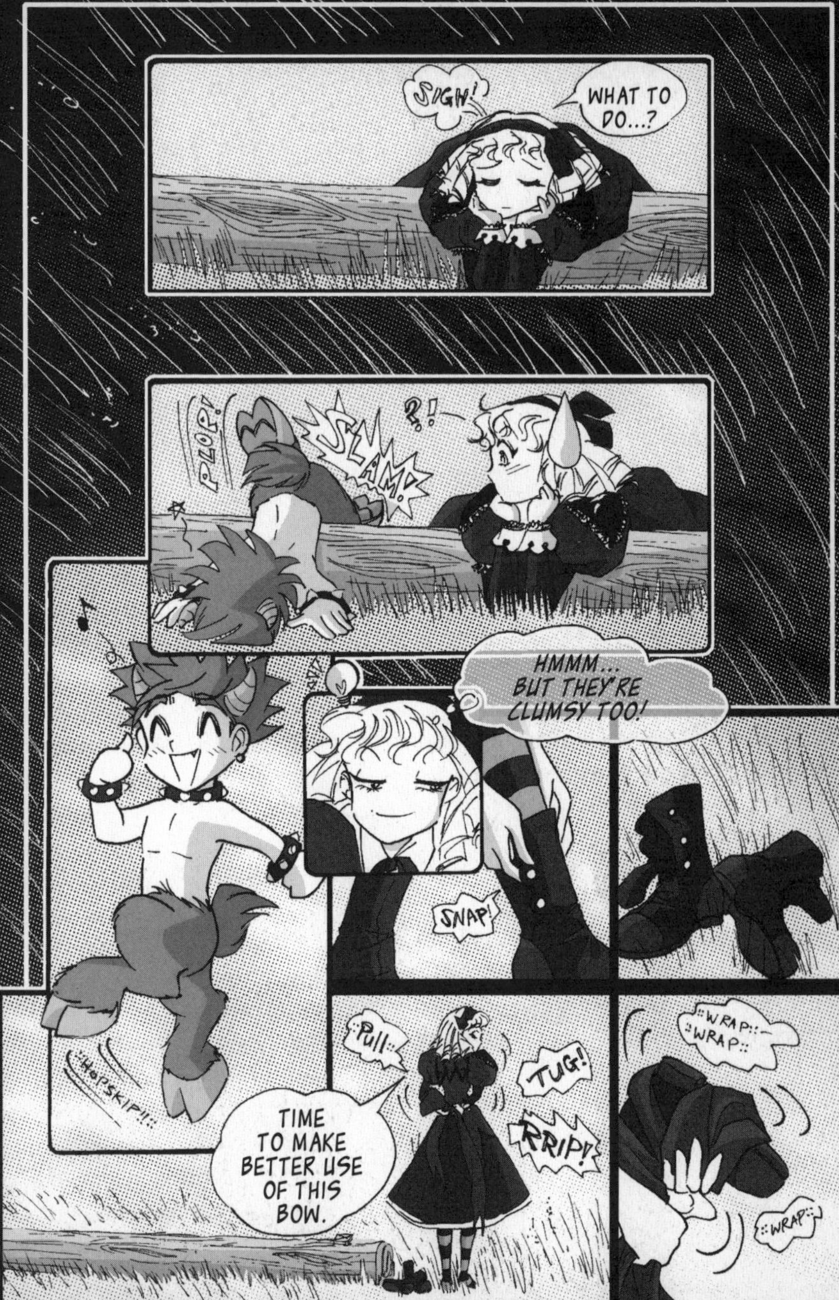
SIGH!
WHAT TO DO...?
PLOP!
SLAM!
?!
HMMM... BUT THEY'RE CLUMSY TOO!
SNAP!
::HOPSKIP!!::
::PULL::
TUG!
RRIP!
TIME TO MAKE BETTER USE OF THIS BOW.
::WRAP::
::WRAP::
::WRAP

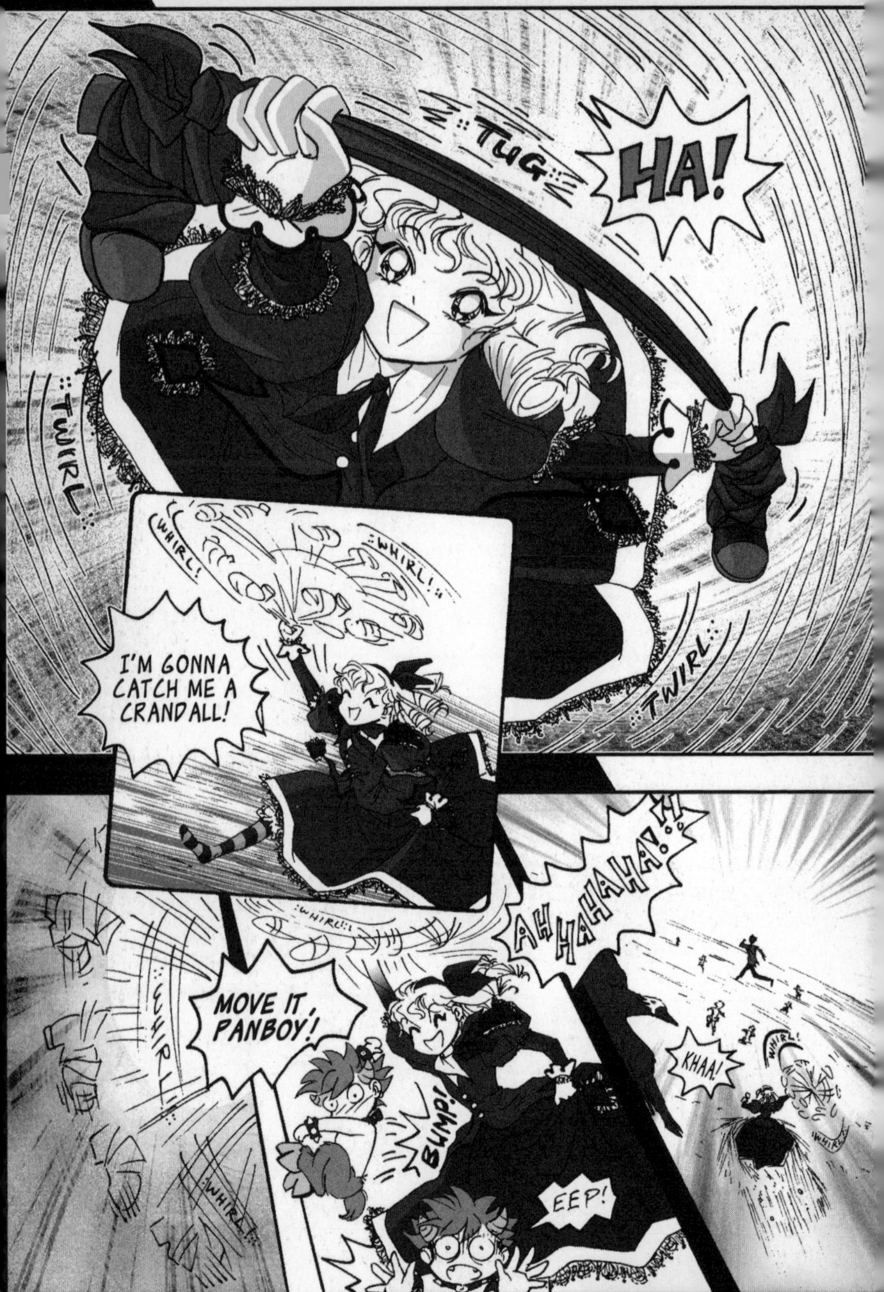
TUG
HA!
TWIRL
TWIRL
WHIRL!
WHIRL!
I'M GONNA CATCH ME A CRANDALL!
WHIRL
WHIRL
WHIRL
AHHAHAHAHA!!
MOVE IT, PANBOY!
BUMP!
EEP!
KHAA!
WHIRL
WHIRL

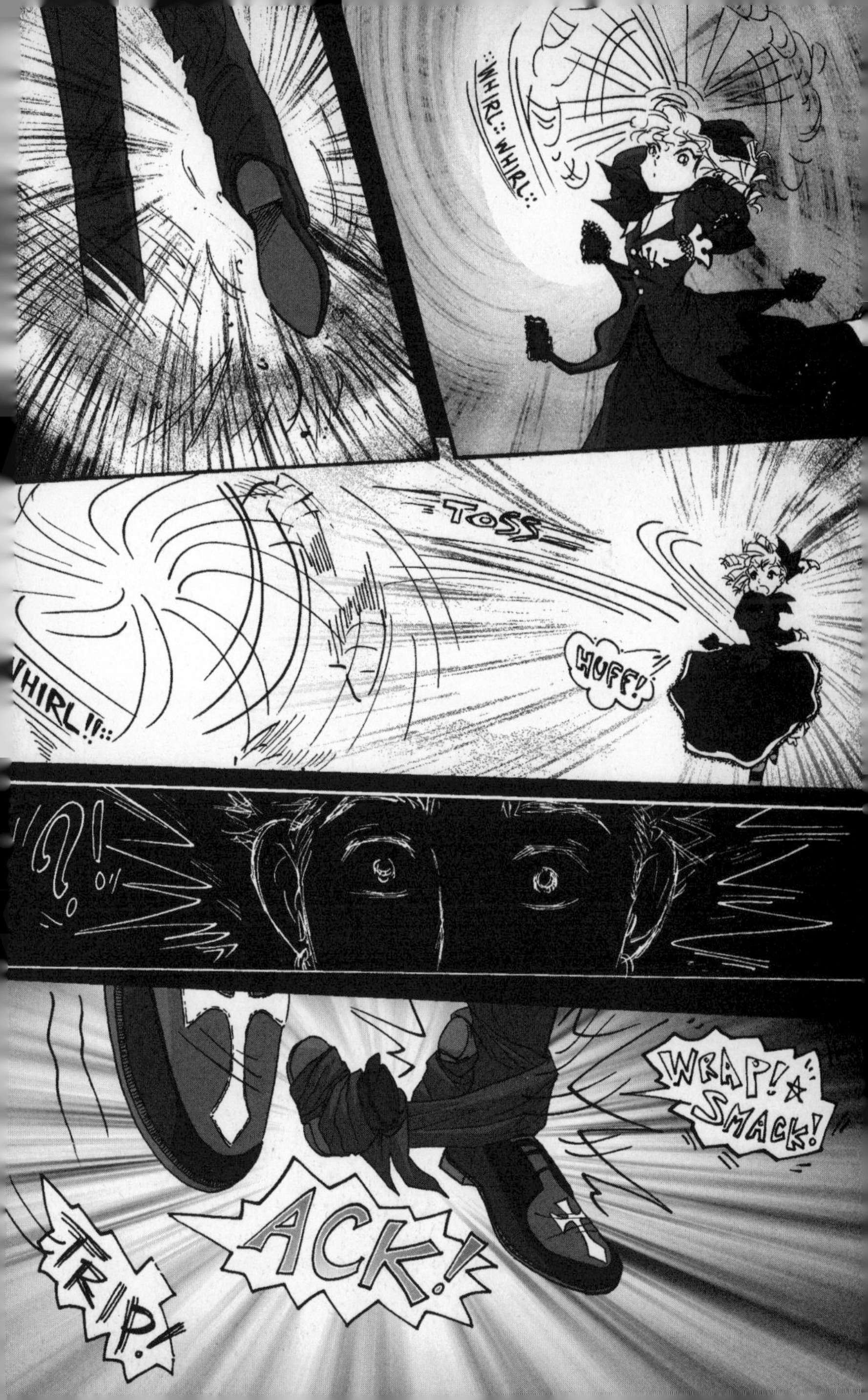
::WHIRL:: WHIRL::
TOSS
WHIRL!!::
HUFF!
?!
WRAP!☆ SMACK!
TRIP!
ACK!

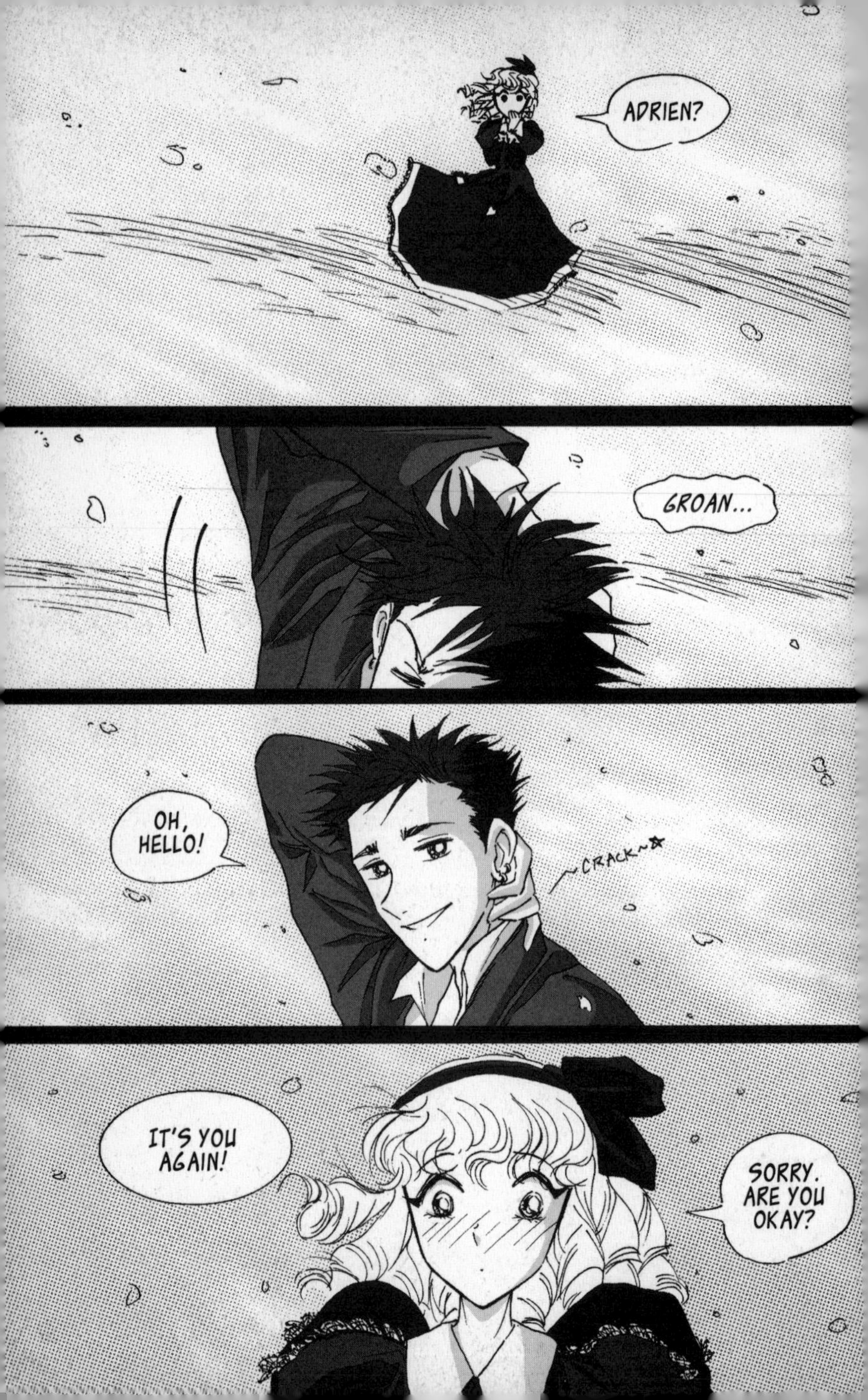
ADRIEN?
GROAN...
OH, HELLO!
~CRACK~
IT'S YOU AGAIN!
SORRY. ARE YOU OKAY?

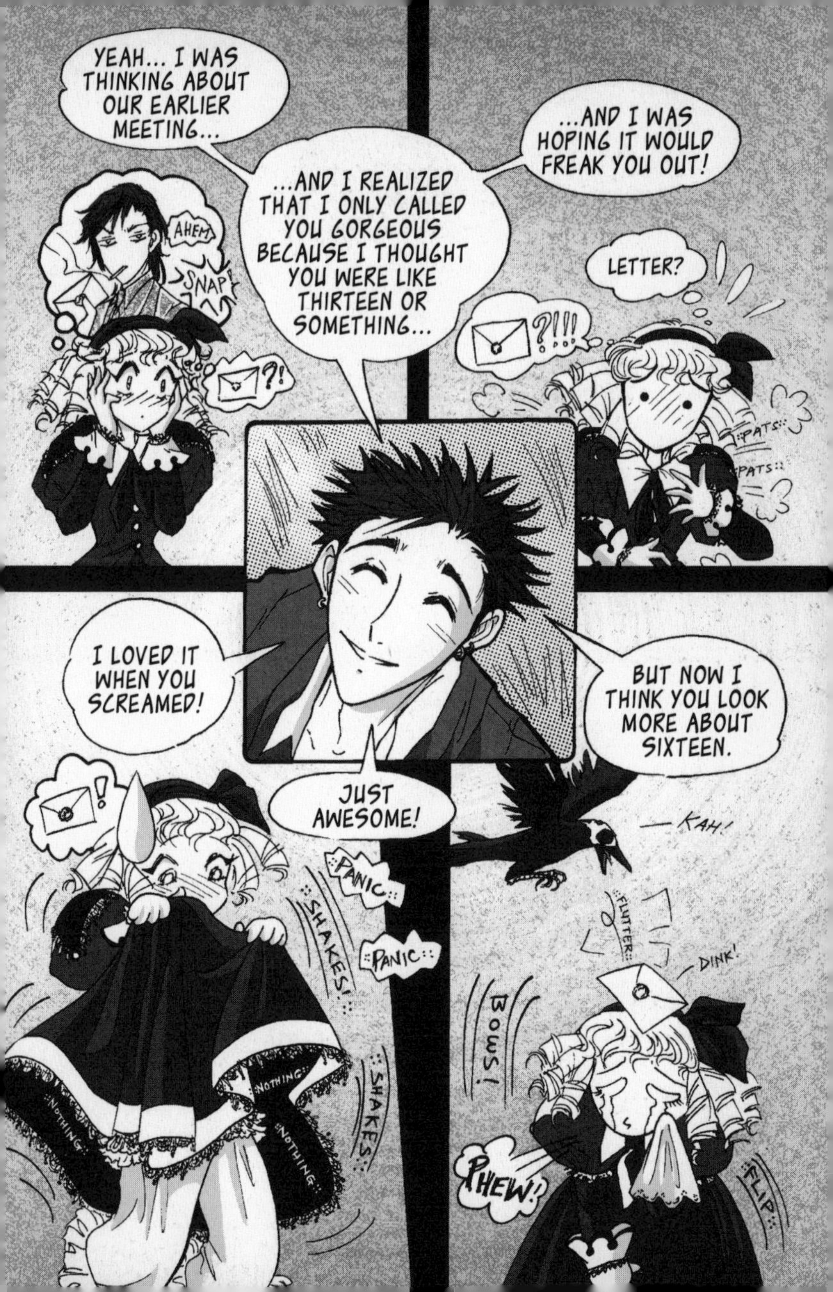
YEAH... I WAS THINKING ABOUT OUR EARLIER MEETING...
AHEM
SNAP!
?!
...AND I REALIZED THAT I ONLY CALLED YOU GORGEOUS BECAUSE I THOUGHT YOU WERE LIKE THIRTEEN OR SOMETHING...
...AND I WAS HOPING IT WOULD FREAK YOU OUT!
LETTER?
?!!!
PATS
PATS
I LOVED IT WHEN YOU SCREAMED!
JUST AWESOME!
BUT NOW I THINK YOU LOOK MORE ABOUT SIXTEEN.
!
KAH!
PANIC
SHAKES!
PANIC
SHAKES
NOTHING
NOTHING
NOTHING
FLUTTER
DINK!
BOWS!
PHEW!
FLIP

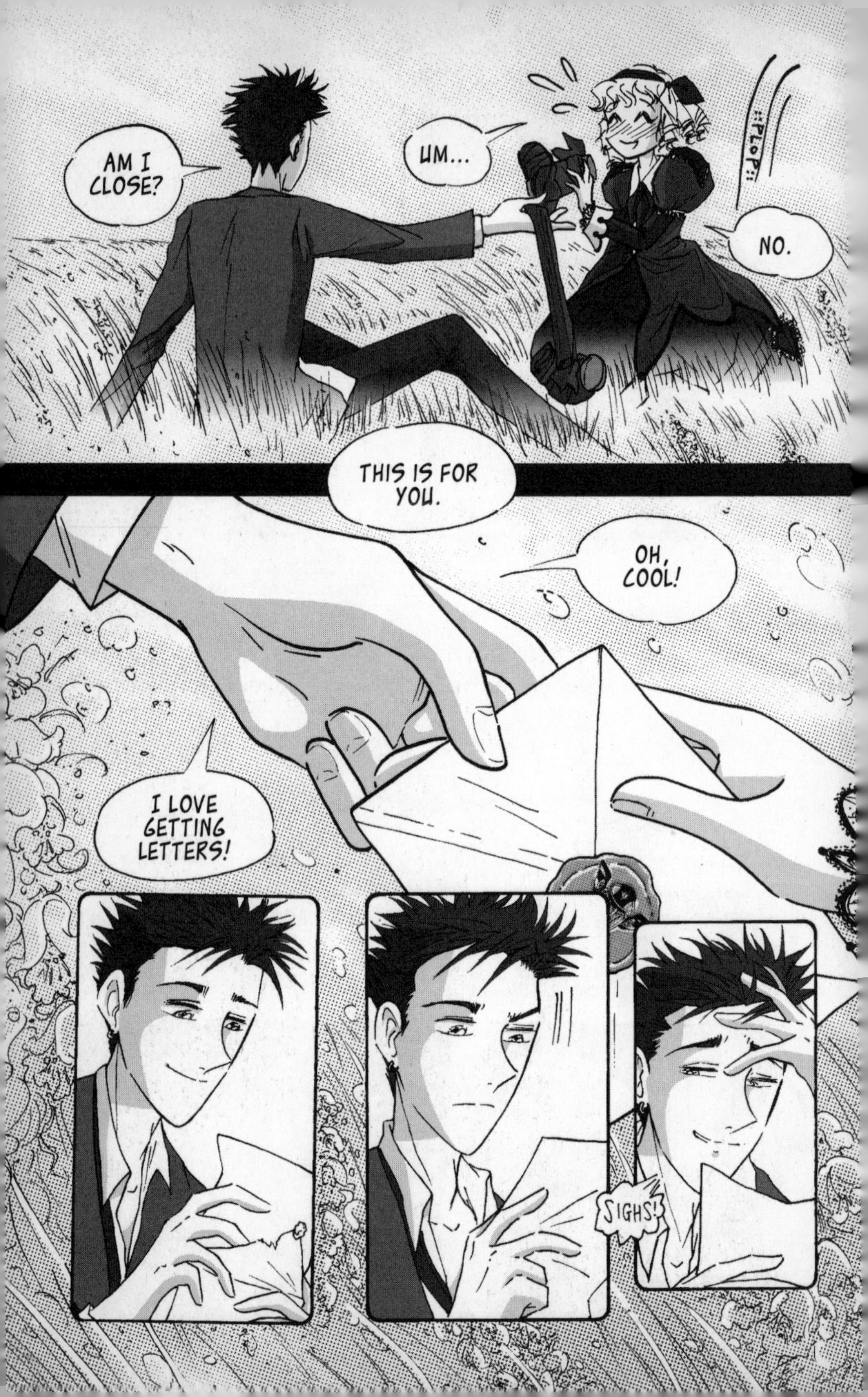
AM I CLOSE?
UM...
::PLOP::
NO.
THIS IS FOR YOU.
OH, COOL!
I LOVE GETTING LETTERS!
SIGHS!

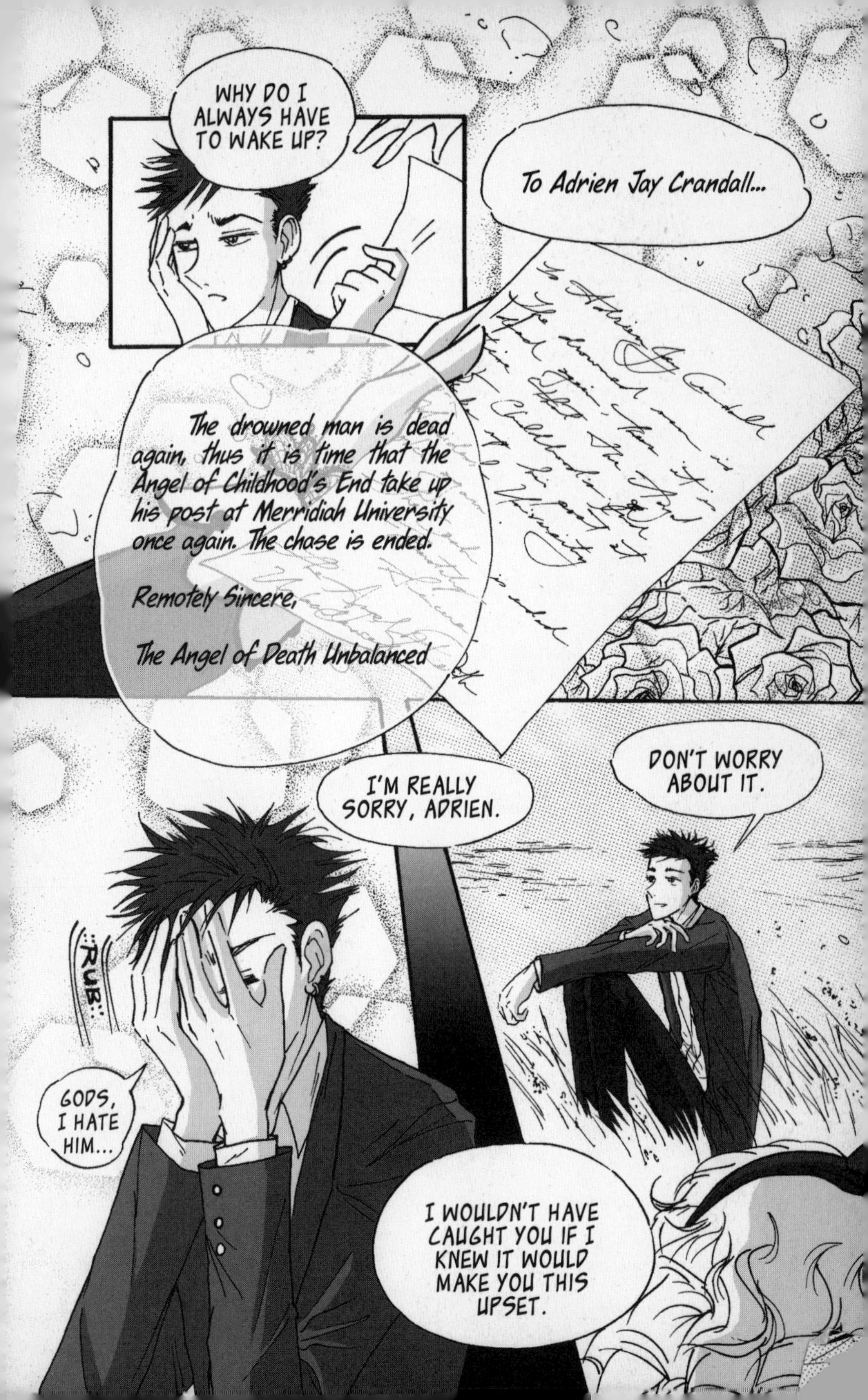
WHY DO I ALWAYS HAVE TO WAKE UP?
To Adrien Jay Crandall...
The drowned man is dead again, thus it is time that the Angel of Childhood's End take up his post at Merridiah University once again. The chase is ended.
Remotely Sincere,
The Angel of Death Unbalanced
I'M REALLY SORRY, ADRIEN.
DON'T WORRY ABOUT IT.
RUB
GODS, I HATE HIM...
I WOULDN'T HAVE CAUGHT YOU IF I KNEW IT WOULD MAKE YOU THIS UPSET.

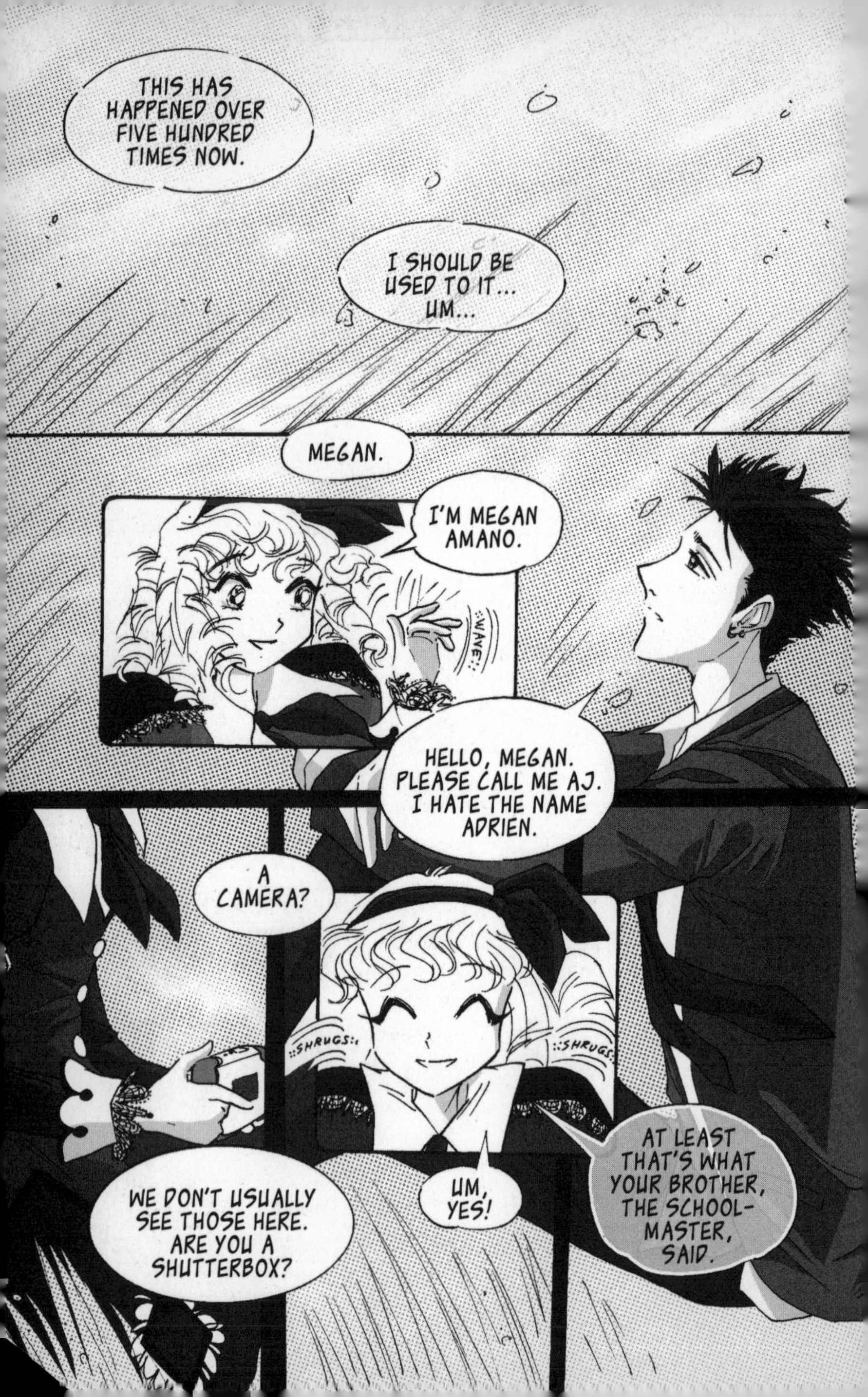
THIS HAS HAPPENED OVER FIVE HUNDRED TIMES NOW.
I SHOULD BE USED TO IT... UM...
MEGAN.
I'M MEGAN AMANO.
::WAVE::
HELLO, MEGAN. PLEASE CALL ME AJ. I HATE THE NAME ADRIEN.
A CAMERA?
WE DON'T USUALLY SEE THOSE HERE. ARE YOU A SHUTTERBOX?
::SHRUGS::
::SHRUGS::
UM, YES!
AT LEAST THAT'S WHAT YOUR BROTHER, THE SCHOOL-MASTER, SAID.

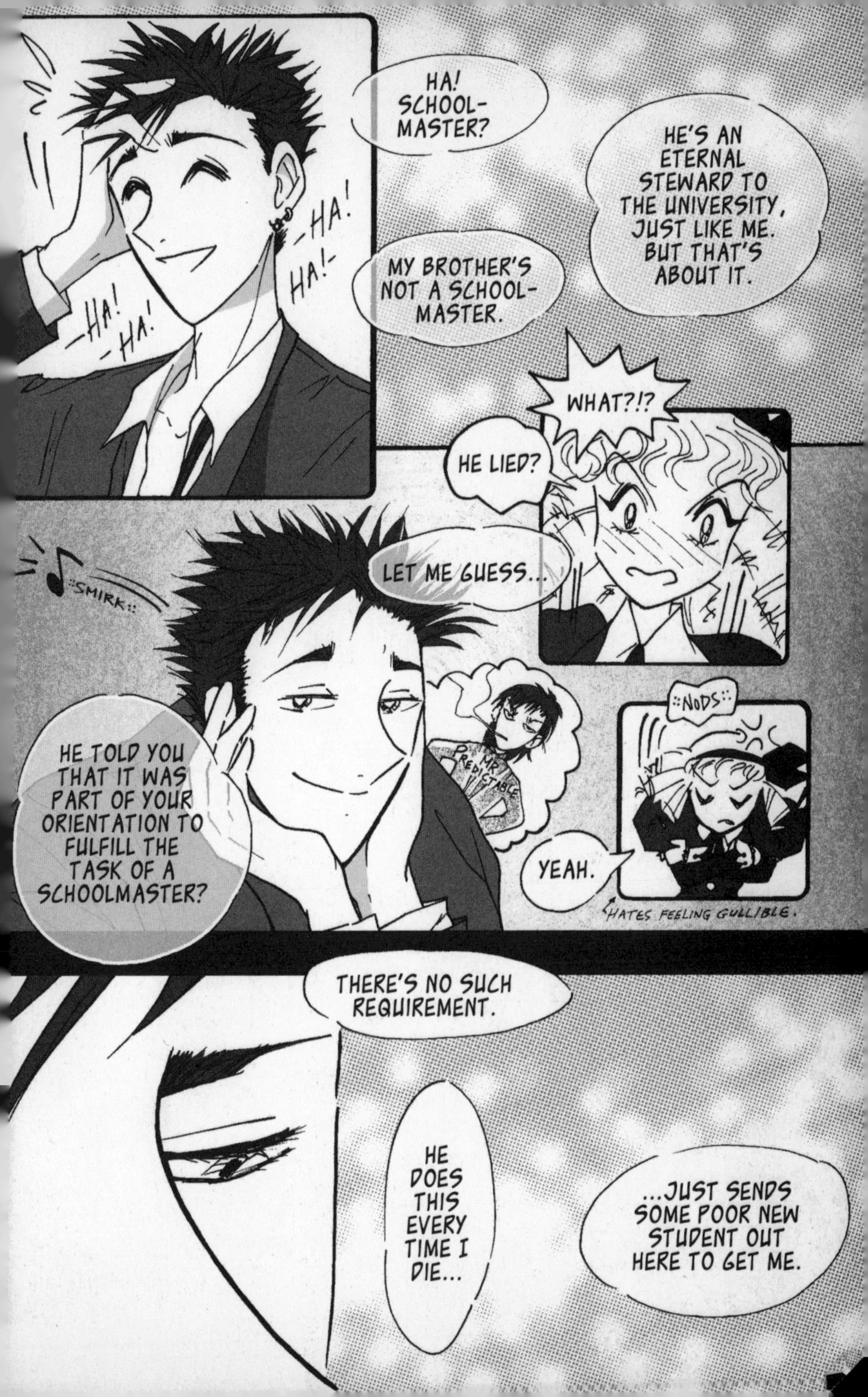
HA! SCHOOL-MASTER?
HA! HA!
HA! HA!
MY BROTHER'S NOT A SCHOOL-MASTER.
HE'S AN ETERNAL STEWARD TO THE UNIVERSITY, JUST LIKE ME. BUT THAT'S ABOUT IT.
WHAT?!?
HE LIED?
::SMIRK::
LET ME GUESS...
HE TOLD YOU THAT IT WAS PART OF YOUR ORIENTATION TO FULFILL THE TASK OF A SCHOOLMASTER?
MR. PREDICTABLE
::NODS::
YEAH.
HATES FEELING GULLIBLE.
THERE'S NO SUCH REQUIREMENT.
HE DOES THIS EVERY TIME I DIE...
...JUST SENDS SOME POOR NEW STUDENT OUT HERE TO GET ME.

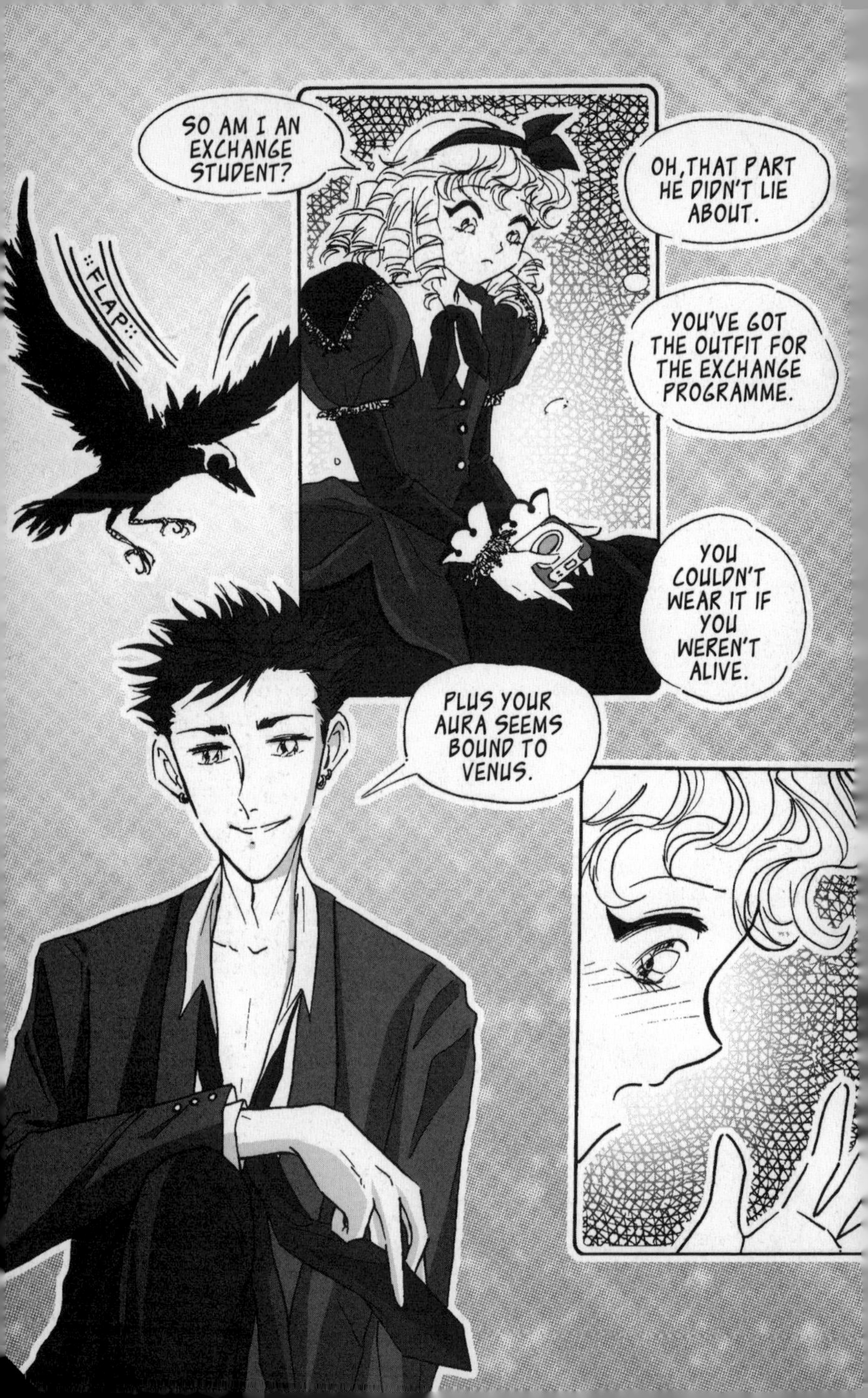
SO AM I AN EXCHANGE STUDENT?
::FLAP::
OH, THAT PART HE DIDN'T LIE ABOUT.
YOU'VE GOT THE OUTFIT FOR THE EXCHANGE PROGRAMME.
YOU COULDN'T WEAR IT IF YOU WEREN'T ALIVE.
PLUS YOUR AURA SEEMS BOUND TO VENUS.

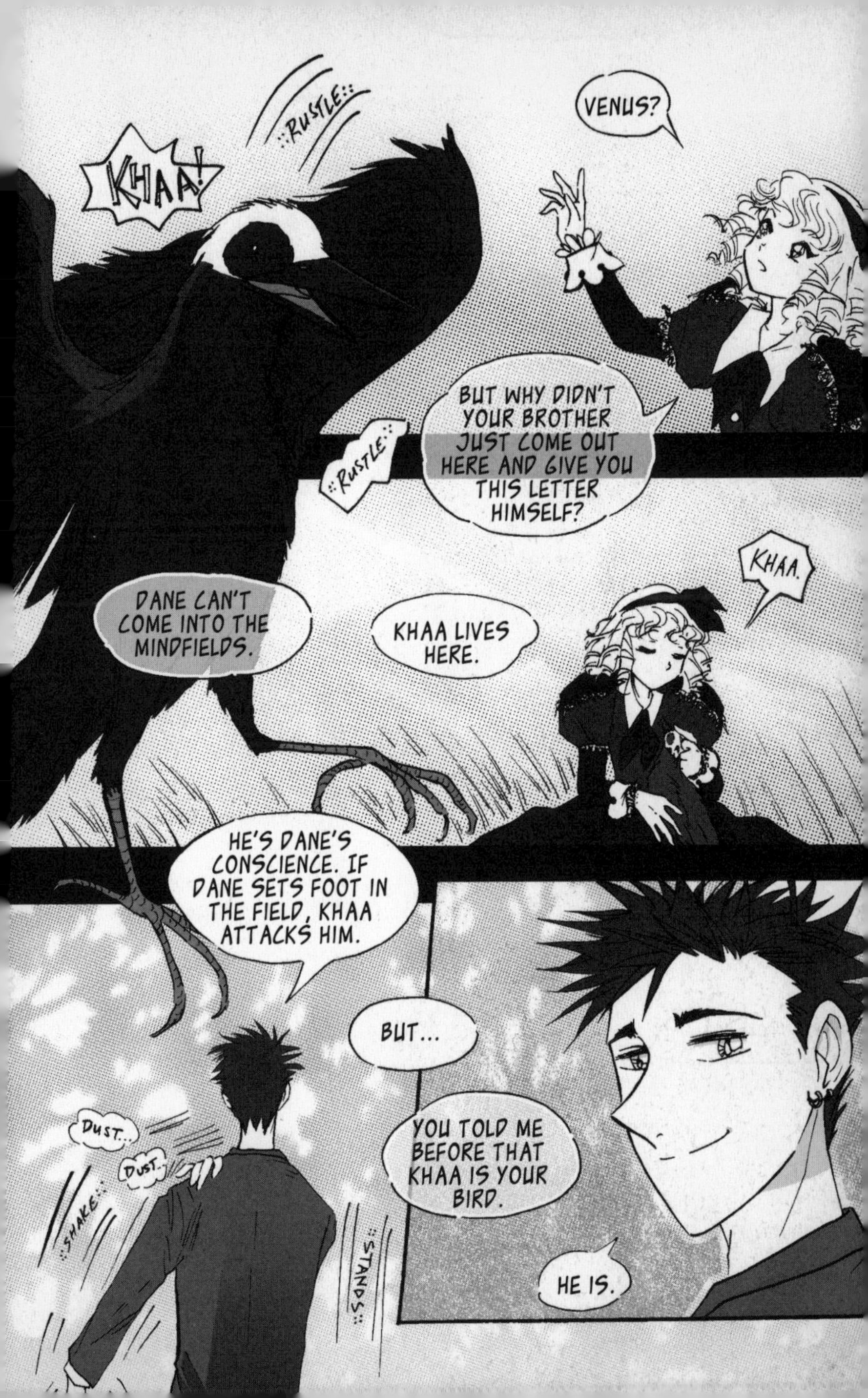
KHAA!
::RUSTLE::
VENUS?
::RUSTLE::
BUT WHY DIDN'T YOUR BROTHER JUST COME OUT HERE AND GIVE YOU THIS LETTER HIMSELF?
DANE CAN'T COME INTO THE MINDFIELDS.
KHAA LIVES HERE.
KHAA.
HE'S DANE'S CONSCIENCE. IF DANE SETS FOOT IN THE FIELD, KHAA ATTACKS HIM.
BUT...
DUST...
DUST...
::SHAKE::
::STANDS::
YOU TOLD ME BEFORE THAT KHAA IS YOUR BIRD.
HE IS.

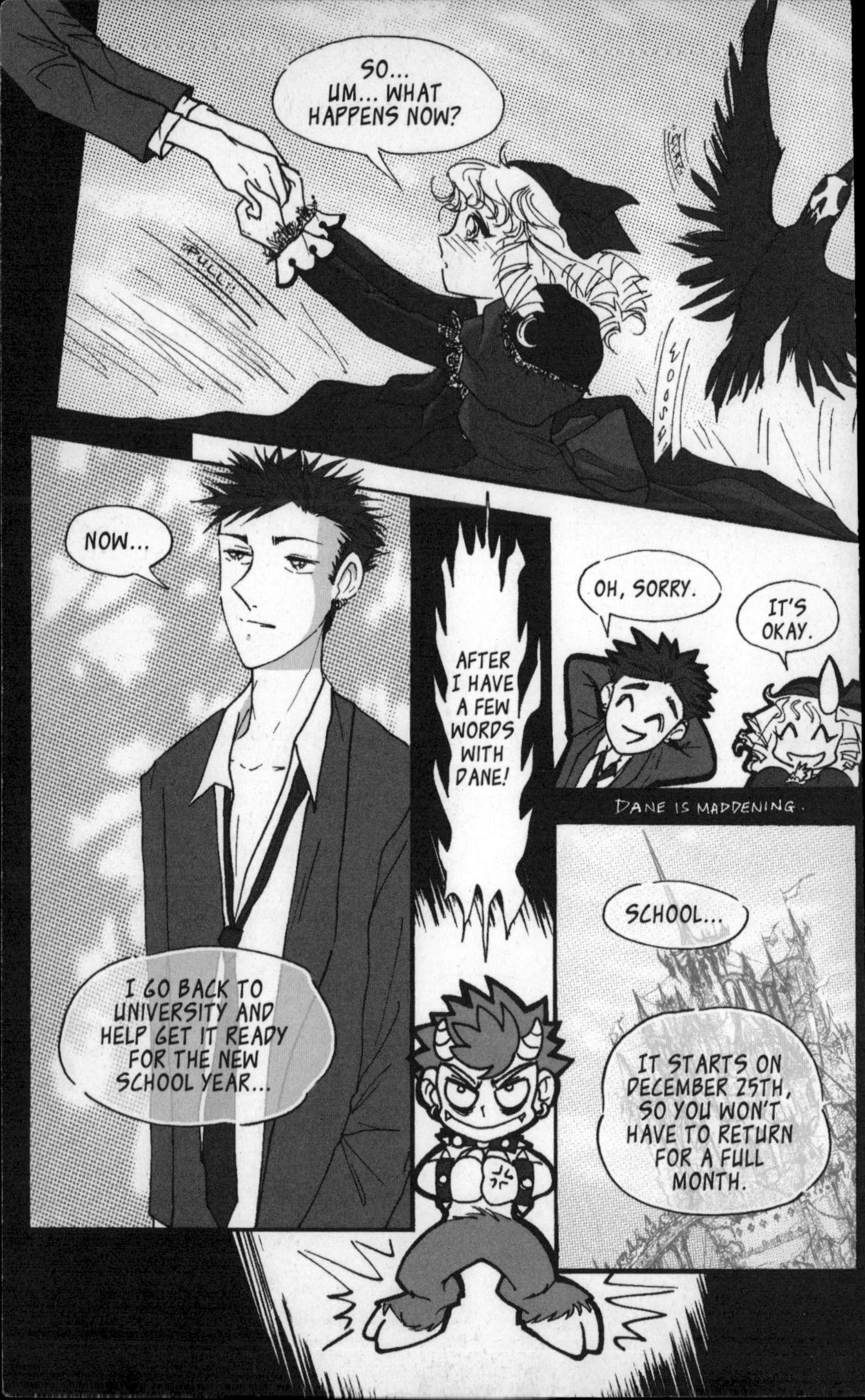
SO... UM... WHAT HAPPENS NOW?
PULL!!
WOOSH
NOW...
I GO BACK TO UNIVERSITY AND HELP GET IT READY FOR THE NEW SCHOOL YEAR...
AFTER I HAVE A FEW WORDS WITH DANE!
OH, SORRY.
IT'S OKAY.
DANE IS MADDENING.
SCHOOL...
IT STARTS ON DECEMBER 25TH, SO YOU WON'T HAVE TO RETURN FOR A FULL MONTH.

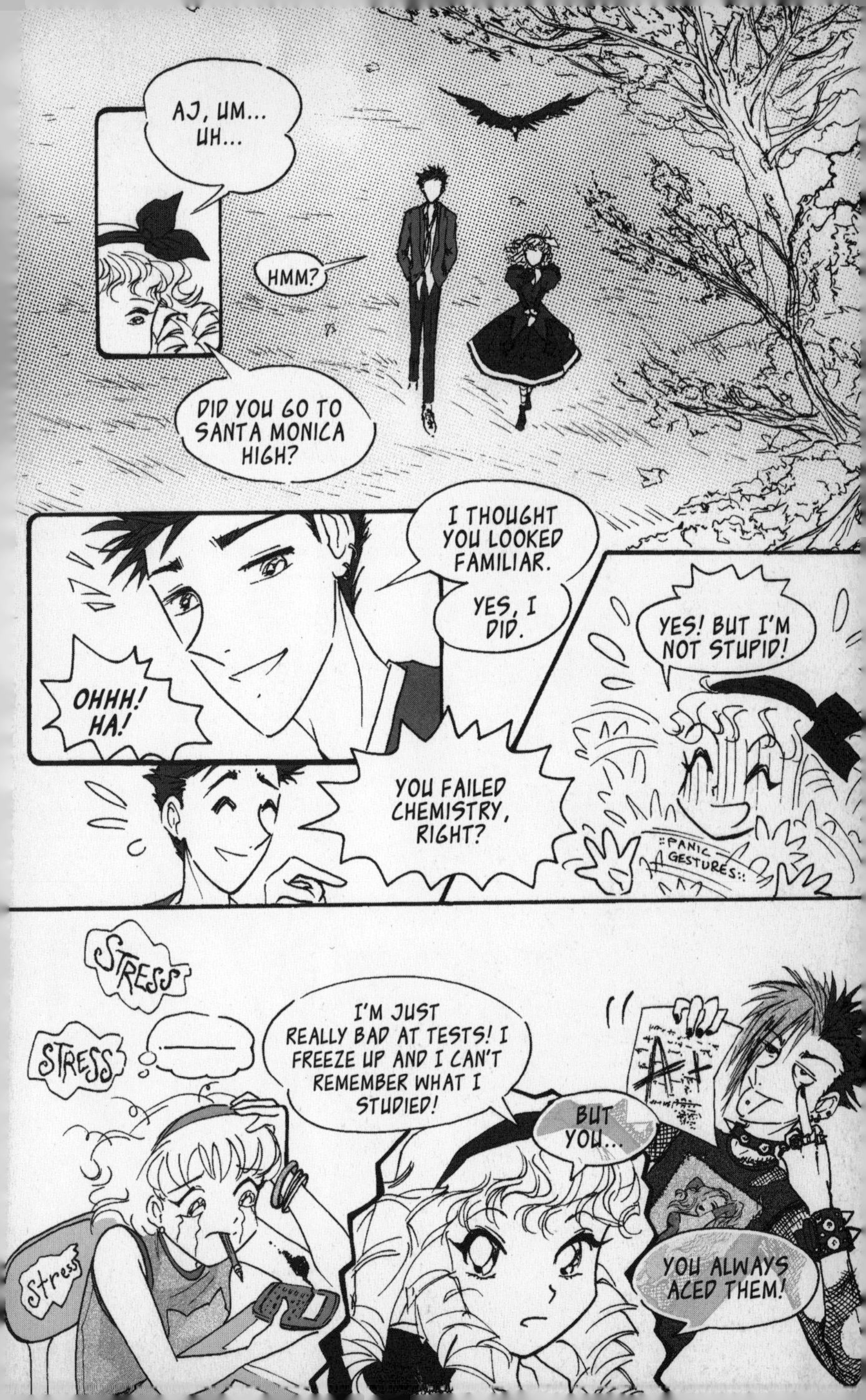
AJ, UM... UH...
HMM?
DID YOU GO TO SANTA MONICA HIGH?
I THOUGHT YOU LOOKED FAMILIAR.
YES, I DID.
OHHH! HA!
YOU FAILED CHEMISTRY, RIGHT?
YES! BUT I'M NOT STUPID!
::PANIC GESTURES::
STRESS
STRESS
I'M JUST REALLY BAD AT TESTS! I FREEZE UP AND I CAN'T REMEMBER WHAT I STUDIED!
stress
BUT YOU...
YOU ALWAYS ACED THEM!

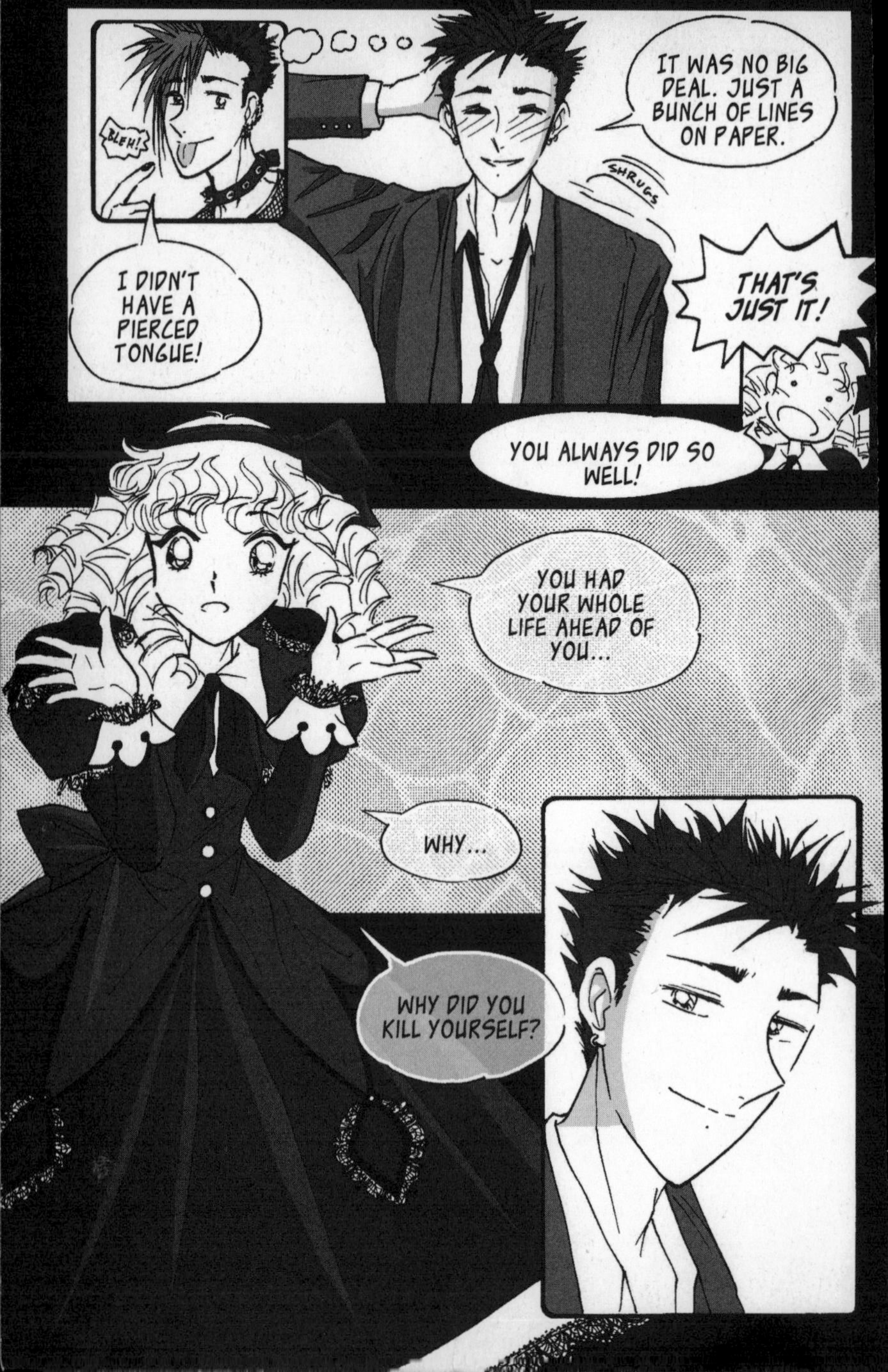
BLEH!
I DIDN'T HAVE A PIERCED TONGUE!
IT WAS NO BIG DEAL. JUST A BUNCH OF LINES ON PAPER.
SHRUGS
THAT'S JUST IT!
YOU ALWAYS DID SO WELL!
YOU HAD YOUR WHOLE LIFE AHEAD OF YOU...
WHY...
WHY DID YOU KILL YOURSELF?

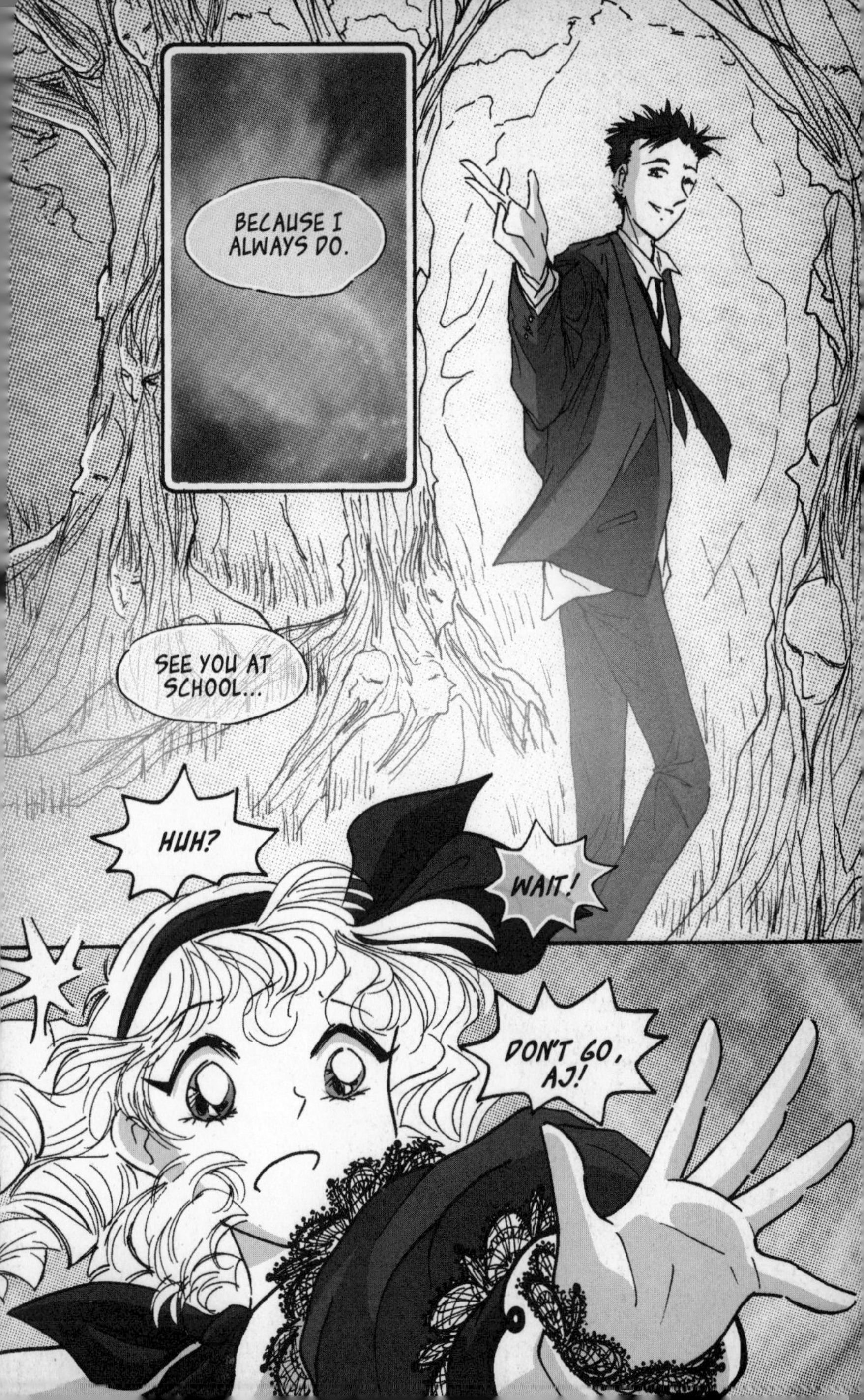
BECAUSE I ALWAYS DO.
SEE YOU AT SCHOOL...
HUH?
WAIT!
DON'T GO, AJ!

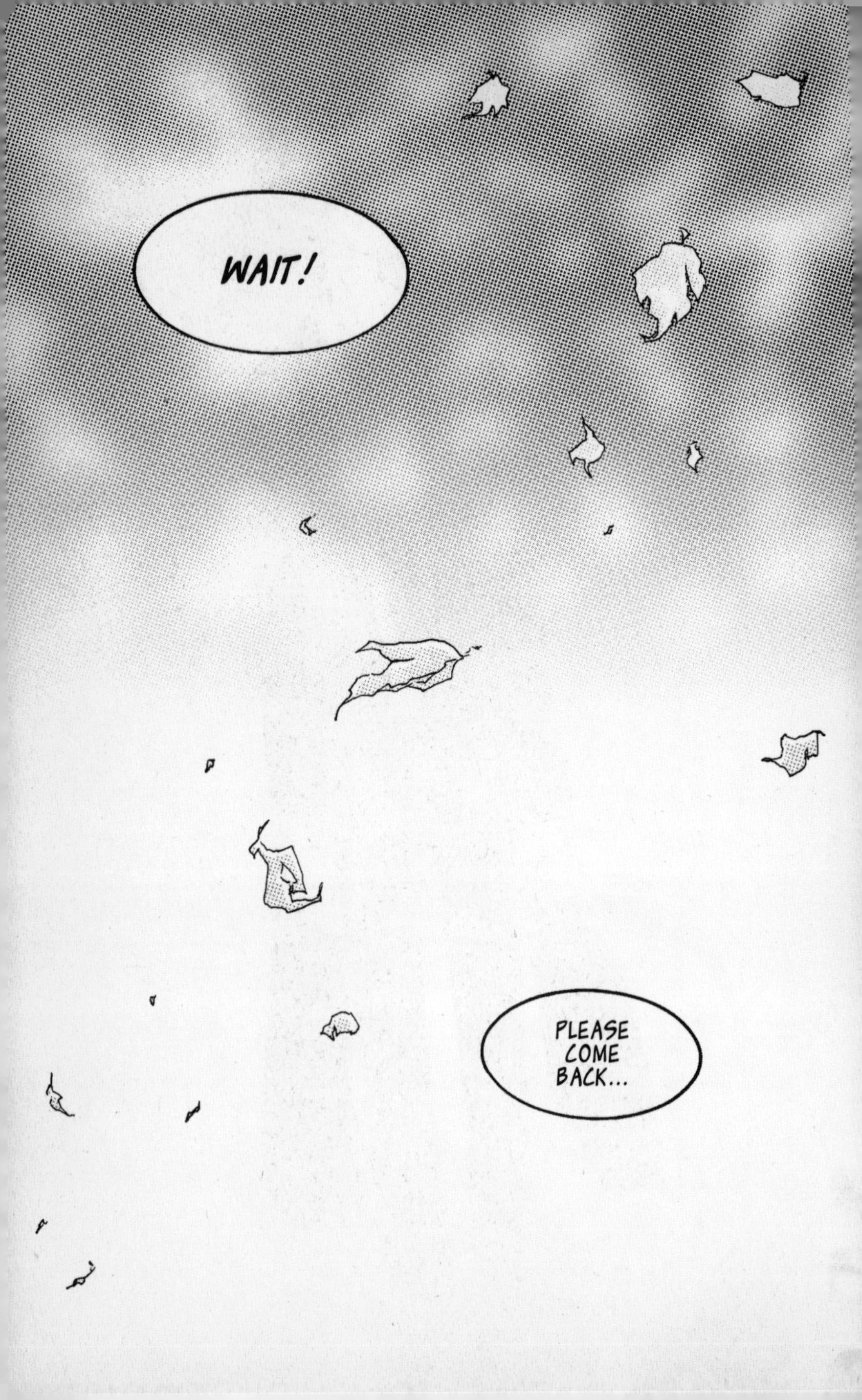
WAIT!
PLEASE COME BACK...

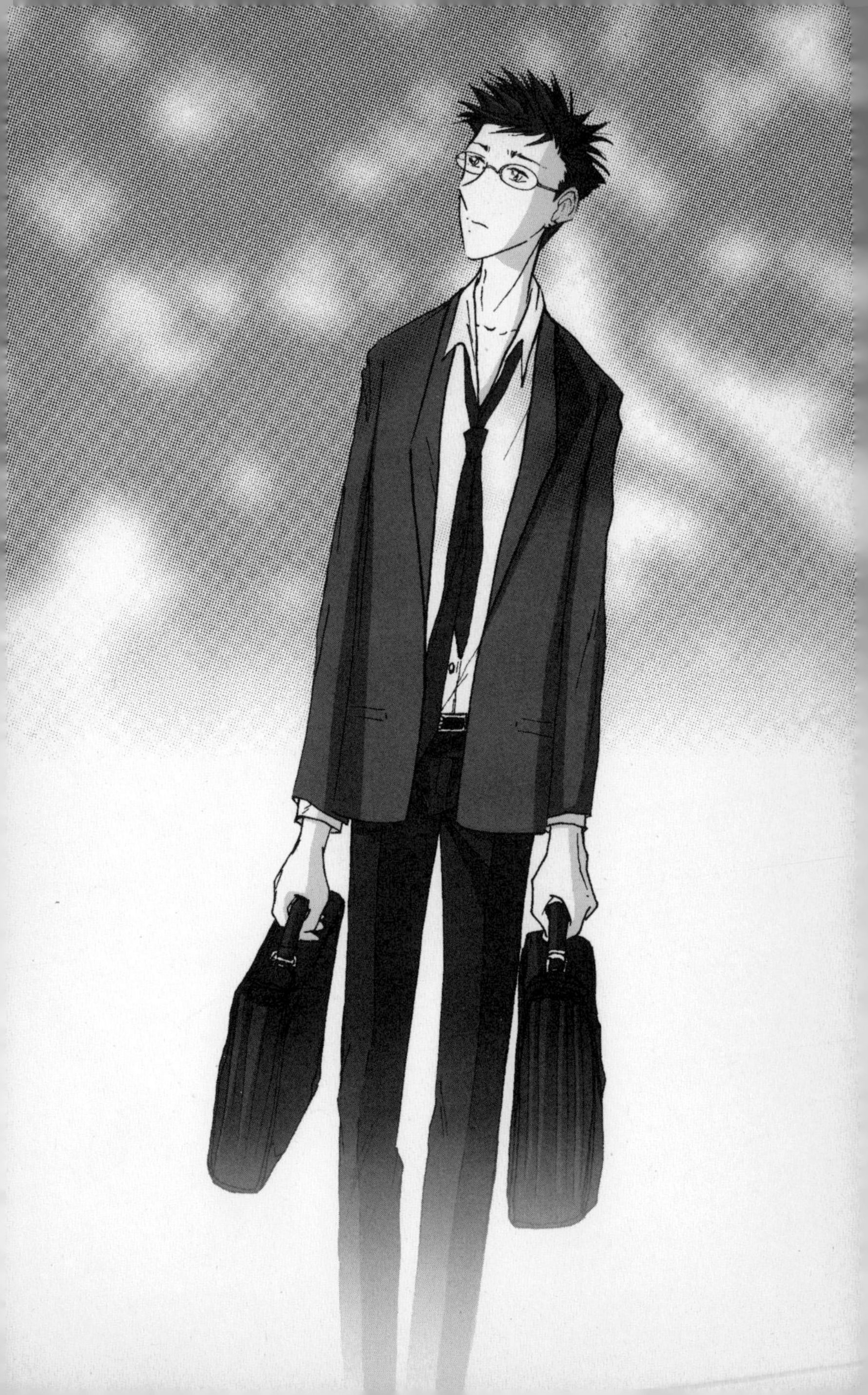

For London,
Los Angeles,
and Tokyo;
the seeds of
influence.

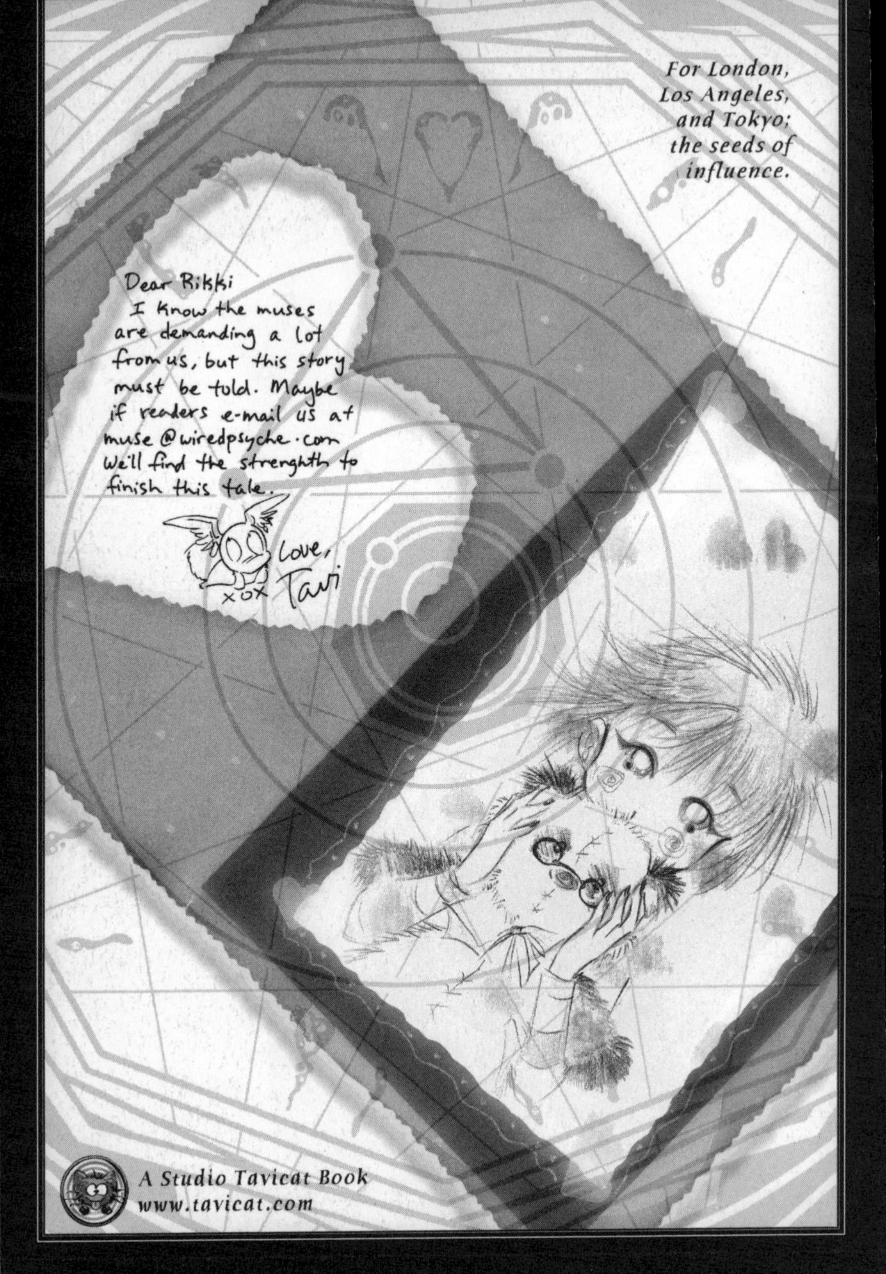
Dear Rikki
I know the muses are demanding a lot from us, but this story must be told. Maybe if readers e-mail us at muse@wiredpsyche.com We'll find the strenghth to finish this tale.
Love,
Tavi
xox

A Studio Tavicat Book
www.tavicat.com

Hello, Diary,
When I woke up this morning, I found a photo of me tacked to my bedroom wall...

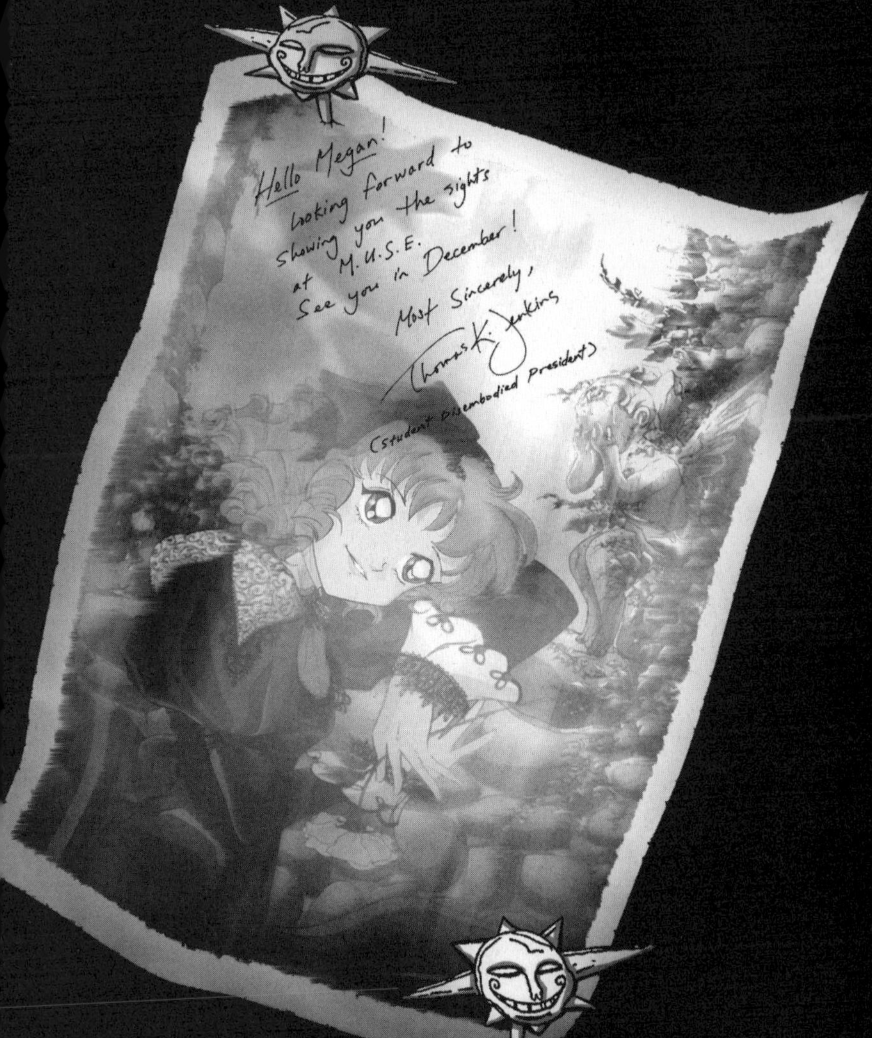
Hello Megan!
Looking forward to showing you the sights at M.U.S.E.
See you in December!
Most Sincerely,
Thomas K. Jenkins
(Student Disembodied President)

I think it's safe to say that my strange story is to be continued...

Afterword

Do you believe in muses? Do you believe in a guiding spirit that takes your hand and helps you maneuver through life's uncertain waters? Or perhaps you believe in Guardian Angels—beings that not only protect you from darker forces and undesirable fates, but sway you towards safety and fortune. I'm not quite sure I do, but I can tell you there have been times in my life that I thought were just too coincidental to have just happened without some kind of intervention...or guidance...or navigation.

Over ten years ago, I met a young couple at an anime convention. Dressed entirely in black, they displayed beautiful, delicate, eye-catching illustrations at their table as they modestly sketched away for curious convention goers. I thought they were pretty darn talented, but as an editor for a superhero publisher at the time, I unfortunately didn't have an opportunity to utilize their abilities. However, I couldn't help but tell my friends in the indie world that there was a great, untapped talent out there, waiting to be unleashed.

As the years passed, I'd run into the couple from time to time at conventions. We would catch up and share stories of where our careers had taken us and where we thought they were going.

Almost ten years later to the day, I now find myself working here at TOKYOPOP. And what do you know, one of the books assigned to me is something called ShutterBox, written and illustrated by Rikki Simons and Tavisha—the very same couple I met at that anime convention a decade past. What a great surprise this was, what a bizarre chance, what an awesome...coincidence?

As a comic book editor, there's no better reward than working with creators like Rikki and Tavisha. They're dependable and imaginative and all-around great people. With ShutterBox, I see a definite progression in their work, but they haven't lost what first made them special. They still have that same sense of magic and wonderment in their stories and illustrations, that same spell that draws you into the worlds they create.

When I finished my final edit of this first volume, I sat back for a moment and wondered...was it a muse that brought our paths together again? Was it someone like Megan, perhaps, who made sure we wound up in this creative collision?

Naw. It was just really great luck. And I'm glad it happened!

-Mark Paniccia

Zodiac P.I.

BY NATSUMI ANDO

TOKYOPOP®

TO SOLVE THE CRIME, SHE NEEDS YOUR SIGN

AVAILABLE AT YOUR FAVORITE BOOK AND COMIC STORES.

www.TOKYOPOP.com

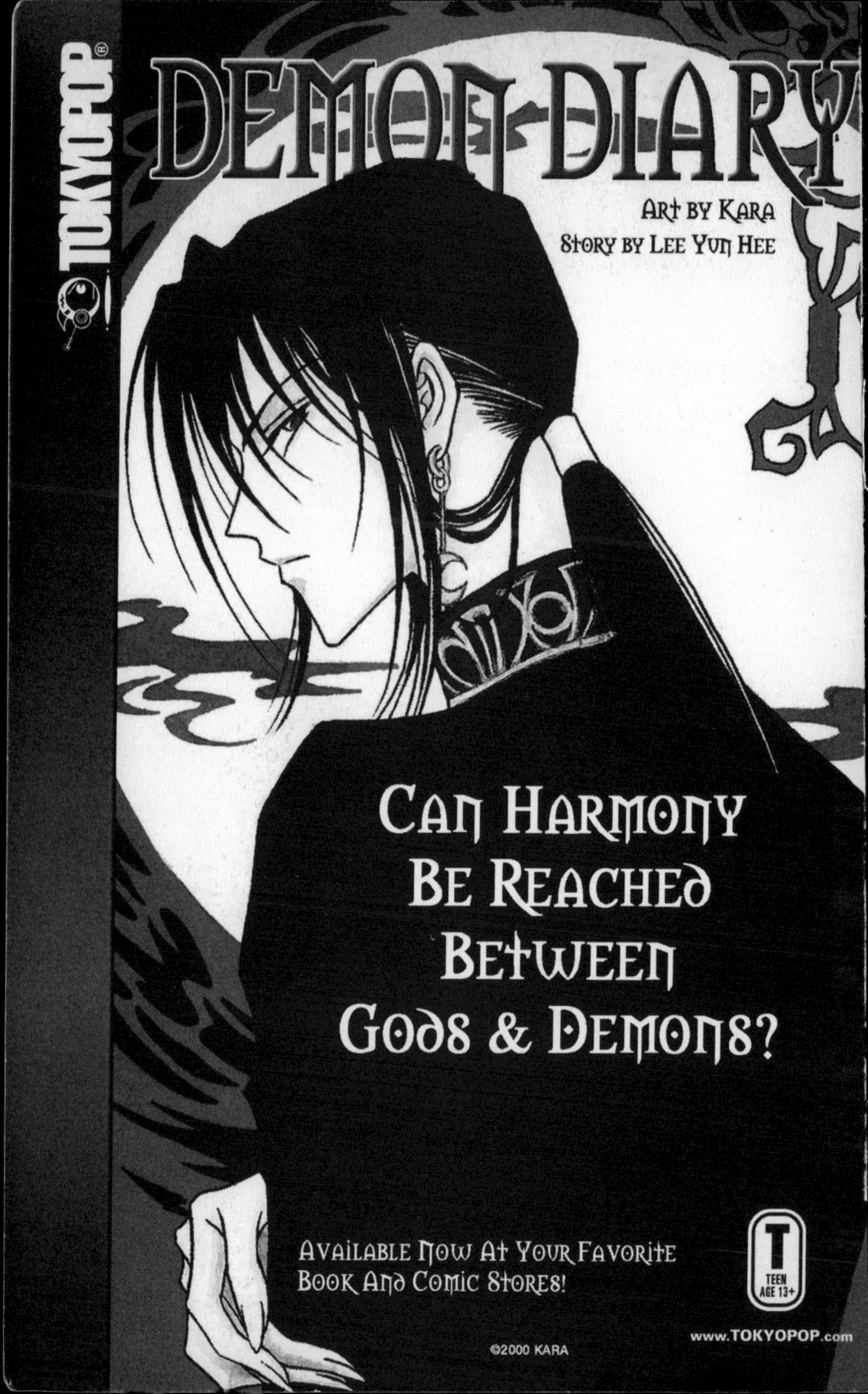
TOKYOPOP
DEMON DIARY
ART BY KARA
STORY BY LEE YUN HEE
CAN HARMONY BE REACHED BETWEEN GODS & DEMONS?
AVAILABLE NOW AT YOUR FAVORITE BOOK AND COMIC STORES!
T TEEN AGE 13+
www.TOKYOPOP.com
©2000 KARA